RENEWALS: 691-4574

DATE DUE

OCT 10			
11.7-92			

D0769290

WITHDRAWN
UTSA LIBRARIES

Facilitating Work Effectiveness

WITHDRAWN UTSA LIB

Issues in Organization and Management Series
Arthur P. Brief and Benjamin Schneider, *Editors*

Facilitating Work Effectiveness

Edited by

F. David Schoorman
Purdue University

Benjamin Schneider
University of Maryland

Lexington Books
D.C. Heath and Company/Lexington, Massachusetts/Toronto

The conference summarized in this book was partially supported by the Organizational Effectiveness Research Programs, Psychological Sciences Division, Office of Naval Research under contract no. N00014-83-K-0551, NR 270-958, Benjamin Schneider and F. David Schoorman, principal investigators.

Library of Congress Cataloging-in-Publication Data

Facilitating work effectiveness.

  Includes index.
  1. Employees, Rating of.   2. Job enrichment.
3. Personnel management.   I. Schoorman, F. David.
II. Schneider, Benjamin, 1938–   . III. Title:
Work effectiveness.
HF5549.5.R3F33   1988   658.3′14   85–46006
ISBN 0–669–12653–5 (alk. paper)

Copyright © 1988 by Lexington Books

All rights reserved. No part of this publication may be reproduced or transmitted in any form or by any means, electronic or mechanical, including photocopy, recording, or any information storage or retrieval system, without permission in writing from the publisher.

Published simultaneously in Canada
Printed in the United States of America
International Standard Book Number: 0–669–12653–5
Library of Congress Catalog Card Number

The paper used in this publication meets the minimum requirements of American National Standard for Information Sciences—Permanence of Paper for Printed Library Materials, ANSI Z39.48–1984. ∞ ™

88 89 90 91 92 8 7 6 5 4 3 2 1

Library
University of Texas
at San Antonio

Dedicated to C. J. (Jack) Bartlett,
mentor, friend, and facilitator

Contents

Part III   Management Issues   145

Part IV   Overview   213

Foreword

Arthur P. Brief
New York University

The primary purpose of Lexington Books' Issues in Organization and Management Series is to call attention to ideas that may fundamentally reshape what we have come to understand about how and why people think, feel, and act at work. The books in the series may serve their attention-grabbing function by addressing matters of theoretical, methodological, or practical concern; and, they may seek to speak principally to academic researchers or practicing professionals. F. David Schoorman and Benjamin Schneider's *Facilitating Work Effectiveness* covers all these bases.

For too many years the idea that willing and able workers encounter obstacles to their performance that they themselves cannot overcome has been grossly underattended to in both the academic and practitioner communities. My bet is that Schoorman and Schneider's book will remedy this oversight.

The book, a tightly edited collection of papers by distinguished scholars, offers a comprehensive examination of work facilitation. Theoretically, the book tackles such concerns as defining the "facilitation" and "effectiveness" constructs and identifying those factors that plausibly could be considered to be facilitators and inhibitors. Methodological concerns discussed include, for example, the measurement of both facilitators and inhibitors and the question of what is the appropriate level of analysis. Practically speaking, in summarizing what is known about work facilitation, the book outlines alternative strategies for enhancing effectiveness.

Because of its emphasis on theory and research, academics will find the book eye-opening, posing many new research questions and suggesting ways to answer them. Given the accessible style in which it is written and its consistent concern with the application of knowledge, professionals will find the book a useful guide to practice.

Preface

Benjamin Schneider
F. David Schoorman

I t was springtime in Maryland on the cliffs overlooking the Severn River at the University of Maryland's Conference Center. We were outside on the veranda drinking beer and eating steamed crabs spliced with Old Bay Seasoning. "Now, this is what I call facilitating work effectiveness," came the insightful comment.

We had brought together a number of insightful commenters. The Office of Naval Research (ONR) had made moneys available to assemble six outstanding academicians and practitioners to address what we know, from a social science perspective, about facilitating work effectiveness. At the time, we were completing our second year of research on the topic and felt the need for up-to-date information about what others were thinking. We also wanted some input from others on our progress and conclusions. We made some calls to the authors of the chapters in this book and each of them accepted the challenge.

All of the chapters here address the issue of facilitating work effectiveness. Each makes the implicit assumption that effectiveness at work requires facilitation; work effectiveness does not just spring full-blown without some attention to its facilitation.

The concept of work facilitation, however, is deceptively simple. What does it mean to facilitate? Is it the opposite of to inhibit? How does one measure the extent to which work effectiveness is facilitated or constrained? How does one manage work so that effectiveness is facilitated? These are the kinds of issues addressed in the present book.

The book is divided into four major sections. Part I presents several conceptualizations of the work-facilitation construct. First, Schoorman and Schneider provide a frame of reference for the research accomplished at the University of Maryland under the ONR contract. Guzzo and Gannett then present the interesting idea that facilitators may be on a different continuum than inhibitors, the former encouraging maximally attainable performance, the latter, in their absence, permitting merely minimally acceptable performance. The next chapter, by Kerr, presents a conceptualization of the role of reward systems as facilitators and inhibitors of work effectiveness. He shows, in essence, how organizations promote behaviors that are inhibitory of work effectiveness while simultaneously espousing the idea that they reward people for effectiveness!

In part II, the focus shifts explicitly to methodological issues in assessing work facilitation. Moeller, Schneider, Schoorman, and Berney describe the heart of the Maryland research effort, the design of a procedure for diagnosing work facilitators and inhibitors. They call the measure (the result of the application of a set of procedures for designing such measures) the work-facilitation diagnostic. Peters and O'Connor then describe their long-term efforts at measuring work inhibitors and add new evidence to the role of inhibitors as valid correlates of some important individual behaviors and attitudes at work. The third contribution to part II, by Roberts and Sloane, presents new vantage points on the aggregation problem in organizational science. A central problem in aggregation concerns the idea that some behaviors need to be described at the level of analysis at which they occur, i.e., that some work-group phenomena are not knowable by aggregating over individuals. Roberts and Sloane describe this issue in detail.

In part III, the issue again changes, this time to the management of work so that work effectiveness is actually facilitated. Schoorman, Schechter, Moeller, and Schneider present results of an attempt to differentiate the roles of leadership and management behaviors in facilitating work effectiveness. Then, Moses and Lyness review their thinking and research about how work effectiveness in the future will be facilitated to the extent that the higher levels of management in organizations are able to cope effectively with the ambiguity of their work worlds. Kaplan then describes a long-term effort at understanding how general managers of organizations actually go about dealing with the high variety, high ambiguity, and scarce information characteristic of their jobs so that effectiveness in their organizations can be facilitated by their own behaviors.

Finally, in part IV, we offer an overview and integration of the papers presented at the conference which became the chapters of this book. The overview is organized around the three major themes of the conference: conceptual, methodological, and management issues.

Our goal in presenting these chapters is to push forward the study and management of work facilitation (and work inhibition). Both our own efforts and the thoughts and research of the contributing scholars indicate that the construct of facilitation may offer a "foot in the door" to conceptualization, measurement, and management that has been very elusive indeed. Our thinking is that the construct of work facilitation offers the potential to serve as a unifying theme for a broad range of theory and research in the study of work.

In this line of thinking, readers should feel encouraged to explore the kinds of issues addressed here but, more importantly, we hope the book will facilitate exploration of additional topics not explicitly covered here. The list is almost endless—socialization, training, job characteristics, groups, and so on as facilitators of work effectiveness. Let us get on with it.

Part I
Conceptual Issues

This part of the book begins to organize the issues requiring attention if the construct of work facilitation is going to have meaning within the larger fabric of the organization sciences. First, Schoorman and Schneider in chapter 1 present their own saga regarding the evolution of their thinking about work facilitation. They show how consideration of the issues to be addressed, the level of analysis at which they will be addressed, and the potential practical utility of the ideas vis-à-vis management all require specification. Indeed, these three issues (what is work facilitation, at what level of analysis should it be assessed, and how can work be managed in ways that facilitate effectiveness) become the organizing themes for the entire book.

Next, Guzzo and Gannett, and then Kerr, present two vantage points on conceptualizing work facilitation. In chapter 2, Guzzo and Gannett lodge the facilitation construct in traditional work-performance theorizing and show that facilitation may be a different idea than inhibition. Kerr presents a conceptualization of work facilitation based on the idea that what people think is rewarded in their work setting is what they are likely to do. The unique element in Kerr's presentation in chapter 3 is the idea that organization rewards can be diagnosed and the diagnosis frequently reveals that organizations reward behaviors they do not desire! The characteristic ways in which organizations defeat their stated purposes by rewarding behaviors they do not desire makes fascinating reading.

1

Grappling with Work Facilitation: An Evolving Approach to Understanding Work Effectiveness

F. David Schoorman
Benjamin Schneider

At the turn of the century, Frederick W. Taylor, an engineer by profession, conducted a series of studies of human behavior in work organizations. The studies focussed on two fundamental questions that were to become the cornerstones of the field of organizational science. The questions were (1) what are the personal qualities of the ideal worker and (2) what are the ideal working conditions? As the field of organizational science evolved, the domain of personal qualities was soon conceived of in multidimensional terms ranging from abilities (cognitive and physical abilities, knowledge, and skills) to motivation of the worker. The general goal of this research was to identify the relevant abilities of the worker as well as the appropriate combination of abilities and motivations that would account for the largest proportion of individual variability in performance. This focus on individual correlates of effectiveness dominated the first 50 years of the study of human performance at work.

Since the 1960s, researchers have begun to focus more on exploring the second question, the issue of working conditions, in their attempts to more precisely account for the variability in performance at work. Here, also, the problem has been one of identifying the variety of facets reflected in performance, this time the organizational conditions that facilitate or inhibit human performance. The issues that have been investigated include the characteris-

This chapter was prepared with support from the Organizational Effectiveness Research Programs, Psychological Sciences Division, Office of Naval Research under Contract No. N00014-83-K-0551, NR 270-958, Benjamin Schneider and F. David Schoorman, principal investigators.

We are indebted to the organizations and the people in them (who will remain unnamed only to protect their anonymity) who collaborated with us in our research efforts and to the infamous ONR research team that has included at various times the following people: Liz Berney, Rosalie Hall, Jocelyn Gessner, Linda Katzman, Andrea Marcus, Anne Moeller, Rene Morales, Dan Schechter, Joe Schneider, and Cindy Staehle.

tics of the task (role ambiguity, task structure, specialization, and task inter-dependence), characteristics of the organization (technology, size, and span of control), organizational policies and practices (reward systems, decision-making styles, communication), and the climate or culture of the organization (climate for service, safety, and so on).

Whereas most of the individual-level research emphasized the role of ability in performance, theoreticians and researchers have focussed on moti-vation as a source for hypotheses about the conditions that will enhance ef-fectiveness. Thus, following writings such as Argyris (1957) and McGregor (1960), this line of research attempts to specify work conditions that will "release" the motivation that all workers are thought to possess. In contrast to the individually focussed research, then, scholars who have emphasized work conditions have taken a more universalist stance on employee motiva-tion: they have assumed that workers *are* motivated and that it is work condi-tions, not a lack of worker motivation, that inhibits employee effectiveness.

Peters and O'Connor (1980) have attempted to integrate the research on both the individual and organizational correlates of individual performance. To this end, they have proposed a rational taxonomy of organizational con-ditions that can constrain individual performance. They argue that situa-tional constraints affect the motivation of the individual worker and have a differential impact on performance by either allowing abilities to be utilized to their fullest or by constraining the expression of worker abilities. Specifi-cally, they argue that the presence of constraints in the work setting will have the greatest negative effect on individuals with the highest ability, resulting in lower performance as well as in more negative affective reactions such as greater dissatisfaction and frustration.

The work of Peters and O'Connor and their colleagues (e.g., O'Connor et al., 1984) provides an excellent review and summary of the research inte-grating the effect of constraints in the workplace with individual attributes in predicting individual performance.

Their work provides a backdrop for describing the present research pro-gram because we and they share a central concern for inhibitors of work effectiveness. However, the conceptual scheme guiding our research program is a fundamentally different one. The present research program is based on the premise that there are facilitators and inhibitors of effectiveness that exist at the unit level and have a significant impact on the performance of the unit. The variability in individual performance of the members of the unit, whether a function of individual differences in skills and abilities or a func-tion of individual differences in reactions to inhibitors, is not of interest in the present research. Thus, the focus of the present research is at a more macro level of analysis, the dependent variable being unit effectiveness, with unit-level inhibitors and facilitators being the hypothesized predictors.

The Unit-of-Analysis Issue

Prior to exploring the conceptual system adapted for classifying facilitators and inhibitors, the issue of the unit of analysis needs to be addressed. As previously noted, our efforts, in contrast to earlier ones, are carried out at the unit level, not the individual level of analysis. This decision affected both the development of the diagnostic survey and the process of data collection. In fact, several interesting (perhaps unconventional) procedures were adopted to accommodate this decision. For example, group consensus data were collected from representatives of the work group (e.g., sales unit, department) and this consensus procedure was contrasted with the usual procedure of aggregating individuals' responses to represent group-level information.

In a tour de force, Roberts et al. (1979) argued that clarity about the level of analysis for any piece of research is essential to avoid an unintentional transgression termed the "ecological fallacy problem" (Robinson, 1950) (also known as cross-level inference). The conceptual, methodological, and data-analytic problems associated with making these cross-level inferences have been raised by other researchers as well (e.g., Blalock, 1964; Firebaugh, 1978; Glick, 1980; Glick and Roberts, 1984; Mossholder and Bedeian, 1983; Schneider 1983a). Glick and Roberts (1984), for example, critiqued a review of equity theory (Vecchio, 1982) to illustrate the problems of interpretation created by crossing levels of analysis:

> The discussion of equity theory was primarily at the individual level of analysis, but previously published data from several studies were reanalyzed at the level of the experimental condition. . . . Thus, the reported correlation coefficients were severely biased upwards. (p. 723)

The authors proceeded to disentangle the mixed levels of analysis, redoing Vecchio's analyses entirely at the individual level. Glick and Roberts's results and conclusions were quite different from Vecchio's.

The level of analysis for this research is explicitly the group level of analysis. This decision was based on the suspicion that the group level of analysis is more appropriate than the individual level of analysis for the study of work facilitation. Earlier works by Peters and his colleagues (Peters et al., 1980; O'Connor et al., 1984) contributed to this suspicion. These researchers conducted experimental and field studies aimed at identifying and categorizing situational performance constraints. (They have identified as many as fourteen major categories of constraints that are neither exhaustive nor mutually exclusive.)

In their research, the individual is the unit of analysis. Despite their careful work, O'Connor et al. (1984), for example, failed to find support for the hypothesized relationship between situational constraints and performance. We reasoned that perhaps groups (be they work groups, departments, stores, organizations, whatever) are the more optimal unit of analysis for the study of situational constraints (or facilitators and inhibitors as they are called in this research) than individuals. Logically, then, situational conditions can be thought to have relatively uniform effects on individuals in a work situation. This hypothesis follows from writings by Schneider (1983a, 1983b) and Schneider and Reichers (1983) on climate as well as a host of writers on organizational culture (e.g., Smircich, 1983; Schein, 1985). Schneider (1983a, 1983b), for example, argued that through vocational and organizational choices into and out of jobs and work settings, similar people end up in similar places, so they tend to share ways of viewing the world. Schneider and Reichers (1983) and various organizational-culture writers add the idea that people working in a particular setting come to share images, impressions, and meanings of the setting through having common experiences and through a process of natural interaction.

There are, then, two cycles of importance: (1) natural attraction to and attrition from settings resulting in similarities among people and (2) involvement in common experiences and the process of natural interaction resulting in a sharing of images, impressions, and meanings. It follows from these two cycles that the work unit is the appropriate focus for research on the effects of work conditions on performance. This follows because the work unit is, in reality, tied together through a common history, a common set of experiences, and common persons (Schneider and Reichers, 1983).

The Conceptual Space of Facilitators and Inhibitors

Given the decision to conduct the research at the unit level, the next conceptual problem we confronted was to grapple with the vast array of potential facilitators and inhibitors of effectiveness that exist in organizations. As was indicated in the opening remarks, prior research suggests that these issues range from characteristics of the task to characteristics of the organization, from policies and practices to climate and culture. The need for a scheme to organize facilitators and inhibitors led to a search for a comprehensive model of organizational functioning by which these issues could be conceptually clarified. The Katz and Kahn (1978) open-systems model provided just such a framework not only for conceptualizing facilitators and inhibitors, but also for conceptualizing organizational functioning in general. The sections that follow describe, first, the general implications of their systems model for organizational functioning and, then, the specific utility of their concept of subsystems as a scheme for classifying work-unit facilitators and inhibitors.

Characteristics of the Systems Model of Organizations

Several characteristics of the open-systems perspective are particularly relevant to the conceptualization of organizations in this research. The system is viewed as a production process that has three stages. The first is the input stage during which raw materials or resources are acquired from the environment and brought into the system. According to Katz and Kahn (1978), all systems, whether biological or social, must derive the energy that is vital to sustaining themselves from the environment around them.

The second stage is the throughput or transformation stage where the raw materials or inputs are acted upon in a prescribed manner that increases their value (or creates a new product with increased value). This is the stage on which most research on inhibitors of performance has been focussed, as shown in table 1–1.

Table 1–1 lists eight "situational resource variables," all of which are clearly in the production-process domain because they explicitly concern the production act itself.

The third stage is the output stage in which the finished product is exported across the system's boundary back to the environment. Due to the

Table 1–1
Situational Resource Variables Relevant to Performance

1. *Job-related information:* The information (from supervisors, peers, subordinates, customers, company rules, policies, procedures and so forth) needed to do the job assigned.
2. *Tools and equipment:* The specific tools, equipment, and machinery needed to do the job assigned.
3. *Materials and supplies:* The materials and supplies needed to do the job assigned.
4. *Budgetary support:* The financial resources and budgetary support needed to do the job assigned, including funds for such things as long-distance calls, travel, job-related entertainment, recruiting new staff, maintaining and retaining existing personnel, and hiring emergency help. This category does not refer to an incumbent's own salary, but rather to the monetary support necessary to accomplish tasks that are a part of the job.
5. *Required services and help from others:* The services and help from others needed to do the job assigned.
6. *Task preparation:* The personal preparation (through previous education, formal company training, and relevant job experience) needed to do the job assigned.
7. *Time availability:* The availability of the time needed to do the job assigned, taking into consideration the time limits imposed, interruptions, unnecessary meetings, non–job-related distractions, and so forth.
8. *Work environment:* The physical aspects of the immediate work environment needed to do the job assigned—characteristics that facilitate rather than interfere with doing the task. A helpful work environment is one that is not too noisy, too cold, or too hot; that provides an appropriate work area; that is well lighted, that is safe; and so forth.

Source: Peters and O'Connor (1980).

cyclical nature of the production process, the value derived from the product in the output stage is critical to determining the value of the inputs in the next production cycle. This model simultaneously suggests that it is important to identify the system of interest by specifying the system boundaries that differentiate it from its environment while at the same time viewing these boundaries as permeable, allowing the system to be affected by, and have an impact on, its environment.

The Subsystems of Activities

According to the Katz and Kahn (1978) framework, the activities or events in an organization can be classified in terms of five generic subsystems. These subsystems are (1) a supportive subsystem, (2) a maintenance subsystem, (3) a production subsystem, (4) a managerial subsystem, and (5) an adaptive subsystem. By adopting this theoretical model, we considerably broaden the domain of issues thought to facilitate or constrain unit effectiveness.

One point requiring attention at the outset is our use of the Katz and Kahn subsystem framework for describing work *units*, not entire organizations. Our impression, then, is that many people think of Katz and Kahn's model as one describing whole *organizations*. However, this is incorrect. The subsystems framework describes how systems work, be they individuals, groups, work units, or even entire nations. So, in what follows it is important to think about *work units*, for it is that unit of analysis to which the subsystems framework will be applied.

Supportive. The supportive subsystem includes all activities and events concerned with the acquisition of resources for the system. These resources consist of the raw materials (including the information) required for the production process. The purchasing function of the unit represents an example of supportive-subsystem activity. The supportive subsystem is also responsible for the disposal of the finished product. This includes activities such as advertising, sales, and delivery of the product. In the context of the model of the stages of production just described, the supportive subsystem represents activities associated with the input stage (acquisition) as well as the output stage (disposal).

Maintenance. The maintenance subsystem is concerned with the acquisition and maintenance of the resources and structures necessary for implementing the production process. There is some ambiguity in the Katz and Kahn discussion of the maintenance subsystem regarding the extent of the acquisition function attributable to the maintenance subsystem, but it is clear that post-acquisition maintenance activities form the core of this subsystem. Some of these ambiguities will be resolved in a later section of this chapter.

The principal resources to be maintained by this subsystem are the human resources as well as the technical resources including the physical environment and equipment. The traditional personnel functions such as selection, staffing, training, performance appraisal, feedback, and rewards belong in this subsystem. Other activities related to the maintenance of the human-resource component include socialization, goal setting, and personal counseling. The maintenance of physical plant and equipment includes regular servicing, updating, and renovations of these resources. The maintenance subsystem activities occur in the input and transformation stages of production.

Production. The production-subsystem activities represent the technical core of the organization where the raw materials acquired by the supportive subsystem are acted upon, thereby creating a new product that inherently has more value than the sum of the raw materials used in its creation. This "value-added" component represents the creative function and central purpose of the unit. The nature of the specific activities of the production subsystem vary greatly as a function of the type of unit, its technology, and service product. For example, welding is an important production-subsystem activity if the unit produces car bodies, lecturing is an important production-subsystem activity in a university department, and making a sale is a critical production-subsystem activity for a telemarketing sales unit. All production-subsystem activities occur in the transformation stage.

Adaptive. The adaptive subsystem is devoted to the long-term survival of the system. The activities of the adaptive subsystem are concerned (1) with monitoring the external environment for changes that would threaten the viability of the unit and (2) with creating mechanisms through which the system can anticipate and adapt to changing environmental conditions.

Typical functions of the adaptive subsystem include long-range planning, research and development, and the gathering of information from the environment.

The concept of an adaptive subsystem is perhaps the most significant contribution of the Katz and Kahn open-systems perspective since it is the relative strength of the adaptive-subsystem activities that most clearly differentiates an open-systems perspective from a closed-systems perspective on unit effectiveness. The adaptive subsystem activities are indirectly relevant to the production process and therefore do not represent any particular stage of production.

Managerial. The managerial subsystem represents the coordination and controlling mechanism for the other subsystems. The managerial subsystem activities tend to exist at a different level than the activities of the other subsystems. In order for the other subsystems to interface efficiently, the managerial subsystem must evolve policies and operating procedures that govern the activities of each of the other subsystems. For example, the information acquired by the adaptive subsystem may dictate the type or quantity of a particular product that is to be created by the production subsystem, which in turn affects the acquisition function of the supportive subsystem. The activities may range in complexity from a simple inventory-control policy to a sophisticated computerized production-scheduling program. Since the managerial subsystem coordinates the activities of all the other subsystems, it exists at each of the stages of production.

Boundary and Leading Subsystems

Two additional concepts related to the subsystems model that are particularly relevant to the present research are (1) boundary subsystems and (2) leading subsystems.

Boundary subsystems refer to subsystems whose activities span the unit's boundary. It is through these activities that the system is able to monitor its environment, change or adapt to its environment when necessary, and obtain needed resources from the environment as well as dispose of its products. As this definition suggests, the supportive and adaptive subsystems are entirely boundary subsystems. Their activities are all directed at the environment of the system. The maintenance subsystem consists of some boundary-spanning activities as in the instance of hiring new personnel. However, the majority of the activities of the maintenance subsystem are directed internally toward maintaining the system. The activities of the production subsystem are focussed exclusively within the system, making it a core subsystem. Since the managerial subsystem consists of the coordination of the other subsystems, its activities are also directed within the system.

According to Katz and Kahn (1978), based on the characteristics of the organization, its product or service, its technology, and its environment, a particular subsystem will gain prominence and exert the greatest influence over the system. This subsystem is called the leading subsystem. The concept of the leading subsystem is interesting in the context of this research in that the process of identifying facilitators and inhibitors in each of the subsystems frequently makes the implicit relative importance of each of the subsystems quite clear. This information can be used as a diagnostic of the system's functioning as well as to corroborate more qualitative perceptions of the strengths and weaknesses of the organization.

Summary

The Katz and Kahn conceptualization of how work systems function was employed as a heuristic for organizing facilitators and inhibitors of unit effectiveness. One goal was to use the Katz and Kahn framework as a vehicle for broadening the conceptual space describing the work conditions that can inhibit or facilitate unit effectiveness. A second, related goal was to then use the framework as a foundation for the design of work-unit diagnostics.

In essence, what we were trying to do was use the Katz and Kahn framework to operationalize Peters and O'Connor's plea:

> Situational constraints relevant to performance outcomes remain a relatively unexplored source of variance of potential importance to researchers and practitioners alike. . . . Future research in this area should be aimed at (1) examining the comprehensiveness of the previously identified dimension space, (2) developing a psychometrically sound measure of the identified situational constraint taxonomy, (3) generating data relevant to establishing the construct validity of the new measure, and (4) using the measure to test hypotheses concerning the direct and indirect effects of the identified taxonomy of situational constraints on both performance and affective work outcomes. (1980, pp. 396–97)

Method: Clarification of Subsystems

In this section, the interviews that served as a foundation for clarifying the subsystem model will be described. This is important to do because we were literally groping for ways to operationalize the various subsystems defined by Katz and Kahn. So, our early interviews in each of the settings in which we have worked serve as the foundation for the later, more systematic, data-collection efforts.

We should say at the outset that the problem of trying to capture all of what may facilitate and inhibit human effectiveness in a work setting is an enormous one. It was only when we "discovered" the Katz and Kahn subsystems model and only after we made it clear to ourselves that unit, not individual, effectiveness was our criterion, that we felt we could achieve our goal.

Here, then, we present what we learned about the Katz and Kahn framework as a vehicle for operationalizing unit inhibitors and facilitators. Chapter 4 by Moeller et al. will provide more details about the actual survey-data–collection procedures and the more formal results relating the diagnostic to unit effectiveness.

Sample 1

Selected faculty of a large mid-Atlantic university were the research participants. Sixteen faculty were interviewed one-on-one for about 45 minutes each to begin to specify the facilitators and inhibitors of teaching effectiveness.

Procedure. Faculty from different departments were asked to indicate the kinds of department conditions that facilitate and/or inhibit them from being as effective as they could be in their classroom teaching role. During the interviews, copious notes were taken about the issues that were raised by the faculty; these notes served as the basis for writing the items to capture the Katz and Kahn subsystems for the design of the eventual work-facilitation diagnostic (WFD).

Interviewers generated about three-hundred items describing department facilitators and inhibitors. Then, through an iterative process, the number of items was reduced to thirty-five. This reduction was accomplished through clarification, condensing, sorting, and deletion of items. Items deleted were those that failed to be consistent with the department level of analysis we retained as our constant focus. For example, items that were written in the first person or were affective (e.g., "I like . . . "; "I am satisfied"), and items descriptive of more macro levels of analysis ("This university . . . ") were all deleted.

Sample 2

In sample 2, the interviews to develop items for the WFD survey were accomplished in a group setting. Participants were sales employees of a national financial-services telemarketing organization. Seven groups of salespersons, each group having between four and six members, were interviewed.

Procedure. Interviewers conducted the group discussions focussing on an exploration of the facilitators and inhibitors of sales-unit effectiveness. Again, interviewers took copious notes and used these notes to write items to capture the issues that were raised during the interviews. This time, about four-hundred items were generated and forty survived the iterative sorting, clarifying, condensing, and discarding process.

Sample 3

The third sample is a manpower unit from one area of the military. Located in metropolitan Washington, D.C., the unit employs both civilians and military personnel. In this sample, the various branches of the manpower unit are the foci of interest.

Procedure. Group interviews were also used in this sample to generate facilitators and inhibitors, this time of branch effectiveness. Seven group interviews of between four and six persons (mostly military) were conducted. Notes taken during the sessions yielded about 450 items, which yielded fifty-eight items after our iterative process.

Summary

The purpose of this analysis is to discuss our conceptual learnings from the interviews and from the process of turning the interviews into surveys. While less formal than the data presented by Moeller et al., these insights into the Katz and Kahn model have been instructive and required documentation because they have implicitly guided our subsequent research.

In summary, the results reported here are based on interview data collected in three different organizations: a large East Coast university, a financial-services telemarketing company, and the manpower-policy component of a military service. In the university, the system of interest was the academic-discipline unit, which in most cases was an academic department. In the telemarketing company, the system was defined as a naturally occurring work unit comprised of a supervisor and approximately eight to ten subordinates. In the military unit, the system was defined as a branch representing a functional work group.

Results

Coding the Facilitators and Inhibitors

One of the earliest observations made in examining the facilitators and inhibitors of effectiveness for the units studied was the preponderance of items related to the acquisition and maintenance of personnel. This may be attributed to the fact that all three organizations in the research program were service organizations where the principal resource needed for effectiveness was the human resource. In order to reflect the relative importance of the personnel and personnel-related facilitators and inhibitors in these organizations, the maintenance subsystem was divided to create a personnel-maintenance subsystem and an equipment-maintenance subsystem. The new personnel-maintenance subsystem now included all activities related to the acquisition and maintenance of personnel. This procedure is completely consistent with the Katz and Kahn (1978) framework since they argue that the five subsystems they proposed were generic subsystems that might require more specific differentiation in particular organizations.

This major reconceptualization of the maintenance subsystem (more details on this are presented later) was not our only learning. We learned something about both the units being studied and the Katz and Kahn framework as we went through the iterative process of reducing 250–400 specific facilitators and inhibitors into one-tenth that number of items for the eventual WFD. Recall that this process is one of clarification, condensing, sorting, and deletion of irrelevant issues.

Supportive. The classification of facilitators and inhibitors as supportive-subsystem activities generally required that they be boundary-spanning activities and activities related to acquiring resources or disposing of a finished product. The fact that all three organizations in the research sample were service organizations had a significant impact on the coding of supportive-subsystem activities.

For instance, since service organizations generally create a service in response to a need or a specific request, the problem of marketing the finished product is not an issue in any of the systems. The complicating factor, however, is that in service organizations, the raw materials that are used to create the final product are much less clear than they would be in a system creating a tangible product. For example, what raw materials are required for telemarketing sales, for teaching a university course, or for developing a personnel policy in the military?

Some of the answers to these questions (as determined by the iterative item review process) were that in the telemarketing organization, a critical raw material is information. Hence, the items, "Supervisors are available to answer questions" and "Salespersons can obtain necessary information from coworkers and/or manuals" were examples of supportive-subsystem items. In the university sample, examples of supportive-subsystem items were "Technical support staff is available to assist faculty in their courses" and "Junior faculty have access to information (discussion with senior faculty, prepared lectures, course syllabi) that help them with their teaching." These items reflect the input necessary for teaching. Similarly, in the military sample, information and technical support were deemed to be critical inputs, as the following examples show: "Information relevant to our jobs is available from other branches," "Our data bases meet our needs," and "Technical support staff (e.g., graphics, computer technicians) is available."

Personnel Maintenance. As discussed earlier, the personnel-maintenance subsystem was created to reflect the added importance this aspect of the maintenance subsystem takes on in service organizations. All activities related to any personnel function were assigned to this subsystem. The generation and identification of personnel-subsystem items proved to be relatively easy. Examples of personnel-subsystem items are: "Attempts to improve sales performance go unnoticed in our section," "Counselors get nonmonetary rewards for good performance," "Quality teaching is an important factor in promotion decisions," and "Our branch is understaffed."

Equipment Maintenance. The equipment-maintenance subsystem reflected the acquisition and maintenance of the facilities and equipment necessary to get the job done. Since information was an important input in each of the organizations in the sample, several items reflect the need for equipment such as personal computers and word processors. Examples of these items are "CRTs are unavailable when needed" and "Our word processing equipment is adequate." Other specific equipment needs were also identified: "Audiovisual equipment breaks down during classes" and "Laboratory facilities and equipment are well maintained." The equipment-maintenance subsystem also addressed issues related to the physical plant and general working conditions. Examples are "Classroom facilities are in poor condition," "Working conditions are unsafe," and "The workplace provides no space for private conversations." As with the personnel-maintenance subsystem items, the issues in equipment maintenance were relatively easy to identify and code.

Production. Production-subsystem activities are concerned with the technical core or the creative component of the system. In most organizations, the identification of production-subsystem activities would seem to be relatively straightforward. However, in the organizations in our sample, the intangible nature of the products created some difficulty in identifying specific items that reflected the production subsystem.

One issue that was common to the three organizations was the workload. Items such as "Faculty teach three or more classes per semester," "We have enough time to do our paperwork accurately," and "We are overloaded with taskings" reflect this concern. Other items coded as production-subsystem activities were autonomy ("We have the autonomy we need to do our jobs" and "Faculty choose the hours they teach"), interruptions and distractions ("Our work is interrupted" and "Too much time is spent running errands"), and pressure ("Deadlines keep us from doing the job well"). As these items all reflect production-subsystem activities, they are directed within the system as prescribed by the theory.

Adaptive. As described earlier, the adaptive subsystem is a boundary subsystem that is directed at the environment and is responsible for monitoring the changes in the environment. This proved to be an interesting subsystem. In two of the samples (the university departments and the telemarketing sales units), the systems of interest did not engage in much adaptive-subsystem activity. Generating the adaptive items in these two organizations proved to be more difficult than for any other subsystem. However, once the items were generated, as you will see in chapter 4 by Moeller et al., they appeared to differentiate between effective and ineffective units in each of the samples. Examples of adaptive items in these organizations are "Faculty members attend workshops, conferences and/or meetings to learn about current methods and issues in teaching their courses" and "We are unaware of changes in company policies or procedures until after they go into effect."

In the military organization, the work of the branches in the study consisted of responding to requests for information from the environment. It was, therefore, very functional for the organization to focus on an adaptive function and anticipate some of the requests it would receive. This led to a relative abundance of adaptive items that were spontaneously generated in the interviews. These items included "We are unprepared to respond to new situations as they emerge," "Other units make policies which conflict with our policies," and "We do not know what the other branches do." As these items reflect the adaptive subsystem, the items are externally focussed and have implications for the future of the system. These items tend to be relatively easy to code.

Managerial. The managerial subsystem is by far the most difficult subsystem to code. Since the activities of this subsystem represent the coordination function for all the other subsystems, the differences between the coordination of an activity and the activity itself are often very subtle. The managerial subsystem achieves its coordination function through policies and procedures. Thus, a policy about acquiring resources is a managerial-subsystem activity while the process of acquiring that resource is a supportive-subsystem activity. A consequence of this is that many facilitators and inhibitors in organizations can be viewed as a particular activity or event that did not occur or, alternatively, as a policy that did not exist. For example, the item "Our supervisor schedules enough counselors to handle call volume" is coded as a managerial-subsystem item even though, with a minor change in emphasis, it could be a production-subsystem item. The general rule used in coding

Table 1–2
Substitutes for Leadership

Characteristics of subordinates
 1. Ability, experience, training, knowledge
 2. Need for independence
 3. "Professional" orientation
 4. Indifference toward organizational rewards

Characteristics of the task
 5. Unambiguous and routine
 6. Methodologically invariant
 7. Provides its own feedback concerning accomplishment
 8. Intrinsically satisfying

Characteristics of the organization
 9. Formalization (explicit plans, goals, and areas of responsibility)
10. Inflexibility (rigid, unbending rules and procedures)
11. Highly specified and active advisory and staff functions
12. Closely knit, cohesive work groups
13. Organizational rewards not within the leader's control
14. Spatial distance between superiors and subordinates

Source: Kerr and Jermier (1978).

managerial items was that they had to reflect a policy or procedure about how things were to be done in the system.

The difficulty in coding managerial-subsystem items is not only a problem in our work. Confusion over what managerial activities are, for example, has led some people to speculate about what leadership and management really are in organizations. Thus, Kerr and his colleagues (e.g., Kerr and Jermier, 1978) have asked whether leaders or what they call substitutes for leadership really determine unit effectiveneses. As shown in table 1–2, which reproduces one list of substitutes for leadership, it is easy to think about facilitators and inhibitors as we have described them.

In fact, our initial conceptualization for this research effort, shown in figure 1–1, was going to be an attempt to test the relative contribution of leadership behaviors (interpersonal superior–subordinate relationships), management behaviors (classical functions of management such as planning, organizing, and decision making), and facilitating work conditions as correlates of work-unit effectiveness. In that model, management behaviors were seen as those most directly related to the creation of facilitators and inhibitors, which in turn were thought to be reflected in unit effectiveness. The role of leadership in the early framework was relegated to handling crises

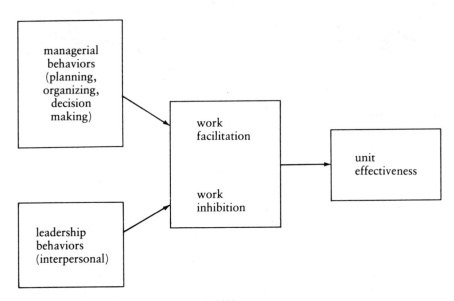

Adapted from Schneider and Schoorman (1982).

Figure 1–1. A Conceptualization of Management, Leadership, and Work Facilitation

arising from poor management (that is, management that created work inhibitors rather than work facilitators).

The Katz and Kahn framework is consistent with our early thoughts about the role of management as the source of facilitators and inhibitors but, for them, leadership behaviors are part of the managerial subsystem. Schoorman et al. present these issues in detail in chapter 7 and describe the handling of the relationships among the variables in figure 1–1.

Suffice it to say here that the issue of management and the managerial subsystem was not and is not a simple one.

Summary

Several general patterns emerged in the facilitator and inhibitor items that seemed to reflect unique characteristics of the organizations from which they were derived. For example, in the university sample, adaptive items (either facilitators or inhibitors) were hard to generate. Perhaps this reflected lack of emphasis on adaptive behaviors in the teaching function of the departments. An interesting footnote to this observation is that, as Moeller et al. show in chapter 4, the data indicate that the adaptive subsystem is the best predictor of teaching effectiveness in this organization. Similarly, in the telemarketing-sales units, items in boundary-spanning subsystems (supportive and adaptive) seemed harder to generate, perhaps reflecting an implicit assumption by the organization that each sales unit functioned relatively independently of the others and of the general environment. In the military organization, a completely different pattern existed with the boundary-spanning items being much easier to generate than items in the production and managerial subsystems. This pattern seemed to verify the researchers' informal assessment of the nature of the organization.

Although the jury is still out on the utility of the subsystem model for classifying facilitators and inhibitors, the evidence presented in this chapter suggests that the subsystem model has furthered our understanding of the functioning of organizations in anticipated ways as well as in unanticipated ways. The systems model provides a scheme for thinking about the organization at a unit level and facilitates maintaining a consistent focus at the unit of interest. It alerts the researchers to the very real issues of system boundaries as well as to the interaction between the system and its environment. The subsystems provide an excellent interview guide for exploring the functioning of various aspects of the system. In addition, an unanticipated benefit is that the subsystems model may serve as an interesting diagnostic of the relative strengths of the units within an organization.

A major learning from our sorting, coding, and clarifying process as we turned hundreds of facilitators and inhibitors into diagnostic items was the apparent utility of the Katz and Kahn subsystems model for describing unit functioning. This means that, while Katz and Kahn's framework has been viewed previously as a vehicle for making *organizational* comparisons, it seems useful for making intraorganization comparisons as well. Within our various samples, this is what we have done.

References

Argyris, C. (1957). *Personality and organization*. New York: Harper.

Blalock, H. M. (1964). *Causal inferences in nonexperimental research*. Chapel Hill, N.C.: University of North Carolina Press.

Firebaugh, G. A. (1978). A rule for inferring individual-level relationships from aggregated data. *American Sociological Review, 43*, 552–57.

Glick, W. H. (1980). Problems in cross-level inference. *New directions for methodology of social and behavioral science, 6*, 17–30.

Glick, W. H., and Roberts, K. R. (1984). Hypothesized interdependence, assumed dependence. *Academy of Management Review, 9*(4), 722–35.

Katz, D., and Kahn, R. L. (1978). *The social psychology of organizations*, 2nd ed. New York: Wiley.

Kerr, S., and Jermier, J. M. (1978). Substitutes for leadership: Their meaning and measurement. *Organizational Behavior and Human Performance, 22*, 375–403.

McGregor, D. M. (1960). *The human side of enterprise*. New York: McGraw-Hill.

Mossholder, K. R., and Bedeian, A. G. (1983). Cross-level inference and organizational research: Perspectives on interpretation and application. *Academy of Management Review, 8*, 547–58.

O'Connor, E., Peters, L., Eulberg, J., and Watson, T. (1984). Performance-relevant situational constraints: Identification, measurement, and influences on work outcomes. Technical report AFHRL-TR-83. Manpower and Personnel Division, Air Force Human Resources Laboratory, Brooks Air Force Base, Tex.

Peters, L. H., and O'Connor, E. J. (1980). Situational constraints and work outcomes: The influences of a frequently overlooked construct. *Academy of Management Review, 5*, 391–97.

Peters, L. H., O'Connor, E. J., and Rudolf, C. J. (1980). The behavioral and affective consequences of performance-relevant situational variables. *Organizational Behavior and Human Performance, 25*, 79–96.

Roberts, K. H., Hulin, C. L., and Rousseau, D. M. (1978). *Developing an interdisciplinary science of organizations*. San Francisco: Jossey-Bass.

Robinson, W. S. (1950). Ecological correlations and the behavior of individuals. *American Sociological Review, 15*, 351–57.

Schein, E. H. (1985). *Organizational culture and leadership*. San Francisco: Jossey-Bass.

Schneider, B. (1983a). An interactionist perspective on organizational effectiveness. In K. S. Cameron and D. A. Whetten, eds., *Organizational effectiveness*. New York: Academic Press.

Schneider, B. (1983b). Interactional psychology and organizational behavior. In L. L. Cummings and B. Staw, eds., *Research in organizational behavior,* vol. 5. Greenwich, Conn.: JAI Press.

Schneider, B., and Reichers, A. E. (1983). On the etiology of climates. *Personnel Psychology, 36,* 19–40.

Schneider, B., and Schoorman, F. D. (1982). Management and work facilitation: An approach to productivity. Working paper and proposal submitted to the Office of Naval Research. College Park: University of Maryland.

Smircich, L. (1983). Concepts of culture and organizational analysis. *Administrative Science Quarterly, 28,* 339–58.

Vecchio, R. P. (1981). An individual-difference interpretation of the conflicting predictions generated by equity theory and expectancy theory. *Journal of Applied Psychology, 66,* 470–81.

Vecchio, R. P. (1982). Predicting worker performance in inequitable situations. *Academy of Management Review, 7,* 103–10.

2

The Nature of Facilitators and Inhibitors of Effective Task Performance

Richard A. Guzzo
Barbara A. Gannett

W ork is performed in a context, an environment. A variety of factors in that environment can influence work performance, some facilitating effectiveness, but others inhibiting it. What are these factors that promote or retard effectiveness? How do they operate? How can they be managed? In this chapter, these and other questions are considered as they relate to individuals and groups at work.

Initially, we address the meaning of effectiveness for both individuals and groups at work. Then, we examine the nature of facilitators and inhibitors of effectiveness. A review of existing evidence concerning these two influences on effectiveness follows, as does a conceptual analysis of the nature of facilitators and inhibitors. The mechanisms by which these factors exert their influence are then discussed, as are practical issues concerning their management. Throughout, the chapter retains a dual focus on the effective performance of both individuals and groups as influenced by contextual factors in the work environment.

Effectiveness

How is effective work performance defined? Or, stated another way, *what* is facilitated or inhibited by various environmental conditions in the workplace?

Effective performance is one of the few outcomes of wide interest in organizational research. It is one of the four most heavily researched outcome variables, according to Staw (1984), the others being job satisfaction, absenteeism, and turnover. Staw asserts, though, that performance effectiveness has not been investigated successfully, due in part to poor research methods and restricted conceptualizations of this outcome variable.

We thank Loriann Roberson and the editors of this book for their helpful comments during the development of this work.

Staw (1984) argues that certain properties of any outcome variable should be made clear when discussing that variable. These properties are the *unit of analysis,* the *optimal level,* and for whom the variable has *utility.* With regard to the unit of analysis, effectiveness is examined in this chapter with reference to the performance of individuals and small groups of employees. We regard the optimal level of effectiveness as its maximal level, though we discuss effectiveness in terms of two benchmarks that establish a range of work performance effectiveness. One benchmark is the ceiling or *maximally attainable* performance. The other is the *minimally acceptable* level of performance. Facilitators and inhibitors are examined as they drive actual work performance toward either of these two end points. Finally, we ask, effectiveness for whom? We adopt the position that the effective work performance of individuals and small groups in an organization is a goal that serves the common interests of all organizational members. We recognize, though, that goals other than effective performance may exist and that the payoffs of effective performance are not evenly distributed among employees. Having specified these properties of our outcome variable of interest, we can now look more closely at effectiveness for individuals and groups.

Criteria of Individual Effectiveness

Organizations are concerned with the adequacy of their members' performance, but often find it difficult to act on that concern. It is not that there is a lack of *means* of assessing performance. Research and practice have identified many methods of assessing performance. These include measures of outputs (quality, quantity, and value), withdrawal (absenteeism, turnover, and tardiness), and disruptions (accidents). Some of the most commonly used means of performance appraisal are ratings and other judgments, as discussed in works by Latham and Wexley (1981) and Bernardin and Beatty (1984). These means of assessing performance effectiveness generally have attained a sophisticated level of implementation. However, as Staw (1984) points out, our conceptualization of the *substance* of effective work performance is impoverished.

Staw's discussion of performance as an outcome variable in organizational research shares much with discussions that have been carried on for some time concerning the "criterion problem" in personnel psychology. Criteria are standards or rules by which a determination of performance adequacy is made. The criterion problem has many facets, one of which is the lack of a generally applicable set of standards that can be used to assess perfomance for all jobs in all settings. Consequently, standards of effectiveness tend to be established anew for each job and organization in which appraisals of performance take place. These situationally derived criteria, as Smith (1976) pointed out, differ in many ways, including their specificity, closeness to organizational goals, and time span. Such differences afford little opportunity to develop a statement about the meaning of effectiveness applicable to a wide variety of jobs.

That criteria of individual effective performance become established situationally is, in fact, advantageous. The most informative, richest indicators of effectiveness are likely to be those that are specific rather than abstract, and a higher degree of specificity is attainable when criteria are developed to reflect the unique qualities of each job and work setting. The development of general criteria would necessarily involve abstraction and come at the cost of specificity. Thus, meaningfulness in criteria of effectiveness is ensured by keeping criteria situationally specific.

In addition to meaningfulness, situational specificity in performance criteria entails other desirable properties. One such property is accuracy. It is likely that appraisals of performance will be more accurate when based on specific rather than abstract criteria (e.g., Latham and Wexley, 1981). Another desirable property relates to the usefulness of performance appraisals for purposes of stimulating high performance. Appraisals of performance allow feedback to be provided to employees and for new performance goals to be set. Evidence indicates that specific rather than general feedback is the more powerful stimulant to increased performance (Ilgen et al., 1979). Also, specific rather than abstract goals are more powerful in generating improved individual performance (Locke et al., 1981) and specific goals can be derived from situationally based criteria of performance.

Note that situational specificity in criteria of performance does not mean that the ingredients of effectiveness in any one job are unique and share nothing with the elements of effectiveness in other jobs. Quality, for example, is an element of effectiveness for most jobs. The importance of quality relative to quantity of work accomplished, though, is likely to differ greatly among jobs. Absenteeism is an ingredient of performance effectiveness, too, that can differ across jobs as well (e.g., exempt versus nonexempt jobs). Thus, situational specificity refers to the necessity of tailoring the measurement, definition, and application of criteria of effective performance to a specific work setting in order to maximize the meaningfulness and usefulness of those criteria.

To summarize, there are few criteria that can be used to assess the level of individual work effectiveness without first tailoring those criteria to specific work situations. Criteria actually used, though, often implicitly reflect the benchmarks of maximally attainable and minimally acceptable performance. Behaviorally anchored rating scales, for example, depict behaviors ranging from near-maximal to at or below minimally acceptable levels for use in evaluating the performance of an employee. Sometimes only one of the benchmarks is important. For example, performance on a professional licensing examination must exceed some mininal value in order for the examinee to qualify for a license. A ceiling (maximally attainable score) exists for such examinations, but the ceiling is of little practical value. What is important is that performance be good enough. Being selected "most valuable player" as a professional athlete, in contrast, requires that performance for a season be at or near the maximally attainable level.

Criteria of Group Effectiveness

In contrast to the literature on individual task effectiveness, literature on effective task performance by groups has explicitly used the concept of maximally effective performance. In large part, this is due to the influence of Steiner's (1972) book on group process and productivity. Steiner presented the following model of group task performance:

$$\frac{\text{actual}}{\text{productivity}} = \frac{\text{potential}}{\text{productivity}} - \frac{\text{process}}{\text{losses}}$$

Potential productivity represents the maximally attainable level of performance by a group. In Steiner's analysis, this ceiling of performance is mainly determined by the resources in a group. Members bring with them many resources, including information, ability, experience, strength, and other qualities that can be applied toward the completion of a task. Note that Steiner's model stresses deviations from the level of maximal performance. Research and theorizing arising from this model have been oriented toward identifying the sources of these deviations, which are termed *process losses*. The sources of process losses identified in Steiner's work are decrements in the effort expended by group members and problems of coordination of member contributions. The size of a group, for example, could be a source of process losses in that coordination becomes more problematic as group size increases (Steiner, 1972).

Interestingly, evidence suggests that the amount of effort expended by group members decreases as group size increases. This phenomenon is labeled *social loafing* (Latané, 1986). Specifically, social loafing refers to the tendency of individuals to exert more effort on a task when performing it alone than when performing it as a member of a group. The larger the group, the greater the tendency toward social loafing. Thus, group size may be a source of process losses related both to effort and coordination.

For Steiner (1972), effectiveness is situationally specific. That is, no attempt is made to specify a meaning of effectiveness applicable to all groups performing all tasks. Other theorists, however, do venture statements about the meaning of effectiveness in work groups intended to apply in almost all situations in which groups work. According to Hackman (1982), effectiveness is defined by the adequacy of a group's outputs and the extent to which group members experience satisfying relations with fellow members. Similarly, sociotechnical theory (Trist, 1981) defines group effectiveness according to criteria meant to apply across the wide range of work settings in which groups exist. Both theoretical perspectives are concerned with the joint optimization of two goals through the performance of work in groups: the achievement of task-related ends and the creation of enjoyable, rewarding social conditions. To the extent that both of these goals are jointly accomplished to as great a degree as possible, groups are regarded as effective.

It is clear that the theoretical statements about the substance of effectiveness by groups and individuals differ. Situationally specific criteria are emphasized in statements about individual effectiveness while both situationally specific and universal criteria are emphasized in statements about work-group effectiveness. We prefer the development of situationally specific criteria for group as well as individual effectiveness because, as previously discussed, situationally specific criteria enhance the informativeness, accuracy, and usefulness of measures of performance. Further, as is true for individual effectiveness, it is fruitful to think of group effectiveness as varying along a continuum marked by two conceptual end points: minimally acceptable and maximally attainable performance.

The Range of Performance Effectiveness

The two end points of the continuum of effectiveness are useful in understanding how facilitators and inhibitors affect work performance. Specifically, facilitators can be thought of as environmental factors that drive performance toward its maximally attainable level, while inhibitors are environmental factors that restrict performance toward the minimally acceptable end point. Let us explore this continuum in some detail.

Minimally Acceptable Performance. Minimally acceptable performance refers to a sort of threshold. If performance dips below it, an employee may incur some jeopardy, such as a demotion, cut in pay, or termination of employment. Subthreshold performance may be redressed through means that are not punitive, such as training or transfer. However, subthreshold performance cannot be maintained in an organization without incurring the risk of penalty. We use the concept of minimally acceptable performance as an aid to depicting levels of actual effectiveness in jobs, realizing that ambiguity usually exists in the identification of any job's minimally acceptable level of performance.

The concept of minimally acceptable levels of performance has a place in organizational theory. For example, in the ideal form of bureaucracy, the specification of minimally acceptable levels of performance was meant to serve as an aid to organizational efficiency. That is, reliable performance from each member of an organization was thought attainable if all members had clear knowledge of exactly what was expected of them in order to be considered as having performed adequately. By establishing steady levels of contribution from employees, bureaucracies could, in principle, efficiently coordinate and combine those contributions into the organization's overall product or service. (See Miner, 1982.) The specification of minimally acceptable levels of performance is only one element in a constellation of characteristics and practices that comprise the true bureaucracy. A true bureaucracy also involves the exercise of rational-legal authority and rules governing behavior, subordination, contractual appointments, depersonalization, division of labor, and other characteristics that, taken together, in theory make organizations efficient.

It did not take long to recognize the discrepancy between what bureaucracy promised and what it delivered. As regards the rigid specification of work rules and minimally acceptable standards of performance, Gouldner (1955) argued that in bureaucratic organizations, standards of minimally acceptable performance become not the standards to be surpassed but the standards to be attained. An unanticipated consequence of bureaucracy, then, is increased *in*efficiency through the specification of minimally acceptable levels of performance.

An example of how the specifications of standards of performance can backfire is the creation of productivity quotas. Productivity quotas specify the minimally acceptable output of a worker or work group during a period of time (such as a shift) or the permissible number of hours to spend on a task. Rather than becoming the standard that differentiates unacceptable from acceptable performance, such quotas tend to evolve into job expectations and entitlements ("the rules say I get eight hours to rebuild this brake so I'm going to take eight hours").

Maximally Attainable Performance. The other end point of the range of work-performance effectiveness is the highest level of performance attainable. As is true for the minimally acceptable level of performance, significant ambiguity characterizes many attempts to specify an exact level of maximally attainable performance for either individuals or groups at work.

As regards individuals, the concept of maximally attainable performance typically is spoken of in only vague terms. An advertising slogan that beckons to recruits to "be all that you can be" hints at the idea of maximally attainable performance by individuals in an organization. It also strongly suggests that people can experience what might be termed self-actualization, a state of complete self-fulfillment. Self-fulfillment and maximally effective performance are distinct concepts, yet it is interesting to speculate about their possible relationship. Can maximally effective performance bring about self-fulfillment and, if so, for whom and under what circumstances? Such questions are beyond the scope of this chapter.

As regards work groups, we discussed earlier that some theories of group effectiveness (e.g., Steiner, 1972) treat the maximal level of effectiveness as an anchor, a reference point for use in explaining how and why groups fall short of that potential level of performance. The orientations toward effectiveness in individual and group literatures thus differ.

We find the distinction between minimal and maximal effectiveness to be useful for both individuals and groups because research on facilitators and inhibitors can be aligned (albeit roughly) according to the end of the performance continuum with which they are most concerned. The following sections review literature on inhibitors and facilitators to illustrate this point.

Situational Factors and Performance Effectiveness

The situational factors of concern (facilitators and inhibitors) are characteristics and conditions external to individuals and groups at work. Inhibitors of individual performance are examined first, followed by a discussion of facilitators of individual performance. Then, inhibitors and facilitators of group performance are discussed, respectively. Presented last are general conceptual issues about the nature of inhibitors and facilitators.

Inhibitors of Individual Performance

Although the dictum that behavior is a function of personal and situational characteristics has long been accepted, it has taken many years to develop theory and empirical findings that substantiate the dictum in the realm of effective work performance. Personal characteristics of interest have included such things as abilities, values, motives, and personality traits, resulting in several taxonomies of these human attributes. There has been no shortfall of personal characteristics that have been cited as potential contributors to effective work behavior.

In contrast, not until the 1970s did movement occur toward a taxonomy of situational characteristics that influence effective work performance. A stimulus to the development of such a taxonomy was the work of Schneider (1978), who focussed on the potential effect of situational variables on the link between ability and performance. In particular, Schneider suggested that situational factors might influence both the strength of the relationship between ability and performance and the average level of performance that appears at work. Schneider's work emphasized environmental factors that prevent people from fully displaying their capabilities, and it suggested that people of the highest levels of ability might be most strongly affected by such situational factors. Incentive systems, job characteristics, and organizational climate were cited as examples of situational factors that could influence the link between ability and performance. A call was made for the development of a taxonomy of situational influences on the ability–performance link.

Peters and O'Connor (1980) responded to the call, developing an empirically verified taxonomy of situational factors relevant to work performance. The focus was on situational *constraints,* defined as characteristics of the situation that interfere with the conversion of ability into effective work performance. Similarly, Naylor et al. (1980) presented a theory of determinants of effective work behavior and emphasized the role of situational constraints. A taxonomy of constraining situational factors proposed by Peters and O'Connor (1980) includes such things as job-related information, tools and equipment, and time availability. (We treat *constraints* and *inhibitors* as synonyms in this chapter.)

A series of studies conducted both in field and laboratory settings tested the ideas formulated by Peters and O'Connor. Laboratory studies (Peters et al., 1980, 1981, as cited by Olson et al., 1984) found situational constraints to be associated with poorer task performance, reduced satisfaction, and increased frustration. However, no support was found for the contention that the effects of constraints are greater for individuals high in ability than for those low in ability. In a field study that investigated the effects of constraints on frustration and satisfaction (but not performance), O'Connor et al. (1982) found that constraints were associated with decreased satisfaction and increased frustration. O'Connor et al. (1984) also found that satisfaction declined as the severity of constraints at work increased. Further, it was found that workers subject to weaker rather than stronger constraints were rated as higher performers and had lower rates of turnover. Relatedly, Peters et al. (1982) demonstrated that situational constraints moderated the relationship between individual differences and performance, such that performance was less predictable from individual characteristics when constraints were strong than when they were weak.

Similar research has been conducted by Olson et al. (1984). In a field study that involved the development of a taxonomy of constraints, they also found environmental constraints to be associated with diminished effectiveness at work. Fourteen situational factors were investigated as constraints by these researchers, including the presence of appropriate resources, tools, and equipment as well as work load, skill training, physical working conditions, and job-relevant authority.

There is some overlap between the lists of situational factors presented by Olson et al. (1984) and Peters and O'Connor (1980). Olson et al. more clearly imply that conditions can be considered either as constraints or facilitators. That is, inhibitors and facilitators are viewed as opposite ends of a single continuum. The issue of whether inhibitors and facilitators are best regarded as opposite ends of a continuum will be again addressed later in this chapter.

Another issue embedded in this body of research is its orientation toward performance. More specifically, the orientation is toward understanding why effectiveness is "low" rather than "high." It is not directed toward understanding how maximal levels of job performance can be attained by individuals at work. Measuring the effects of constraints on performance recalls the charge that Maslow (1970, p. 288) made against mainstream psychology's proclivity to study people and their behavior in highly constrained, limited settings. By way of analogy, he suggested that much of psychological research sought to measure people bent over in low rooms. He argued that such investigation tells us only about the limiting room and ignores the heights that people can attain. He further challenged psychology to concern itself with understanding those heights.

In a sense, then, research on situational constraints on individual performance tells only part of the story. It does not consider those situational factors that induce maximally attainable levels of performance. The partial story told by research on constraints, though, is substantial. The research has broadened our theoretical understanding and provided new data about determinants of individual work performance. Also, the research has great practical importance. It has identified barriers and obstacles to effective performance, making it easier to remove them from the environment.

Facilitators of Individual Performance

The bulk of existing research on facilitators of individual performance does not share a singular theme as does research on constraints. However, research on facilitators can be loosely collected under the rubric of productivity research. Using this rubric, a rather large body of literature can be located. This literature concerns how various practices and conditions in the work environment facilitate the attainment of high levels of effectiveness. (In this discussion, we treat *effectiveness* and *productivity* as synonyms.)

Reviews of this literature include Cummings (1982), Guzzo (in press), Guzzo and Bondy (1983), Katzell and Guzzo (1983), Katzell et al. (1977), and Locke et al. (1980). In them, situational factors that facilitate performance have been identified. Some are similar to factors cited by Schneider (1978) as important to the link between personal ability and performance (e.g., incentive systems). A number of other organizational conditions and practices have been identified as well. The typology of facilitating practices and conditions adopted by Guzzo et al. (1985) is used here.

Guzzo et al. investigated the effects of various intervention programs designed to raise worker productivity. The interventions consisted of planned, monitored attempts to create conditions or establish practices in organizations that would foster increased work effectiveness. The typology of interventions included realistic job previews, training programs, provision of feedback, management by objectives, goal setting, the use of financial incentives, work redesign, work rescheduling, changes in supervisory methods, and large-scale organization-development activities. Further description of the substance of these interventions is provided by Guzzo et al.

Evidence from ninety-eight studies concerning the impact of these interventions on productivity was reviewed through meta-analysis, a quantitative technique for summarizing the results of many studies. The use of meta-analysis permitted the calculation of estimates of the magnitude of the impact of the interventions. Such quantitative estimates of strength of impact made it possible to compare directly the various programs' power for changing productivity.

Overall, these interventions had a significant positive impact on productivity. (See table 2–1.) The weighted (by sample size) average effect of .44 for all intervention programs can be interpreted roughly as indicating that the average level of productivity of workers exposed to the interventions exceeded by almost one-half standard deviation the performance of workers not exposed to the interventions. Not unexpectedly, certain interventions had more powerful effects than others, as table 2–1 shows. Note that the measures of productivity used in this study were quite encompassing: any quantitative assessment of a change in the quantity, quality, rate, or cost efficiency of performance at work was included as a measure of a change in productivity, as were changes in turnover, absenteeism, and disruptions to work performance.

Table 2–1
Magnitude of Effects of Interventions to Facilitate Productivity and Effectiveness

Intervention	Average Effect Size	95% Confidence Interval
Realistic job preview	−.03	−.08 to .04
Training	.78	.56 to 1.00
Appraisal and feedback	.35	.08 to .62
Management by objectives	.12	.10 to .14
Goal setting	.75	.57 to .93
Financial incentives	.57	−.10 to 1.24
Work redesign	.42	.28 to .56
Supervisory practices	.13	.05 to .21
Work rescheduling	.21	.09 to .33
Sociotechnical changes	.62	.54 to .70

Source: Adapted from Guzzo et al. (1985).

The research reviewed by Guzzo et al. frames the question of situational influence on effectiveness as "how can current levels of effectiveness be raised by changing situational factors?" Research on inhibitors frames the question of situational influence on effectiveness as "how do situational factors hold back effectiveness?" Returning to Maslow's (1970) analogy of doing research in rooms with low ceilings, research on facilitators of effectiveness changes the dimensions of the room and observes the consequences, although the research cannot tell us what is maximally attainable effectiveness at work.

Inhibitors of Group Performance

Inhibitors of group effectiveness have not been identified and studied as such. However, through research, a number of situational factors have been identified.

Theoretical work on group effectiveness by Hackman (1982), for example, cites technological constraints as an important mediator of the degree to which a group can convert its resources into effective task performance. Also cited as a determinant of effectiveness in the Hackman model is the degree to which the organizational context supports group task performance by providing the group with appropriate information, education, and rewards. These factors resemble several of the constraints on individual performance cited by Peters and O'Connor (1980). Similarly, Shiflett (1979) also acknowledges the existence of constraints. Shiflett's work provides a formal model of effectiveness in which constraints are one element, although the work does not specify the substance of constraints. Thus, several situational factors that constrain individual performance also can be expected to constrain group performance.

Certain conditions that bring about process losses (Steiner, 1972) and thus suboptimal performance by groups can be considered inhibitors, although some of these conditions may be better regarded as properties of a group, not of its context. Group size, for example, is often negatively associated with group effectiveness, but size is an attribute of a group, not of the context in which a group performs. However, a communication network may be considered an aspect of a situation, and the type of communication network that exists for a group can inhibit its performance on a task (Davis, 1969). Communication networks determine which group members can communicate and the nature of the flow of such communication.

Other theorizing emphasizes the importance of a group's task in determining effectiveness. Considering a group's task as a contextual factor, the shared idea in this line of theorizing is that the contribution of other situational factors to group effectiveness differs according to characteristics of the group task (Shea and Guzzo, 1987; Steiner, 1972). This contingency perspective suggests that situational factors (e.g., reward systems) may act as constraints on group performance for some tasks but not others.

Facilitators of Group Performance

Although most research on task performance by groups has been oriented toward the identification of factors that prevent groups from attaining maximal effectiveness, some research exists that is oriented toward the identification of factors that act to push actual levels of group effectiveness toward maximally attainable levels. This literature on facilitators of group performance embodies a suggestion made by Hackman and Morris (1975) that researchers investigate the effects of having groups perform tasks in unconventional ways. By doing so, we reject the commonplace experiences in groups to learn if new means of organizing and managing groups enhance effectiveness. Many of the findings referred to shortly are based on reports of attempts to alter the way groups typically go about their work.

Several of these attempts focus on changing the social circumstances in which groups perform their tasks. Examples of team building for the purpose of creating greater trust among group members illustrates this approach (Woodman and Sherwood, 1980), as do various forms of process consultation (Kaplan, 1979). Broadly speaking, though, interventions of this particular sort have not been demonstrably beneficial in generating higher levels of task performance (Kaplan, 1979; Woodman and Sherwood, 1980), although such practices do induce changes in the interpersonal relationships among group members. It thus appears that social relations among group members often have little bearing on the effectiveness with which a group performs its task.

Task effectiveness does appear to be enhanced by interventions that are highly specific to the task at hand. Woodman and Sherwood (1980) report that the more task-specific an intervention, the more likely it is to pay off in greater task effectiveness in a group. In the realm of group decision making, a large number of interventions exist that facilitate increased effectiveness (Guzzo, 1986). These include procedures such as brainstorming to stimulate creative ideas, the use of the nominal group technique to integrate group members' ideas and reach decisions by voting, and quantitative methods for representing points of view in a group, thus helping groups overcome potentially disabling conflict and disagreement. The utility of these procedures is highly situationally specific. Brainstorming is not needed, for example, when good solutions to a decision problem are known. Thus, it appears that the facilitation of task performance by groups is often best accomplished through changes in practices tailored to specific contexts.

Not all facilitators of group effectiveness need to be considered situationally specific, however. Reward practices for recognizing effective groups and autonomy given a group to carry out its work may serve as facilitators in a wide range of contexts. Autonomy is emphasized both by Hackman's (1982) theory and sociotechnical theory (Trist, 1981) as an essential ingredient in the creation of effective task-performing groups in all contexts. Other trans-situational facilitators may be identifiable as well.

Note that, as with analyses of individual performance, investigations of inhibitors and facilitators of group performance frame the question of situational influence in different ways. Research on constraints largely concerns "subtractions," emphasizing process losses and situational handicaps. Research on facilitators of group performance, in contrast, tends to concern "additions" in the sense of learning what can be changed to enable groups to raise their level of performance. Thus, for both individuals and groups, factors identified as inhibitors differ from those identified as facilitators.

The Relationship between Facilitators and Inhibitors

Contextual factors that detract from the effectiveness of individuals and groups performing tasks are inhibitors or constraints. Those that foster increased effectiveness are facilitators. But what is the relation between facilitators and inhibitors? Is the absence of an inhibiting condition necessarily facilitating? Are facilitators and inhibitors opposites?

As mentioned earlier, previous work has addressed the conceptual distinction between facilitators and inhibitors, although we believe it has done so only in a limited way. Olson et al. (1984), for example, developed a taxonomy of situational influences on performance in the military. In the taxonomy reported, facilitators and inhibitors mostly are represented as opposites. Thus, for example, the lack of tools and equipment needed to do a job is considered an inhibitor of performance and the presence of necessary tools and equipment is considered a facilitator. The same is true for other situational factors such as time available and amount of job-related information. Deficits in either of these factors are regarded as inhibitors of performance, while a sufficiency of either is regarded as a facilitator.

We believe that it is wiser to regard inhibitors and facilitators as distinct entities, not as opposites. Thus, the absence of needed tools, time, information, and so on surely inhibit performance for individuals and groups. However, their sufficiency should not be necessarily regarded as a facilitator. We find it useful to regard inhibitors as situational factors that restrict performance, constraining it to minimally acceptable levels. Facilitators, on the other hand, are regarded as situational factors that drive performance toward the level of maximal effectiveness. Such conditions need not drive performance completely to its maximally effective level, though, to be considered facilitators.

Conceptualizing inhibitors and facilitators, not as opposites, but as distinct situational factors (with inhibitors' effects constraining performance to be near the minimally acceptable end of the performance effectiveness continuum and, on the other hand, facilitators' effects elevating performance toward the maximally attainable end of the effectiveness continuum) has certain advantages. One advantage is a degree of conceptual clarity. With this distinction in mind, it is possible to develop unique taxonomies of inhibitors (constraints) and facilitators, thus simplifying the taxonomic task and yielding concrete rather than abstract categorizations of situational factors that affect performance.

A further advantage of the present conceptualization of inhibitors and facilitators is its practical value. In organizations, the question "why isn't performance up to standards?" will likely generate a different response than the question "how can we improve performance around here?" To answer the former, look to the role of constraining factors in the environment and remedy the situation by acting on identified deficiencies. To answer the latter, look to what is known about potential facilitators and add them to the situation. Thus, the present conceptualization has diagnostic value when making efforts to change the level of work effectiveness in an organization.

How Facilitators and Inhibitors Affect Performance

The preceding section provided evidence that a variety of situational factors influence the level of effectiveness of individuals and groups at work. Not addressed in the preceding section, however, is *why* facilitators and inhibitors influence effectiveness. In particular, no attention was given to possible mediating processes through which facilitators and inhibitors affect performance. The objective of this final section of the chapter is to present an analysis of such mediating processes.

A Model of Individual Performance

A model of individual performance formulated by Campbell and Pritchard (1976) is a useful device for understanding why facilitators and inhibitors affect performance. Although the model was explicitly devised with regard to individual performance effectiveness, elements of the model are useful, by analogy, to understanding the performance effectiveness of groups at work as well. The model is shown in table 2–2.

Before using the model in table 2–2 to interpret the effects of facilitators and inhibitors, a few explanatory comments are in order. For present purposes, we shall regard *performance* as used in the model as equivalent to *effectiveness* in the work context. In the model, *aptitude* refers to the potential of an individual to perform well on a job and *skill* refers to the present

Table 2–2
A Model of Individual Performance

Performance	=	f (aptitude level	×	skill level	×	understanding of the task
		×	choice to expend effort	×	choice of degree of effort to expend	
		×	choice to persist	×	facilitating and inhibiting conditions not under the control of the individual)	

Source: Campbell and Pritchard (1976).

capability of an individual to perform a job. The term *understanding of the task* refers to the knowledge a person has about the level of performance expected, goals and objectives to be attained through the task, and methods and procedures for executing the work at hand. Conflicting or ambiguous information about one's role at work affects the understanding of the task. This term of the model represents informational determinants of performance. The model also cites three types of choices made by individuals. These choices, reflecting the role of motivation in performance (Campbell and Pritchard, 1976, p. 65), deal with the initiation, amount, and persistence of effort expended toward task performance. The final term of the model concerns environmental factors that affect performance: facilitators and inhibitors.

Note that the model defines facilitators and inhibitors as causes of performance that are separate and conceptually independent of the other terms in the model. We take issue with this. We suggest that facilitators have their effects on performance through their impact on the other terms of the model. That is, the effects of facilitators on performance are indirect and mediated. Facilitators affect performance because they change the skill levels, choices to persist, and other factors that, in turn, directly affect performance.

On the other hand, we hypothesize that inhibitors have *both* direct and indirect effects on performance. That is, inhibitors directly contribute to restricted effectiveness at work as well as bring about changes in the other direct determinants of performance effectiveness. These points are elaborated shortly with reference both to individual and group effectiveness at work.

Effects and Characteristics of Facilitators

In addition to the assertion that the effects of facilitators are mediated, there are three additional points we wish to convey. First, facilitators simultaneously affect several of the direct causes of performance effectiveness identified in the Campbell and Pritchard (1976) model. That is, the effects of facilitators tend to be mediated by multiple rather than single direct causes of performance effectiveness. Second, there is great uncertainty about the effects of facilitators. It is possible to know precisely neither the strength of the effect of a facilitator nor which of several immediate causes of performance a facilitator will affect in any instance. Third, because of the considerable uncertainty in the effects of facilitators, it is important to be *redundant* (that is, to use several facilitators) when attempting to raise performance effectiveness through the use of facilitators. These three points are elaborated next.

Multiple Effects. Consider the facilitators of performance identified in table 2–1 and how their effect is mediated by the direct causes of performance cited in the Campbell and Pritchard (1976) model. It is apparent that the facilitators of table 2–1 simultaneously affect more than one direct cause of performance appearing in the model. Goal setting illustrates this point.

Goal setting can affect motivation, according to the terms of the model in table 2–2. Specifically, the presence of goals can make a person more likely to choose to expend effort to accomplish a task. Goal difficulty has been shown to be positively related to performance (Locke et al., 1981), indicating that the choice of the degree of effort to expend is influenced by goal difficulty. Similarly, persistence at a task can be influenced by the presence of identifiable goals.

In addition, goals can affect the understanding one has of the task. One of the postulated effects of goals is the stimulation of planning and strategic thinking about how best to attain a goal and thus complete a task (Locke et al., 1981). Further, attaining or failing to attain goals is a source of feedback that can develop one's understanding of one's job in a way that aids effectiveness. The effects of goals on performance are thus mediated by several immediate determinants of performance. These determinants are both motivational and informational in nature.

Other facilitators listed in table 2–1 also can be regarded as having their overall impact mediated by multiple direct determinants of effective performance. Financial incentives, for example, can affect multiple motivational determinants. Changes in supervisory practices, such as the adoption of participative decision making, also can affect motivational and informational determinants of effectiveness. Training can be employed to change skills, information, and motivation. The effects of factors identified as facilitators, then, are mediated by direct causes of performance and the effects of any one facilitator tend to be mediated by more than one direct cause of performance.

Uncertainty. Uncertainty exists regarding the effects of facilitators. Uncertainty exists both about the magnitude of the effect of facilitating conditions and about which direct causes of effectiveness are affected at any time by facilitators.

The use of economic incentives as facilitators of performance illustrates uncertainty of magnitude of effect. Table 2–1 shows that, on average, financial incentives serve as facilitators of effectiveness, but that there is wide variation in the magnitude of the effect of financial incentives. The confidence interval reported in table 2–1 shows this, and, as Guzzo et al. (1985) report, the effect of financial incentives was strongly positive in some cases and in others nonexistent or negative. It appears that the effect of financial incentives depends on several yet-to-be-understood situational factors. The same is true for other facilitating conditions—there is substantial variation in their effects. The picture of facilitators is this: facilitators are events and circumstances whose contribution to effective task performance is carried by several direct causes that themselves are affected in varying ways by facilitators. With additional data and continued development of theory, the uncertainty surrounding the effects of facilitators may be reduced. At present, though, the existence of uncertainty has a distinct implication for practice: the need for redundancy.

Redundancy. Redundancy refers to duplication and repetition. When creating facilitating conditions, redundancy is a means of countering the uncertainty inherent in the effects of facilitators. Rather than implementing a single change of circumstances or a single new practice, either of which is thought to be a facilitator or performance, the "doctrine of redundancy" calls for several changes of circumstances or practices since it is never certain whether any one change will actually have its intended impact or what magnitude its impact might be. Just as redundancy in communication ensures accurate transmissions and redundancy in the design of mechanical systems of airplanes ensures successful flights, so, too, can redundancy in the use of facilitators ensure the successful enhancement of performance.

There is, frankly, little evidence for this assertion, although we are not alone in making it. (See Hackman, 1985.) Relatively few studies exist of the effect of attempts to create redundant conditions designed to enhance performance. And rarely is the importance of redundancy directly investigated. However, in their review of the literature of interventions designed to affect productivity, Guzzo et al. (1985) found that the impact of multiple simultaneous interventions tended to be more strongly positive than interventions designed to alter only one aspect of the workplace. Further, what Guzzo et al. classified as sociotechnical interventions typically involved several changes in workplace conditions and practices. This type of intervention was found to have strong favorable effects on performance. Thus, what little evidence exists indicates that redundant (or at least partially redundant) interventions designed to create facilitating conditions are likely to be successful.

Effects and Characteristics of Inhibitors

It was stated earlier that inhibitors are hypothesized to have indirect effects on performance effectiveness. That is, inhibitors can affect any of the several direct causes of performance cited by Campbell and Pritchard (1976). Conditions identified by Peters and O'Connor (1980) and Olson et al. (1984) such as inadequate job information and insufficient tools are interpretable in terms of their effects on informational determinants of effective performance while inappropriate workloads and other conditions can be understood in terms of their motivational impact. Thus, the effects of inhibitors are, in part, mediated.

Additionally, inhibitors directly affect performance. Barriers to performance such as shortages of tools and too little time can make it physically impossible to complete tasks effectively. Severely inhibiting conditions may have psychological consequences such as anger, frustration, and dissatisfaction (see Olson et al., 1984) in addition to their effects on motivational and informational determinants of performance. But impairment of performance can be directly attributable to such inhibitors, not just to their mediated effects. The more severe the inhibitor, the more easily its direct effects may be observed.

A final interesting possibility to consider is that constraints in the environment may actually have *beneficial* effects on performance. For example, this would be true if the constraints were regarded as posing a challenge to be overcome. Countless examples exist of jerry-built solutions resulting from opportunistic use of limited resources. It is probably the case that only in the short term can inhibitors be a stimulus to effectiveness; effective performance could not be maintained in the presence of enduring inhibiting conditions.

Conclusion

The ideas presented in this chapter are hypotheses, often quite speculative in nature, about the nature and operation of facilitators and inhibitors. These environmental conditions are not viewed as opposites. Instead, facilitators are viewed as distinct features of a work environment that tend to push the performance of individuals and groups toward levels of maximal effectiveness. Further, the effects of facilitators are regarded as mediated by direct causes of performance such as information, motivation, and skill level. There are perhaps more differences than similarities among facilitators of individual and group effectiveness, but facilitators exist for each and operate in an analogous fashion. For both groups and individuals, the effects of facilitators are imbued with uncertainty. This uncertainty demands redundancy in the creation of facilitators to ensure their success in raising performance effectiveness.

Inhibitors, on the other hand, tend to restrict performance toward minimally acceptable levels of effectiveness by individuals and groups. Like facilitators, inhibitors have indirect effects on performance but, unlike facilitators, inhibitors also directly affect performance. Recognizing inhibitors that exist in a workplace has great practical value, as does recognizing the opportunities to create facilitating working conditions.

References

Bernardin, H. J., and Beatty, R. W. (1984). *Performance appraisal.* Boston: Kent.

Campbell, J. P., and Pritchard, R. D. (1976). Motivation theory in industrial and organizational psychology. In M. D. Dunnette (ed.), *Handbook of industrial and organizational psychology.* Chicago: Rand McNally.

Cummings, L. L. (1982). *Improving human resource effectiveness.* Berea, Ohio: ASPA Foundation.

Davis, J. (1969). *Group performance.* Reading, Mass.: Addison-Wesley.

Gouldner, A. W. (1955). *Patterns of industrial bureaucracy.* New York: Routledge and Kegan Paul.

Guzzo, R. A. (1986). Group decision making and group effectiveness in organizations. In P. S. Goodman (ed.), *Designing effective work groups.* San Francisco: Jossey-Bass.

Guzzo, R. A. (in press). Productivity research in review. In J. P. Campbell and R. J. Campbell (eds.), *Individual and group productivity in organizations.* San Francisco: Jossey-Bass.

Guzzo, R. A., and Bondy, J. S. (1983). *A guide to worker productivity experiments in the United States, 1976–81.* New York: Pergamon.

Guzzo, R. A., Jette, R. D., and Katzell, R. A. (1985). The effects of psychologically based intervention programs on worker productivity: A meta-analysis. *Personnel Psychology, 38,* 275–91.

Hackman, J. R. (1982). A set of methods for research on work teams. Technical Report 1. New Haven, Conn.: School of Organization and Management, Yale University.

Hackman, J. R. (1985). Doing research that makes a difference. In E. E. Lawler, A. M. Mohrman, S. A. Mohrman, G. E. Ledford, and T. G. Cummings (eds.), *Doing research that is useful for theory and practice.* San Francisco: Jossey-Bass.

Hackman, J. R., and Morris, C. G. (1975). Group tasks, group interaction process, and group effectiveness: A review and proposed integration. In L. Berkowitz (ed.), *Advances in experimental social psychology,* vol. 8. New York: Academic Press.

Ilgen, D. R., Fisher, C. D. and Taylor, M. S. (1979). Consequences of individual feedback on behavior in organizations. *Journal of Applied Psychology, 64,* 349–71.

Kaplan, R. E. (1979). The conspicuous absence of evidence that process consultation enhances task performance. *Journal of Applied Behavioral Science, 15,* 346–60.

Katzell, R. A., and Guzzo, R. A. (1983). Psychological approaches to productivity improvement. *American Psychologist, 38,* 468–72.

Katzell, R. A., Bienstock, P., and Faerstein, P. H. (1977). *A guide to worker produc-*

tivity experiments in the United States, 1971–75. New York: New York University Press.

Latané, B. (1986). Responsibility and effort in organizations. In P. S. Goodman (ed.), *Designing effective work groups.* San Francisco: Jossey-Bass.

Latham, G. P., and Wexley, K. N. (1981). *Increasing productivity through performance appraisal.* Reading, Mass.: Addison-Wesley.

Locke, E. A., Feren, D. B., McCaleb, V. M., Shaw, K. N., and Denny, A. T. (1980). The relative effectiveness of four methods of motivating employee performance. In K. D. Duncan, M. M. Gruneberg, and D. Wallis (eds.), *Changes in work life.* New York: Wiley.

Locke, E. A., Shaw, K. N., Saari, L. M., and Latham, G. P. (1981). Goal setting and task performance: 1969–1980. *Psychological Bulletin, 90,* 125–52.

Maslow, A. H. (1970). *Motivation and personality,* 2nd ed. New York: Harper and Row.

Miner, J. B. (1982). *Theories of organizational structure and process.* Chicago: Dryden.

Naylor, J. C., Pritchard, R. D., and Ilgen, D. R. (1980). *A theory of behavior in organizations.* New York: Academic Press.

O'Connor, E. J., Peters, L. H., Rudolph, C. J., and Pooyan, A. (1982). Situational constraints and employee affective reactions: A partial field replication. *Group and Organization Studies, 7,* 418–28.

O'Connor, E. J., Peters, L. H., Pooyan, A., Weekley, J., Frank, B., and Erenkrantz, B. (1984). Situational constraint effects on performance, affective reactions, and turnover: A field replication and extension. *Journal of Applied Psychology, 69,* 663–72.

Olson, D. M., Borman, W. C., Roberson, L., and Rose, S. R. (1984). Relationships between scales on an Army work questionnaire and measures of performance. Paper presented at the 92nd Annual Meeting of the American Psychological Association, Toronto.

Peters, L. H., and O'Connor, E. J. (1980). Situational constraints and work outcomes: The influence of a frequently overlooked construct. *Academy of Management Review, 5,* 391–97.

Peters, L. H., O'Connor, E. J., and Rudolph, C. J. (1980). The behavioral and affective consequences of performance—relevant situational variables. *Organizational Behavior and Human Performance, 25,* 79–96.

Peters, L. H., Chassie, M. B., Lindholm, H. R., O'Connor, E. J., and Rudolph, C. J. (1981). The joint influence of situational constraints and goal setting on performance and affective outcomes. Paper presented at the Meeting of the Southwest Academy of Management, Houston.

Peters, L. H., Fisher, C. D., and O'Connor, E. J. (1982). The moderating effect of situational control of performance variance on the relationship between individual differences and performance. *Personnel Psychology, 35,* 609–21.

Schneider, B. (1978). Person—situation selection: A review of some ability—situation interaction research. *Personnel Psychology, 31,* 281–97.

Shea, G. P., and Guzzo, R. A. (1987). Groups as human resources. In K. M. Rowland and G. R. Ferris (eds.), *Research in personnel and human resources management,* vol. 5. Greenwich, Conn.: JAI Press.

Shiflett, S. (1979). Toward a general model of small group productivity. *Psychological Bulletin, 86,* 67–79.

Smith, P. C. (1976). Behaviors, results, and organizational effectiveness: The problem of criteria. In M. D. Dunnette (ed.), *Handbook of industrial and organizational psychology.* Chicago: Rand McNally.

Staw, B. M. (1984). Organizational behavior: A review and reformulation of the field's outcome variables. In M. Rosenzweig and L. W. Porter (eds.), *Annual review of psychology,* vol. 35. Palo Alto, Calif.: Annual Reviews.

Steiner, I. D. (1972). *Group process and productivity.* New York: Academic Press.

Trist, E. (1981). *Evolution of socio-technical systems.* Toronto: Ontario Quality of Working Life Centre.

Woodman, R. W., and Sherwood, J. J. (1980). The role of team development in organizational effectiveness: A critical review. *Psychological Bulletin, 88,* 166–86.

3

Some Characteristics and Consequences of Organizational Reward

Steven Kerr

Many theories and models of human motivation have established their place in the organizational behavior literature. Achievement motivation theory, two-factor theory, expectancy theory, reinforcement theory, cognitive dissonance theory, and articulations of various needs hierarchies disagree in many important respects, but share a belief in the guiding force of hedonism—Man as a seeker of pleasure, however pleasure is defined, and as an avoider of discomfort, stress, and pain (Bentham, 1875; Spencer, 1899). Within this context, it seems safe to conclude that people join work organizations for private, even selfish reasons; they hope that through membership in an organization and participation in its activities, a variety of personal needs will be satisfied. Largely as a result, modern organization theory has come to grips with the premise that member agreement on what constitutes an organization's goal is usually limited to agreement about highly ambiguous, general statements. Such vague agreement typically conceals considerable dissensus about strategies and subgoals, with the result that organizations usually appear to pursue many different, even conflicting goals at the same time. Once this is understood, it is easy to see why "ultimately it makes only slightly more sense to say that the goal of a business organization is to maximize profit than to say that its goal is to maximize the salary of Sam Smith, Assistant to the Janitor" (Cyert and March, 1963, p. 30).

That people have personal needs is a constraint, but not necessarily a critical one, upon the ability of an organization—or those who act in its name—to make plans and take action in pursuit of collective outcomes, however vaguely defined. A major determinant of the degree of criticality of this constraint is whether the organization's reward and punishment systems encourage or discourage its members from pursuing these collective outcomes. This problem is often identified as one of "motivation," which is usually defined in terms of behavior that is purposive (Bindra, 1959), goal-directed (Lawler, 1973; Chung, 1977), and reflective of people's choices among alternative forms of voluntary activity (Vroom, 1964). A glance at these definitions is sufficient to see, however, that the problem is not one of motivation, but of *goal congruence*. With the exception of reflexive actions and, to a certain extent, frustration-instigated actions, nearly all behavior is purposive and reflective of some degree of choice among alternatives. An employee who for example:

sneaks down the back steps to get coffee, in violation of the rules,

calls in sick every Monday morning,

goes home at night with half the firm's office equipment

is engaging in highly motivated behavior, according to almost anybody's definition. The essential truth is not that such employees are not motivated; it is that such personal need fulfillment by some organization members is incongruent with, and likely to frustrate, the (public or personal) needs of other members. To the extent that these other members are desirous of accomplishing the ambiguous, general outcomes that have been labeled organizational goals, they will probably conclude that coworker behaviors of the kind just described are disloyal and undesirable, and they will therefore seek to prevent such behaviors from occurring. For such prevention, they will probably depend upon selection (whereby people with the "wrong" goals and motives are kept from becoming members), training (by which goals and motives are, presumably, improved by means of orientation or indoctrination), and assimilation through gentle exposure to the organization's myths, norms, and values.

Such methods are well conceived, but are not wholly adequate for the task. Our tools of selection are imperfect and becoming more so under the growing barrage of government constraints. Training for the purpose of altering skills and knowledge is far more reliable than training to change goals and values, and assimilation is often a time-consuming, unpredictable process. As a result, many organization members retain incongruent goals and motives despite selection, training, and exposure to culture. (Occasionally, as a result of these experiences, they even develop new incongruities.)

Therefore, an effective reward and punishment system may be defined as one that takes as given the existence of incongruities in member goals and motives, and seeks to reduce these through intelligent use of quid pro quos. Rather than regarding people's tendencies toward selfishness as an insurmountable barrier, an effective reward–punishment system takes the personal goals of people as a fact of life, and it uses these personal goals to stimulate participation and performance. If a reward–punishment system could be made to operate perfectly, people would pursue common objectives neither because they have been selected as martyrs nor because they have been made noble through training, but for that most reliable of all reasons—the perception by all employees that it is in their personal best interests to do so.

Yet we shall argue that most reward systems are so far from perfect that they often encourage behaviors antithetical to organizational goals and undesired by the rewarder, while ignoring—and sometimes even punishing—desired behaviors. Rather than *facilitating* goal-oriented organizational behavior, rewards dispensed by such systems actually serve as *inhibitors* of performance.

Is this argument valid? How can it be determined whether an organization's reward system is malfunctioning in this manner? The next section of this chapter will describe one method of collecting, organizing, and interpreting data so as to address these questions.

Describing the Reward System: An Organizational Diagnostic

Step 1: What Are the Rewards?

Strictly speaking, we ought to be thinking not of rewards but of reinforcers—things that maintain or strengthen behavior. However, as has been pointed out by Luthans and Kreitner (1975), it is impossible to know in advance which intended reinforcers will, in fact, prove reinforcing. In any case, managers are accustomed to think and speak about rewards, not reinforcers, so we shall do the same here.

Consistent with motivation theories and with the practice of most organizations, it is possible to identify three reward types that, though they possess overlapping elements, may be considered to be relatively distinct. These three types of rewards are financial, prestige, and job content.

Financial. Among practicing managers, the belief is widespread that money and things closely related to money are the most powerful facilitators of subordinate effort and performance. As Lawler (1971, p. 62) has pointed out, "the evidence indicates that managers consistently tend to overestimate the importance of pay to their subordinates," compared to subordinates' self-estimations of its importance. By *pay* is meant "the money, fringe benefits, and other commodities that have financial value which organizations give to employees in return for their services" (Lawler, 1971, p. 1).

To assemble an inventory of pay-related rewards is for most organizations a simple, straightforward exercise. Far more difficult is to assign a weight to each reward that accurately reflects the extent to which it is valued by subordinates. When management makes assumptions about such values without subordinate input, the results may be calamitous. For example, one midwestern manufacturer spent a fortune each year on a showcase, industry-leading program of insurance and retirement benefits, only to eventually learn that the program was grossly undervalued by most employees. Even employees in poor health or fairly close to retirement were often unapprecia-tive of the firm's benefit program and in some cases were even leaving the company for what management considered to be inferior opportunities else-where. (Eventually the firm commissioned research on the subject and learned that few workers understood the program well enough to place an accurate value upon it; translating the program's provisions into simple words and cartoons alleviated the problem.) Meanwhile, the firm ended its support of an infinitely smaller financial reward—support for some after-hour employee organizations—only to promptly find itself the target of a wildcat walkout in one if its Canadian subsidiaries. Though the financial cost to the company was low, the felt value of the firm's hockey team was appar-ently quite high! This example illustrates one of the more interesting research findings about organizational reward systems—that the power of a reward to "motivate" (that is, to create goal congruence) is virtually unrelated to its cost.

Prestige. These rewards usually incur some financial cost to the organization and, because they add to recipients' prestige, can have a subsequent effect upon their earning power. Nevertheless, the distinguishing feature of pres-tige-related rewards is that, unlike financial rewards, their receipt has no di-rect effect upon the recipient's financial well-being. Their intended purpose is to increase the respect, acceptance, and envy of the recipient by other indi-viduals, either within or outside the organization.

Job Content. As Lawler (1973, p. 153) has pointed out, "Individual re-sponses to enriched jobs may vary, but . . . depending on how the work is arranged, jobs can provide various kinds of opportunities for employees to satisfy important needs and to achieve important goals." Research on job enrichment (cf. Steers and Porter, 1979, pp. 406–7) suggests that job content can act as a reward to the extent that it provides an incumbent with:

> experienced meaningfulness—a feeling that the work is important and worthwhile;

> experienced responsibility—a feeling of personal accountability for the outcomes of work performed; and

> knowledge of results—an understanding of whether effort has been suc-cessful, and performance effective.

In general, job content is an important determinant of the extent to which organization members will experience these psychological states.

Step 2: What Behaviors Are Facilitated by Rewards?

After cataloguing the various financial, prestige, and job-content rewards, the next step in performing the diagnostic is to obtain information concerning member perceptions of how (that is, for what sorts of behaviors) rewards are obtained. Depending on how organizational rewards are distributed, they may—either intentionally or inadvertently—inhibit or facilitate individual and/or group performance.

Individual Performance. For a reward to be labeled as facilitating individual performance, recipients must believe that they are more likely to receive it (or to receive more of it) if they as individuals perform well than if they perform poorly.

Group Performance. For a reward to be labeled as facilitating group performance, organization members must believe that they will all share in its distribution if the group performs well. The term *group* may refer to a small work team or task force, an operating plant or subdivision, or the organization as a whole.

There is a tendency for U.S. organizations to rely—some would say over-rely—upon individual rewards, even when they are probably inappropriate, just as Japanese firms depend much more heavily upon group rewards. Actually, whether group performance is superior to individual performance as a determinant of rewards depends upon many factors, including the nature of the task being performed, the size of the work group, the social environment, and the particular incentive plan employed (Opsahl and Dunnette, 1966). In general, individual performance is a superior basis for rewards from the standpoint that workers can more readily see the relationship between their efforts and the rewards they receive. On the other hand, rewards for group performance are more likely to foster collaboration than competition.

Making rewards dependent upon performance—whether individual or group—is consistent with most prevailing views of motivation, including operant and expectancy theories. Nevertheless, it is all too seldom practiced in ongoing organizations. The truth of this statement may seem suspect since, for example, nearly all organizations claim to implement "pay for performance" and label their reward and punishment mechanisms as merit systems. In truth, however, "the contingency connection between performance and pay is slowly but steadily being eroded" (Luthans and Kreitner, 1975, p. 105). Even when the distribution of rewards does take recipients' performance into account, many organizations violate the principle that rewards must be dispensed in such a way as to be perceived as meaningfully greater—in magnitude and/or likelihood of attainment—for high than for low performance. In this respect, Lawler (1971, p. 72) found that "by far the most common sin committed by organizations is to offer too small . . . a financial reward when pay is used to motivate performance." The same conclusion was reached by Hamner (1975) and by Meyer (1975) with respect to economic rewards. The allocation of nonfinancial rewards has been less often studied, but it is probably even more true of such rewards that their administration is usually governed more by other factors than by recipients' performance.

Attendance. There is an old saw that organizations nearly always set out to measure and reward performance but, if the task proves too onerous, attendance—being on time, appearing every day, shuffling papers, and "walking busy"—tends to be focussed on instead. Remember that business firms almost never own up to the fact that attendance is a major determinant of rewards. Even blatant disregarders of performance often claim to operate a merit system. For example, in the group health claims division of a large eastern insurance company that boasted to new hires of its pay-for-performance system, the salary increase formula was as follows:

1. If the worker is "outstanding" (a select category, into which no more than two employees per section may be placed): 5 percent

2. If the worker is "above average" (normally all workers not "outstanding" are so rated): 4 percent. . . .

Now, since . . . the difference between the 5 percent theoretically attainable through hard work and the 4 percent attainable merely by living until the review date is small . . . many employees are rather indifferent to the possibility of obtaining the extra 1 percent reward. . . .

However, most employees are not indifferent to the rule which states that, should absences or latenesses total three or more in any 6-month period, the entire 4 or 5 percent due at the next "merit" review must be forfeited. In this sense, the firm may be described as *hoping* for performance, while *rewarding* attendance. (Kerr, 1975, pp. 78–79)

Membership. The old saw goes on to say that if measuring and rewarding attendance also proves too onerous a chore, then rewards tend to be distributed for mere membership in the organization. Some membership rewards are *fixed* in that all members are offered them upon entry as a reward *for* entry. Thus, university employees are granted library rights, members of the military have immediate access to low-cost consumer goods at base exchanges, and many organizations sponsor after-hour athletic and social clubs that all employees may join. Other membership rewards are *variable,* which means that one must be a member for a specified time to receive the reward (e.g., a 20-year pin), or that the longer one has been a member, the more of the reward one is entitled to. (Vacation days are usually of this type.)

We are not arguing here that all rewards ought to be distributed solely for group or individual performance. Most people prefer to have some solid flooring, some base they can rely upon. Particularly in light of the dubious credibility of many performance-appraisal systems in the eyes of those who must live under them, few employees would prefer to have all their rewards wholly determined by how well they were judged to be performing. It is probably desirable that some rewards, (for example, insurance and retirement benefits) accrue primarily for membership.

Nevertheless, making rewards dependent upon membership is inconsistent with nearly all modern theories of motivation, and it tends to result in erratic and frequently dysfunctional member behavior. For example, Bandura (1969, p. 28) has pointed out that under such conditions, "the response output following reinforcement is very low but accelerates rapidly as the time for the next reinforcement approaches. . . . The fixed-interval schedule is likely to generate only the minimum output expected in a given situation, particularly if the activity itself is somewhat unpleasant."

Despite these theoretical and empirically observable disadvantages, membership-based reward systems are highly prevalent among modern organizations. (Cf. Luthans and Kreitner, 1975.) Boosted directly by many unions and indirectly by many judges and government agencies, their use is steadily increasing as well.

Hierarchical Level. Sometimes rewards are made available to all employees who advance to a particular level within the organization. Authorization to travel first class, rather than coach, and admission to a firm's executive dining room are examples of this type of reward. Whether or not such rewards are performance-based depends upon the extent to which performance plays a major role in determining which employees are promoted. Even when promotions are largely performance-based, they may still be of limited usefulness as reward-system components. This is because (1) in most cases, they can be awarded to a particular individual only infrequently and (2) because promotions have such a major impact on the work lives of most recipients—typically causing changes in authority, responsibilities, job duties, and so on—they are often regarded by potential recipients with mixed emotions and in some cases may actually be resisted or refused.

Other. Organizations sometimes present rewards for reasons other than those just described. Race, sex, common school ties, hazards and unpleasantries of job duties, incentives offered by the overall job market or by particular competitors, and numerous other factors all serve to influence the distribution of valued rewards.

Step 3: Who Controls the Distribution of Rewards?

The next step in the reward system diagnostic is to obtain data about people's perceptions of where control resides over each organizational reward. In general, control of rewards tends to be exerted by some combination of the following individual and power centers:

Organization Policy. In some cases, rewards are distributed in strict accordance with prearranged rules and policies and can only be altered, if they can be altered at all, through actions initiated at the highest organization levels. Often sick leave, retirement benefits, and insurance coverage are of this nature, as may be various prestige-related rewards such as those pertaining to office size and location. To grant a new hire five weeks vacation, for example, or to locate a low-level worker in a vice-presidential office would require that changes be made in many organizations' official policies.

High-Level Management. In other cases, a reward can be distributed without change in policy but, from the vantage point of any particular respondent, such a distribution requires action by someone at a higher level than the respondent's immediate supervisor. For example, to close the office at noon on New Year's Eve would probably not be a violation of official policies but, for most employees, would require that a decision be made by someone at a level above their superior's.

The Union. In unionized organizations, a number of rewards are usually specified in contracts and cannot be altered during the life of the contracts except through complex renegotiations.

Personnel Division. The extent to which Personnel (or Human Resources) exerts influence over the distribution of rewards varies greatly from firm to firm, but in some places Personnel enjoys considerable discretion over the magnitude, and even more discretion over the timing, of a wide variety of organization rewards.

Immediate Superior. This category encompasses all rewards that, from the vantage point of a respondent, can be administered at the discretion of the respondent's direct superior.

Self. In this category are included all rewards that a particular respondent feels he or she controls personally.

Automatic Receipt over Time. Rewards falling into this category consist of those described earlier as being dispensed for either fixed or variable "membership." They are listed here among the "who controls" categories although, since they accrue either immediately upon entry or automatically over time, they are only within an organization's control to the extent that it has the ability to terminate employees. In many cases, union contracts, civil service regulations, company tradition, or other forces make it all but impossible to invoke the power of discharge. In other cases, a termination can be effected, but the severed employee retains rights to certain organization rewards. (Thus, many discharged baseball managers continue to collect salary, and U.S. ex-presidents continue to enjoy the benefits of Secret Service protection.) It can therefore be argued that rewards that are dispensed automatically over time are "controlled" by the organization in only the loosest sense of the word.

Step 4: What Organizational Consequences Are Facilitated by Employee Behaviors?

Step 2 used the menu of rewards identified in step 1 as its reference point, and it sought information about how (for what behaviors) each reward was obtained. Step 4 proceeds from the opposite perspective, starting with a menu of employee behaviors and seeking to learn what employees believe will happen to them if they carry out those behaviors.

To be maximally informative, it is important that the menu of behaviors be established not by the researcher/consultant, but by organization members themselves, as they attempt to address the following questions:

1. What are the most important goals and objectives of your organization and of your work group?
2. What are the employee behaviors you feel are most important in *facilitating* the goals and objectives you mentioned? Describe them.
3. What are the employee behaviors you feel are most important in *inhibiting* the goals and objectives mentioned? Describe them.

Respondents are told to be as explicit as they can and to make the lists as long as they can. They are encouraged to be behavioral in their descriptions if they prefer (e.g., "it's important that employees be willing to take risks") or to be quantitative if that is their preference (e.g., "we have to increase our sales calls at least 25 percent").

Responses to questions 2 and 3 are then combined into a single list, with responses mixed together so that nobody but the researcher and the contributor of each item know whether a response was offered as a facilitator or as an inhibitor of performance. The consolidated list is then presented to subordinates of those who have contributed items to the list, and these subordinates are asked to predict whether they would receive rewards or punishment, approval or disapproval if they performed each of the actions described (or whether the organization's reward system is so opaque to them that they can make no prediction).

Appendix 3–A1 contains a representative listing of responses to steps 1 and 4, taken from actual administrations of the diagnostic questionnaire.

Collecting the Data

Reward-system diagnostics of the kind just described have been performed by the author in approximately thirty-five organizations during the past ten years. It is reasonable to suppose that so many administrations, over so long a period, would have produced a data-collection tool with acceptable psychometric properties. Such a supposition would be false for several reasons.

First, the methodology has varied considerably from administration to administration. In many cases, data have been collected during various management training programs of half-day to one-day duration. In some of these programs, the information was reported verbally, with no hard-copy accompaniment. In other programs, participants turned in written analyses of their reward systems. In addition to the data obtained during these programs, questionnaires were administered in eighteen organizations, including two Veterans Administration hospitals, one large state university, and eight large (Fortune 500) and seven small corporations. Data from three other corporations were obtained solely through interviews.

Data from the early questionnaires were useful chiefly to demonstrate the virtual worthlessness of the original version of the instrument. A second version proved better, but was also eventually discarded in favor of the third, present form. This version has been subjected to various tests of reliability and validity.[1] However, these are made more difficult by the fact that each organization that has used the diagnostic has—for the best of reasons—altered its contents. In the form most often used, it is comprised of seven detailed modules, and thus far no organization has proved gullible enough to permit administration of all seven. Furthermore, the two modules most often used—the menu of rewards (obtained in step 1) and the list of desired and undesired employee behaviors (step 4)—are always tailored to fit particular organization interests and requirements. Considered together, these methodological no-nos mean that adequate normative data do not yet exist for the present version of the diagnostic, and the questionnaire used to obtain reward-system data is still a somewhat unknown quantity with respect to its psychometric properties.

The four key modules of the present version of the questionnaire are illustrated in appendix 3A–2.

Some General Truths about Organizational Reward Systems

Because of the methodological limitations of the research instrument, it is necessary to be careful when analyzing data obtained through its use and when drawing conclusions from these data. One of the best safeguards against being misled by any paper-and-pencil instrument is to present what it says respondents are thinking and feeling to the respondents, and then to ask if the data accurately reflect their views. This procedure was routinely followed in the training programs and in six of the questionnaire administrations. It is in the reactions of respondents to results that the instrument's power to capture important organizational realities has often been made most clear. Its effect upon participants has sometimes been so dramatic as to call to mind the light bulb that appears over cartoon characters' heads as they have sudden insight. (In fact, that same metaphor has been suggested on two occasions by participants, in discussions following survey feedback.)

If one central truth can be said to emerge from repeated utilization of the diagnostic, it is this: organizations often do not get the subordinate behaviors their leaders claim to want, but they invariably get the behaviors that subordinates believe are rewarded. What goes on in a particular organization may look like Disneyland or an asylum to an outsider—and sometimes to insiders who have not thought systematically about their de facto reward and punishment systems—but it is coherent and predictable from the standpoint of what Simon (1957) has described as personal and subjective rationality.

Reward-System Profiles

One way to organize the information obtained through use of the diagnostic is to construct reward-system "profiles," which are then presented to respondents so as to validate the data and to provide a basis for subsequent discussion. These profiles are crude, essentially nonstatistical devices that probably do minimum harm to data from an instrument that has not proved itself psychometrically. The profiles are usually derived by calculating means, standard deviations, and frequency distributions from modules 1, 2, and 3 of the questionnaire.

Separate profiles are usually constructed for each organizational unit and level, though different units and levels may be combined if response patterns are similar. Of course, supplementary analyses of the data from modules 1–3 are often performed, and information pertinent to module 4 is analyzed separately, as will be explained shortly.

Figure 3–1 presents an illustrative reward-system profile. The response pattern shown in this figure is not reflective of data from any one organization, but is a composite of several administrations of the diagnostic instrument. It is considered to constitute a "healthy" profile for a number of reasons. First, we know from our empirical work with the instrument that organizations whose profiles resemble figure 3–1 typically report fewer problems with attendance, motivation, morale, and other dysfunctions consistent with goal incongruence as described earlier. Second, from a conceptual standpoint, figure 3–1 is consistent with various guiding principles offered by op-

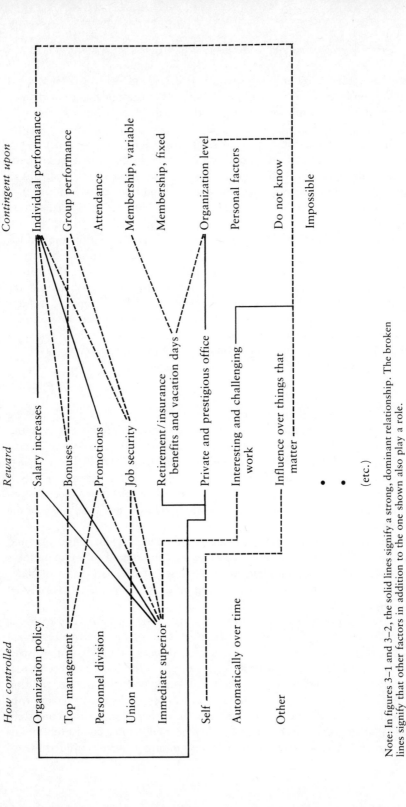

Note: In figures 3–1 and 3–2, the solid lines signify a strong, dominant relationship. The broken lines signify that other factors in addition to the one shown also play a role.

Figure 3–1. Typical Profile (Partial) of a Healthy Organization

erant and expectancy theories. As depicted in figure 3–1, (1) attractive rewards are available to organization members, and a fair number of these are controlled by subordinates' immediate supervisors, (2) a number of attractive rewards are believed to be attainable through individual and/or group performance, (3) respondents view themselves as well as their superiors as active elements in the reward system rather than as mere passive recipients of rewards, (4) respondents also view themselves as able to exert influence over things that matter to them, and (5) the organization is seen as attending to the content of jobs as well as to more material rewards.

Figure 3–2 depicts an "unhealthy" organizational reward system. This figure is a composite of two distinct profiles obtained through actual use of the diagnostic. One profile was constructed during a management training program for commissioner-level employees of a medium-sized Midwestern city. A fascinating incident during this program occurred during the break immediately prior to the session where they were to construct the profile. These senior officials—nearly all in their early sixties or late fifties—congregated in the hall to lament "the lack of good young people in city government." They then marched back into the classroom and proceeded to draw up the profile shown on the right side of figure 3–2. It was not until late in the day that the connection was made and the irony noted. The irony is, of course, that these senior leaders had, however unwittingly, helped to create a reward system that was destructive to youthful ambition. As can be seen from figure 3–2, nearly everything good that can happen to you as an employee of this city (salary increases, bonuses, promotions, and so forth) will happen through mere membership. The reward system created no incentive for employees to perform; among those employees who did have other incentives to perform, the city's reward system created no incentive to remain in the city's employ. Yet the city's leaders, having participated in the creation of this reward system, spoke of the problem of disappearing young talent as though some diabolical, unfathomable force was conspiring against them!

The left side of figure 3–2 is a partial reconstruction of a profile obtained as a result of administering the instrument in a midsized Southeastern Veteran's Administration hospital. Respondents were heads of services, their immediate subordinates, and other middle- and high-level administrators. The profile closely resembled their mood during the administration—in their own words, depressed and defeated. During the feedback system, one manager ventured his opinion that the system they operated under "made them all into eunuchs," stripping them of power by denying them influence over promotions, raises, discharges, and other attention-getters they felt they needed to be effective and seen as powerful by their subordinates.

Figure 3–3, another "unhealthy" organizational profile, also portrays a composite reconstruction of actual administrations of the diagnostic. It can in fact be said that, whereas figure 3–1 depicts "actual" reward systems as

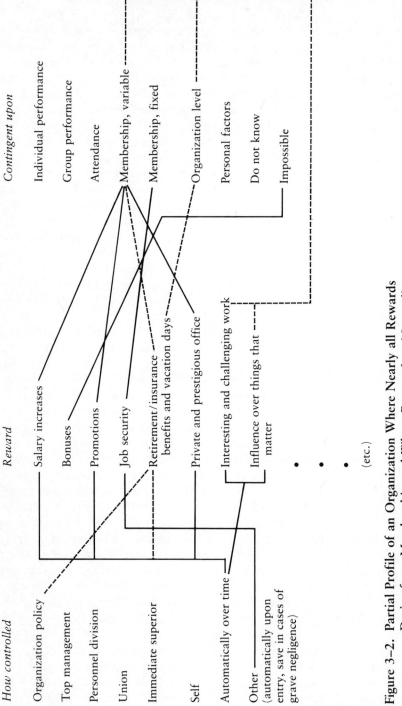

Figure 3–2. Partial Profile of an Organization Where Nearly all Rewards Derive from Membership and Where Respondents' Immediate Superior Is Seen as Powerless to Influence Rewards

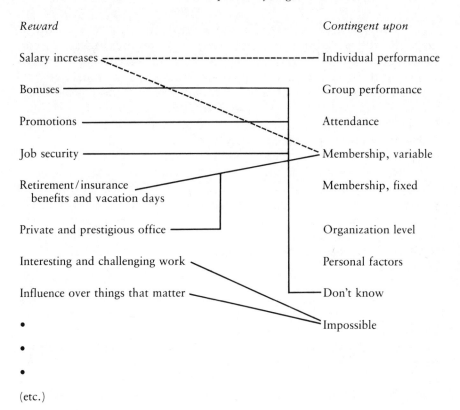

Reward   *Contingent upon*

Salary increases — Individual performance

Bonuses — Group performance

Promotions — Attendance

Job security — Membership, variable

Retirement/insurance benefits and vacation days — Membership, fixed

Private and prestigious office — Organization level

Interesting and challenging work — Personal factors

Influence over things that matter — Don't know

• — Impossible

•

•

(etc.)

Figure 3–3. Partial Profile of a "Theory X" Organization: Responding Members Lack Content Incentives and Information about Rewards

often described by employees at or near the top of an organization, figure 3–3 depicts the identical "actual" reward systems as viewed by many employees nearer the bottom. One of the most durable findings from this research has been the systematic disintegration of the reward system as the source of data shifts from organizational leaders to organizational followers. This disintegration usually takes the following forms:

1. Whereas high-level management tends to describe their reward system as rich in opportunity for the meritorious, lower-level workers are much less likely to perceive a clear connection between performance and reward.

2. High-level management tends to be much clearer and have far more confidence about how their reward system works. The lower the level of respondents, the more likely they are to circle the "don't know" response in replying to questions.

3. Lower-level employees also seem particularly sensitive to contradictions and cross-pressures in the implementation of rewards as well as to the existence of competing norms and sources of rewards. (For example, an early version of the diagnostic asked employees to complete the statement: "If I work especially hard around here . . . " This statement was repeated three times, and respondents were instructed to answer it differently each time. One hourly worker first answered "I would make my boss happy" and then "none of the other guys would even talk to me.")

4. Employees at low levels are far more likely than their leaders to perceive that various rewards, particularly job-content rewards, are "impossible." To be told by a department head that it is impossible to receive a twelve-month sabbatical is probably uninteresting; on the other hand, to be told that it is impossible to obtain job challenge, feedback about performance, and opportunities to participate is definitely interesting—particularly when, as often happens, a boss constructs a far different portrait of organizational "reality."

This last point probably deserves some embellishment. Figure 3–3 illustrates another oft-replicated finding from repeated use of the diagnostic, namely the tendency for organizations to underattend to job content in favor of more tangible rewards. Perhaps this is changing as a result of increased emphasis placed in recent years upon job enrichment and quality of working life. If this is the case, however, for some reason the diagnostic has not been able to document the change. Respondents from high organizational levels almost never claim, but low-level employees often claim that the organization denies freedom, recognition, job challenge, and so on. Of course, such differences may largely reflect actual differences in job content at various organizational levels. However, it is interesting to note that, when high-level participants in multilevel training programs have been asked to complete the diagnostic "as you believe your subordinates would," they almost always describe an organization far richer in job-content rewards than the actual descriptions of these subordinates. Perhaps, paradoxically, it is the relative abundance and availability of content rewards that causes many rewarders to take them for granted. According to nearly everyone's responses to module 3 of the questionnaire, feedback, recognition, opportunities to participate, and the like are *not* part of any union or civil service agreement, *not* hoarded and grudgingly dispensed by Personnel, and *not* seriously constrained by company policy. In this sense they have, potentially, unique value. Yet, though the power of these rewards to motivate—that is, to increase goal congruence—is well established in the research literature, they are used in most organizations, if at all, haphazardly and inconsistently. (For example, during the Veterans Administration survey-feedback session following their construction of the profile shown in the left side of figure 3–2, they owned up to the fact that, while organization policy and high emphasis on "variable membership" robbed them of the opportunity to influence most financial and prestige-related rewards, the only constraint upon job-content rewards was their own ignorance about how to use them effectively.)

Conclusions from Module 4

As mentioned earlier, the fourth major component of the diagnostic focusses on respondent perceptions of what organizational consequences are facilitated by employee behaviors. This module is usually tailored quite a bit to ensure that items described are key contributors to desired outcomes or particularly exasperating inhibitors of performance. For purposes of analysis, items are often clustered according to a common theme and similarity of response pattern. As is the case with respect to the profiles constructed of data from the other modules, module 4 data are always fed back to participants so as to validate responses and catalyze discussion.

Among the oft-replicated findings from repeated use of module 4 are several that are already well established in the organizational literature. For example, data from module 4 show clearly that:

1. Most U.S. organizations tend strongly to reward successful short-run firefighting, even if success is achieved at the expense of the firm's fitness for future action. In many of the organizations studied, it is personally rational, in light of the perceived reward system, for members to willfully mortgage the firm's future against a few flashy short-run statistics.

2. Organizations often encourage competition among subunits, inadvertently to the point where subunits consciously sabotage each other's objectives in pursuit of their own. To some extent, such competition represents the embodiment of conscious philosophy—as occurs, for example, when General Motors permits Pontiac to compete with Chevrolet. Far more common, however, is the case where high-level management does *not* want subunits to compete, does *not* intentionally create a reward system that fosters competition, and often does *not* claim to have any understanding of why it is happening (A senior vice president of one of the United States's larger companies scornfully remarked that he "really can't understand why they pull against one another as they do. They act as though they're a lot of little [name of company]s. I can't seem to make them realize that they've got to pull together." Meanwhile, employees in this firm from lower-level vice presidents down to department managers were indicating on the diagnostic questionnaire that keeping information from other departments and achieving their unit's goals even at other units' expense were rewarded, that seeking to build good relations with other departments was ignored, and that investing time to create opportunities for other departments was routinely punished!)

3. Organizational leaders are fond of pointing up the need for employees to attend to various thankless tasks. Yet, some of these same leaders create reward systems that assure that these tasks will *literally* be thankless. Team building, conducting performance appraisal and feedback, initiating plans for managerial succession, community involvement, and engaging in career and retirement counseling are among the most cited examples of ignored activities, even though these actions are included in module 4 only as they are deemed critical to the organization's success by those who decide how the instrument should be tailored—usually top management or its representatives.

4. Watching prices, staying within budget, and generally keeping costs to a minimum are rewarded activities in some organizations, but are highly risky in others. It is often the case that, should a manager demonstrate ability to operate efficiently with fewer workers, a typical "reward" is that the manager's budget will be cut the following year, vacant positions will be permanently reassigned to another unit, and the manager's power base will soon erode. As another example, many reimbursement formulas—including Medicaid, Medicare, and Blue Cross, though this has been changing—historically have punished hospitals financially for keeping treatment costs down and discharging patients in the minimum time possible. Hospital administrators have, therefore, often been rewarded for performing needless tests, running up patient bills, and admitting and subsequently retaining people who could be treated equally competently and far less expensively as outpatients.

5. Doing honest, accurate performance appraisal is often punished, whereas submitting appraisals so inflated as to be nonsensical is often rewarded. For example, the Marine Corps defined the performance category "excellent" as "qualified to a degree seldom achieved by others of his grade." This is not even the most favorable category! That honor belongs to "particularly desirable to have." Yet in 1976, 97 percent of all lieutenant colonels and majors on active duty were marked excellent or higher in their regular duties. Ninety-six percent of this group were rated as particularly desirable to have, as were 95 percent of the captains and 93 percent of the lieutenants. (During one of the training programs, a participating Marine Corps physician described his early days in a position of authority when he attempted to accurately describe the strengths—and limitations—of those men and women working under him. Not only were several of his subordinates passed over for promotion, but he himself received written criticism of his "failure to come to grips with deficiencies in staff under his care." After upping his ratings in the next reporting period to resemble Corps averages, he received verbal praise for having gotten his area under tighter control.)

6. There is a fairly consistent though complex relationship between goal difficulty and rewards. The extreme cases are unsurprising: achieving hard goals is universally rewarded, and failing to make what are perceived as easy

goals is always punished. The more interesting data pertain to what is likely to occur if (1) "hard" goals are narrowly missed and (2) "easy" goals are attained. Respondents seldom agree on the likely consequences of narrowly failing to attain difficult goals. When they do agree, it is usually to say that they might be rewarded or might be punished. (Some respondents claim to be well aware of the determining factors; others claim no such awareness. Since respondents always agree that their firms encourage them to set difficult goals, and since difficult goals are by definition subject to failure, the question is not an idle one, and it often generates rather heated discussion.)

The companion question also tends to generate heat, but the discussion invariably takes a different tack. Respondents readily concur that setting goals perceived by others as easy is punished, even if the goals are subsequently attained.[2] The disagreement occurs with respect to the likelihood that the easy goals they set will be perceived as easy by others. In cases where consensus is reached that fudging (secretly building in slack, so as to cause easy goals to appear as hard goals) is possible, then agreement usually follows that setting and attaining easy goals is rewarded. Since research exists to show that easy goals are usually made, but seldom exceeded by very much, this is an important finding.

Caveats and Conclusions

Some of the most replicated findings from use of the diagnostic instrument described in this chapter are summarized in appendix 3–A. The research described in this chapter is ongoing; it is in no sense a finished product. Several questions pertinent to methodology were raised earlier; at this point, some additional caveats are probably in order.

First, the diagnostic is concerned with perceptions of reward systems, not directly with reward systems themselves. Fortunately, the two are not wholly unrelated. As Lawler (1973, p. 55) has pointed out, the single most important determinant of most people's performance-outcome expectancies is the objective situation. Furthermore, nothing in the philosophy of the diagnostic described here precludes collection of more "objective" data to use as an aid in interpreting results, and this collecting has been done on several occasions. Nevertheless, the diagnostic's underlying assumption is that organizational behavior is more accurately predicted and described from knowledge of people's perceptions of the reward system than from cognizance of its "actual" properties.

Second, this chapter has been written as though it were true that employees respond only to the organization's formal reward–punishment system. Of course this is not the case! People come to the workplace already equipped with a myriad of ethics, norms, and values, and it is therefore entirely possible that "a person may be self-motivated, that is, may carry out assigned tasks with an enthusiasm both of compulsion or inborn desire, or early parental training, or life experiences and reinforcement histories that predate organizational membership" (Kerr and Slocum, 1981). People practicing self-motivation typically set their own standards and evaluation systems, and they administer their own rewards (Thoresen and Mahoney, 1974).

Researchers disagree about the extent to which systems that depend upon self-motivation can be effective. Manz and Sims (1980) and Manz (1986) discussed some conditions under which self-reinforcement works fairly well, and Lawler (1976, p. 1251) has argued that "the evidence is mixed, but it does suggest that under certain conditions people can exercise self-control and that when they do, self-control can eliminate many of the problems that occur when control systems operate solely on the basis of formal rewards and punishments." On the other hand, Miner (1975) concluded from his review of the literature that primary reliance on self-control and self-motivation typically produces intermediate levels of satisfaction, but output quality and concentration on work usually suffer. His conclusion was that "organizations that utilize few external sanctions tend to be consistently less effective" (1975, p. 198). As pointed out by Thoresen and Mahoney (1974) and by Manz and Sims (1980), even when behavior is self-controlled, the absence of external reinforcements will usually cause such behavior eventually to be discontinued.

It therefore seems safe to conclude that self-reward and information rewards by significant others in the work setting are important shapers of people's on-the-job actions. (cf. Porter et al., 1979, for a discussion of peer-group effects upon individual motivation and behavior.) Even so, the fact remains that for a reward system to be effective, it must encourage people to work toward outcomes desired by the rewarder, rather than acting as an obstacle to be overcome. Therefore, this chapter does not deny the fact that additional forces beyond the formal reward system are at work—but does deny the relevance of the fact. Managers responsible for persuading subordinates to work in collective pursuit of organizationally desired outcomes must *cause* these subordinates to care about those outcomes. It is preposterous that so many managers create irrelevant, even destructive reward systems (as identified by the diagnostic) and then hope that organization members will, despite the formal system, strive to perform.

A third caveat is that the diagnostic described in this chapter focusses extensively upon rewards and hardly at all upon punishments. This emphasis on rewards has increased with each passing year and each new version of the questionnaire, largely at the instigation of the organizations studied. There does not seem to be much conceptual or empirical justification for such overemphasis on rewards. Until recently, it was widely argued in the organizational behavior literature that punishment-based incentive systems were so ineffective (and immoral?) as to be unworthy of implementation or serious study. Bandura wrote in 1969, for example, that "the use of aversive control is . . . frequently questioned on the grounds that it produces a variety of undesirable by-products. This concern is warranted" (p. 294). Bandura went on to say, however, that "many of the unfavorable effects . . . that are sometimes associated with punishment are not necessarily inherent in the methods themselves but result from the faulty manner in which they are applied" (p. 294). In recent years, this distinction has been understood by more and more people, and a great deal has been learned about the best manner to apply punishment and the conditions under which it is most likely to be effective. (cf. Arvey and Ivancevich, 1980; and Sims, 1980). It will undoubtedly be advantageous for further administrations of the diagnostic to pay greater attention to punishment as well as rewards.

Numerous other caveats could be, but will not be, dwelt upon. For example, it is well known that people's needs and aspirations change over time. A dynamic methodology is required to track these changes and their consequences for organizational reward systems. It is also known that not only the nature and magnitude of rewards, but also their timing, exert an important influence upon people's behavior. Yet this version of the diagnostic does not seek to measure *when* rewards and punishments are administered. Another variable of interest concerns whether rewards and punishments are public or private, formal or informal. It will probably be necessary in the future to take cognizance of this dimension also.

In conclusion, what can be said to be the most important lesson learned so far from this research? Let me preface a reply with a passage from Skinner's *Walden Two,* in which the character Frazier reveals something about himself that many readers have taken to be autobiographical of Skinner. Frazier states: "In my early experimental days . . . I remember the rage I used to feel when a prediction went awry. I could have shouted at the subjects of my experiments, 'Behave, damn you! Behave as you ought!" (1948, p. 289).

The most important learning point to me from this research is an awareness of the tremendous extent to which *we* do today what Skinner was chiding himself for four decades ago. To an alarming extent, according to results from the diagnostic, we (however inadvertently) create systems of reward and punishment that encourage—Skinner would say "force"—other people to conceal and distort information, conspire against our goals, mortgage our future for trivial present advantage, avoid risk taking and challenges, neglect important responsibilities, and engage in other acts that make us want to cry out, "Behave, damn you! Behave as you ought!"

Can we learn from our past mistakes? Specifically, can we learn to stop "blaming the rat" for behaving as *any* personally rational employee (or spouse or child) would, given the reinforcement contingencies *we* have established? It is some comfort to know that Frazier did. In *Walden Two,* Skinner permits Frazier the following insight: "Eventually I realized that the subjects were always right. They always behaved as they should have behaved. It was I who was wrong. I had made a bad prediction" (p. 289).

Frazier's insight, much later, is our own. That is the essential truth, for all its flaws, communicated by the diagnostic. Our subjects, like Skinner/Frazier's, *are* "behaving as they ought." They have figured out our system—or so they think—and are doing the best they can for themselves, and no amount of mourning for the supposed death of the Protestant Ethic will change this. What *will* change this is for all of us to think more seriously about our existing systems of reward and punishment, how they are perceived by others, and how they can be improved so as to create greater goal congruence. In our everyday behavior we do this already. When, for example:

> we tell our child that she can't watch television if her homework is not finished,
>
> we offer the neighbor kid $2 to cut our lawn and another $2 after we inspect it,
>
> we tell our friends at the *start* of the meal that the waiter will bring separate checks at the end,
>
> we inform the child who is to cut the cake that his brother will choose the first piece,

we are using prospective rewards and punishments to cause others to care more about something that is important to us. Our organizations are more subtle, more varied, and infinitely more complex—but the principle is the same.

Notes

1. Some of these have been by the author and some by Erik Jansen, as part of a 1986 Ph.D. thesis, using data from one of the largest U.S. health care organizations.

2. The only exceptions to this finding occur in organizations that practice a strange breed of MBO whereby "goals missed" are subtracted from or divided into "goals made," so as to derive an "efficiency score" that is then used for salary decisions.

References

Arvey, R. D., and Ivancevich, J. M. (1980). Punishment in organizations: A review, propositions, and research suggestions. *Academy of Management Review, 5,* 123–32.

Bandura, A. (1969). *Principles of behavior modification.* New York: Holt, Rinehart and Winston.

Bentham, J. (1875). *An introduction to the principles of morals and legislation.* Oxford, England: Clarendon.

Bindra, D. (1959). *Motivation: A systematic reinterpretation.* New York: Ronald.

Chung, K. H. (1977). *Motivational theories and practices.* Columbus, Ohio: Grid.

Cyert, R. M., and March, J. G. (1963). *A behavioral theory of the firm.* Englewood Cliffs, N.J.: Prentice-Hall.

Hamner, W. C. (1975). How to ruin motivation with pay. *Compensation Review, 7,* 17–27.

Kerr, S. (1975). On the folly of rewarding a, while hoping for b. *Academy of Management Journal, 18,* 769–83.

Kerr, S., and Slocum, J. W., Jr. (1981). Controlling the performances of people in organizations. In W. Starbuck and P. Nystrom (eds.), *Handbook of organizational design.* New York: Oxford University Press.

Lawler, E. E., III (1971). *Pay and organizational effectiveness.* New York: McGraw-Hill.

Lawler, E. E., III (1973). *Motivation in work organizations.* Monterey, Calif.: Brooks/Cole.

Lawler, E. E., III (1976). Control systems in organizations. In M. Dunnette (ed.), *Handbook of industrial and organizational psychology.* Chicago: Rand McNally, 1247–91.

Litwin, G. H., and Stringer, R. A., Jr. (1968). *Motivation and organizational climate.* Boston: Division of Research, Graduate School of Business Administration, Harvard University.

Luthans, F., and Kreitner, R. (1975). *Organizational behavior modification.* Glenview, Ill.: Scott, Foresman.

Manz, C. C. (1986). Self-leadership: Toward an expanded theory of self-influence processes in organizations. *Academy of Management Review, 11,* 585–600.

Manz, C. C., and Sims, H. P., Jr. (1980). Self-management as a substitute for leadership: A social learning theory perspective. *Academy of Management Review, 5,* 361–67.

Meyer, H. H. (1975). The pay for performance dilemma. *Organizational Dynamics, 3,* 39–50.

Miner, J. B. (1975). The uncertain future of the leadership concept: An overview. In J. Hunt and L. Larson (eds.), *Leadership frontiers.* Kent, Ohio: Kent State University Press, 197–208.

Opsahl, R. L., and Dunnette, M. D. (1966). The role of financial compensation in industrial motivation. *Psychological Bulletin, 66,* 94–118.

Porter, L. W., Lawler, E. E., III, and Hackman, J. R. (1979). Ways groups influence individual work effectiveness. In R. Steers and L. Porter (eds.), *Motivation and work behavior,* 2nd ed. New York: McGraw-Hill, 355–64.

Simon, H. A. (1957). *Administrative behavior.* New York: Free Press.

Sims, H. P., Jr. (1980). Further thoughts on punishment in organizations. *Academy of Management Review, 5,* 133–38.

Skinner, B. F. (1948). *Walden two.* London: Macmillan.

Spencer, H. (1899). *Principles of psychology.* New York: Appleton.

Steers, R., and Porter, L. W. (1979). *Motivation and work behavior.* New York: McGraw-Hill.

Thoresen, C. E., and Mahoney, M. J. (1974). *Behavioral self-control.* New York: Holt, Rinehart and Winston.

Vroom, V. H. (1964). *Work and motivation.* New York: Wiley.

Appendix 3–A1
Typical Responses to Steps 1 and 4
of the Organizational Diagnostic

Financial rewards

increases in salary

bonuses for performance relating to budgets and schedules

bonuses for quality work

increases in number of paid vacation days

organization-sponsored life and health insurance benefits

free physical examinations

organization-sponsored retirement benefits

stock options

discounts on company securities

discounts on company products

free tickets to plays and sporting events

free membership in luncheon, social, and athletic clubs

sabbatical leaves with pay

Christmas gifts and bonuses

automobile mileage allowances

tuition refunds for college courses

Prestige rewards

office size, location, and furniture

access to executive clubs, washrooms, and dining rooms

right to fly first-class

assignment of a private secretary

membership in high-status task forces

titles

formal commendations and awards

favorable mention in company publications

authorization to wear particular clothing or jewelry (e.g., twenty-year pin)

Job-content rewards

freedom concerning job duties

freedom concerning working hours

organizational sponsorship of programs related to personal growth and individual development

access to information about what others (boss, coworkers, outsiders) think of an individual's performance

private, informal recognition for jobs well done

challenging duties

varied, interesting work

important, meaningful duties and responsibilities

having influence in setting goals and making decisions

Combination of financial, prestige, and job-content rewards

job security

career, personal, and financial counseling

in-house training programs

promotions to higher-level positions

access to company facilities and equipment for personal use

Employee behaviors pertaining to creativity and initiative

coming up with new, untested ideas

taking a chance, based upon the best information available at the time, that turns out badly

never questioning organization rules and policies

questioning the old, established ways of doing things

anticipating and worrying about problems that have not yet arisen

displaying entrepreneurial skills

learning and talking about new management techniques and philosophies and being willing to try them out in practice

Teamwork and cooperation

keeping information from other departments

achieving your own goals at the expense of others in your work group

achieving your own goals at the expense of other departments in the organization

not volunteering information to higher levels unless you are asked for it

identifying opportunities for other departments

investing time to pursue opportunities for other departments

building good relationships with other departments

Risk orientation

avoiding responsibility

avoiding risky situations

always going along with the majority

agreeing with the boss even when the boss is wrong

breaking rules when necessary to get the job done

exceeding your authority when necessary to get the job done

setting extremely high and challenging goals and then narrowly failing to make them

setting easy goals and then making them

putting off making a decision when large stakes are involved

being willing to throw away the game plan when conditions warrant

"Dirty jobs"

designing and recommending human-resource processes and programs

maintaining a continuing program of appraisal and counseling

worrying about the price of things and keeping costs down

giving feedback to your supervisors about their job performance

investing time to develop a managerial succession program

Miscellaneous other

admitting mistakes when you have made them

criticizing managers in other departments

setting no goals

spending beyond budget

letting it be known that you are considering job opportunities outside the organization

developing measures for improving the organization's cost effectiveness

Appendix 3–A2
Key Modules of the Reward-System Questionnaire

Module 1: What Is Rewarding to You?

To help you pin down this difficult question, we have listed some features that many people consider to be attractive. Some of these may not currently exist at this firm. (Of course, you personally may be indifferent to many of them. You may also find that rewards of great value are missing from the list.) Place a number from 1 to 4 alongside each feature listed to indicate that:

1. It is *extremely important* to you, one of the most valuable of all organizational rewards.
2. It is of *high value* to you.
3. It is of *some value* to you.
4. It is of *no value* to you, and you would care nothing about getting it or keeping it.

Remember to answer *without* considering whether it is possible to get these things on your job and in this organization. Later questions will be concerned with organizational realities. Now we are interested in your general feelings about each of the features listed.

1. Bonus for quality work   _____
2. Bonus for performance relating to budgets,
   schedules, etc.   _____

Module 2: How Are Rewards Obtained?

(Note: This module began with a tear-out page of instructions that clarified terms in a manner consistent with the discussion in step 2 and acquainted respondents with the following response codes.)

1. This is *the only factor* that determines whether I receive this reward or more of this reward.

2. This is *one of the major factors* that determines whether I receive this reward or more of this reward.

3. This has *some bearing, but is not a major factor* in determining whether I receive this reward or more of this reward.

4. This has *no bearing* on whether I receive this reward or more of this reward.

For each of the rewards listed next, paying careful attention to the definitions and answer codes, please indicate to what extent *each* factor on the right influences how people receive this reward. You should have a number from 1 to 4 for *each* of the factors labeled a, b, c, d, e, and possibly for factor f. The only exceptions would be if the answers are IMPOSSIBLE or DON'T KNOW.

1. Bonus for quality work
   _____ POSSIBLE
   - a. individual performance _____
   - b. organizational or work-unit per-   _____
     formance
   - c. length of tenure (variable) _____
   - d. being an employee (fixed) _____
   - e. organizational level _____
   - f. other (describe below) _____

   _____

   _____ IMPOSSIBLE
   _____ DON'T KNOW
2. Bonus for performance relating to budgets, schedules, etc.

Module 3: At What Level Are Organizations Controllable?

(Note: This module also began with a tear-out page of instructions that clarified terms in a manner consistent with the earlier discussion in step 3 and acquainted respondents with the following response codes.)

1. Means that the person, or the level, has *total control* over the reward; it is the only opinion or decision that really matters.

2. Means that the person or level has *some control* over the reward; it is one of the opinions that really matters.

3. Means that the person or level has *little or no control* over the reward.

For each reward listed next, please enter a number in *each* box in column a, b, c, d, e, or f to indicate whether, for *you* personally to receive this reward, a decision would have to be made by top management, your immediate superior, or others in the organization, or whether the reward would be based on time with the company.

Reward	*(a)* Company Policy/top Management	*(b)* Immediate Supervisor	*(c)* Self	*(d)* Union	*(e)* Other	*(f)* Time	*(g)* Don't Know	*(h)* Impossible
Bonus for quality work								
Bonus for performance relating to budgets, schedules, etc.								

(Respondents were instructed to place a check mark in columns g or h, rather than a number in any other column, if they did not know how a particular reward was controlled or if they felt that receipt of a particular reward was, for them, impossible.)

Module 4: Which Actions are Approved and Which Are Disapproved?

Next are a series of actions, both general and specific, that to varying degrees may bring approval or disapproval. For each item, place a number (from 1 to 5) on the right side to indicate whether *you* would probably receive approval or disapproval from above if you did what was described.

In deciding which number to enter on any line, please use the following code:[1]

a. The action would probably bring disapproval.

b. The action would probably bring neither approval nor disapproval.

c. The action would probably bring approval.

d. The action would bring approval or disapproval, depending upon circumstances I am aware of and can predict.

e. The action might bring approval or disapproval, depending upon circumstances I am not aware of and cannot predict.

1. Coming up with new, untested ideas   _____
2. Avoiding responsibility   _____
3. Always going along with the majority   _____

Note

1. I am indebted to Litwin and Stringer (1968) for the original idea of constructing such a scale.

Appendix 3A–3
Oft-Replicated Results from Using the Diagnostic

1. When respondents are asked to rank the available rewards in order of their attractiveness, most of the top ten rewards are inevitably "job-content" rewards (what Herzberg called "motivators"). Irrespective of job level or type of industry, people invariably select interesting work, challenge, job freedom, and opportunities for performance feedback as among the valued organizational rewards. Salary increase and job advancement (promotion) are also on most people's list of top ten rewards.

2. "Job-content" rewards tend to be underutilized in most organizations, particularly in the perceptions of lower-level employees.

3. "Membership" remains an exceedingly important basis for distribution of organizational rewards. This is true not only in civil service and union-dominated organizations, but everywhere else in the private sector. (Public-sector managers and those in unionized establishments typically imagine that membership would not be important elsewhere but, according to results from the diagnostic, such is not the case.)

4. Most organizations (inadvertently) create a circumstance whereby one or more levels of management are rendered all but powerless by the reward system in that the distribution of rewards is mostly beyond their control or discretion. In a variation of the "responsibility-without-authority" dilemma, these levels of management are expected to carry out their responsibilities without having influence over the organization's reward and punishment systems.

5. Most reward systems are seen as far less coherent and credible at lower organizational levels than at higher ones. Low-level respondents are less likely to claim to understand the system, are more likely to claim that various rewards are impossible to attain, and are far more likely to provide data that suggest important incongruencies between the reward system and organizational goals and priorities.

6. Among the most important incongruencies typically described are:

rewarding short-run activities and successes, even at the expense of the organization's ultimate well being;

rewarding dysfunctional competition among subunits or among individuals within subunits, while inadvertently punishing attempts by units or individuals to interact cooperatively or to identify opportunities for one another;

ignoring, or even punishing, attempts by employees to perform necessary training, appraisal, and counseling activities;

punishing people who set risky, challenging goals, while rewarding those who set and attain easy goals;

punishing people who bring minority (possibly unpopular) opinions to their boss, while rewarding those who agree with the boss and go along with the majority; rewarding conformity while punishing risk taking.

Part II
Methodological Issues

This part presents ideas about the level of analysis at which work-facilitation constructs can be operationalized. The three chapters take different units of analysis as their focus. Peters and O'Connor in chapter 5 focus on individual behavior. In chapter 4 Moeller et al. conduct their research at the work-unit level of analysis. Roberts and Sloane in chapter 6 present the position that all levels of analysis need to be simultaneously considered.

Each chapter attempts to substantiate its position through data collection and analysis with effectiveness as the criterion of interest: individual, work-unit, and system effectiveness.

4
Development of the Work-Facilitation Diagnostic

Anne Moeller
Benjamin Schneider
F. David Schoorman
Elizabeth Berney

This chapter develops the methodology used in the operationalization of the Katz and Kahn (1978) framework described by Schoorman and Schneider in chapter 1. The goal of the operationalization of the Katz and Kahn subsystem conceptualization of unit effectiveness was a measure, the work-facilitation diagnostic (WFD), useful for diagnosing inhibitors (also known as constraints or barriers) and facilitators of unit effectiveness. In this chapter, the rationale and procedures used for data collection are presented. In addition, some evidence comparing two collection procedures and some evidence for the validity of the operationalization attempts are presented.

Schoorman and Schneider note in chapter 1 that a central feature of our research program was the decision to emphasize unit, not individual, correlates of effectiveness. This decision had several important consequences for the design of the WFD, for the collection of the WFD data, and for the analysis of the data (some of which were already presented by Schoorman and Schneider in chapter 1). Perhaps the central issue of concern, they suggest, is the idea that when studying *situational* facilitators and inhibitors, the criterion of interest is the effectiveness of the unit, not the individuals.

Once we decided to conduct this research effort at the unit level, however, important yet unresolved data-collection issues surfaced to plague us. Questions still remained about from whom diagnostic data should be obtained. Should the data be collected from individuals in the situation, from observers, or from *groups* of individuals? In this introduction, we present some of these issues and our reasoning for proceeding the way we did.

Without the cooperation of the two organizations we investigated (and the people in them), the research reported here would not have been possible. We want to name them, but we cannot because of our promise to them of anonymity. Other people contributed to our efforts as part of the soon-to-be legendary Office of Naval Research (ONR) research team—and we can name them: Jocelyn Gessner, Andrea Marcus Konz, Joan Rentsch, Dan Schechter, and Cyndy Staehle.

Unit-Level of Analysis Data

The literature on organizational climates provides guidance for the design of a diagnostic survey that would be suitable to collect and then evaluate unit-level information. Within this literature, an active discussion of the issues of aggregation has emerged (James and Jones, 1974; Jones and James, 1979; Schneider, 1983; Schneider and Reichers, 1983). Schneider (1983), for example, advocated that researchers collect their data at the level to which they choose to aggregate. In other words, if individuals' responses are to be aggregated to represent department-level information, then participants should be responding to survey items (or interview questions and so on) that reflect this future transformation, as in "Untrained employees are being sent to *this department*."

Also included in the climate literature is a discussion of the data-analytic techniques used to evaluate the appropriateness of the aggregation procedure (James et al., 1984; Jones and James, 1979). James et al. (1984), for example, argue that estimating within-group interrater reliability according to their methods provides more accurate and interpretable estimates of agreement among group members. They demonstrated that other methods used to estimate agreement (for example, intraclass correlations) were less sensitive to *degrees* of agreement, especially when the data are restricted in range "which is likely to occur if judges in a single group agree on responses to essentially parallel items" (p. 9). In our work, the James et al. procedure, among others, was used to estimate interrater reliability of WFD responses whenever individual responses were aggregated to the unit level.

The climate literature, while helpful in specifying some of the relevant issues, fails to exhaust the potential range of data-collection issues or procedures. Another procedure that we employed was the "group-consensus procedure." Briefly, this procedure involved two steps. First, selected members of the work unit were asked to complete a survey individually. Then, they were asked to complete another, identical, survey as a group. In other words, they were asked to come to consensus on the best responses to the survey items. A member of the research team was present to facilitate discussion among the work-unit participants when consensus was problematic.

The group literature suggests that the consensus procedure may be more legitimate than the aggregation procedure for obtaining valid unit-level data. Aggregation assumes that individual responses can be averaged to give valid unit-level information. However, Alderfer and Brown (1972) and Alderfer et al. (1984) argue that averaged individual responses may not be the most valid measure of unit functioning.

Alderfer et al. (1984), for example, propose that individuals' responses need to be understood in the context of a variety of intergroups (gender, age, and race, for example) in which respondents are embedded. With the consensus procedure, group members are encouraged to discuss the meaning behind their differing individual responses (which may have been engendered by their differing intergroup identities). This discussion perhaps provides members with new perspectives and/or stimulates the consideration of new issues as they respond to the survey items. Thus, in the ideal case, the groups' consensus response is more than a simple arithmetic average; it is a unique blend of perspectives.

An analogy to vision illustrates the hypothesized conceptual advantage of the group-consensus procedure (Maruyama, 1978). The perception of depth cannot be achieved by averaging the experience of monocular vision of the left eye with that of the right eye. Rather, it is the interaction of both eyes operating in tandem that results in the perception of depth. In the same way, averaging group members' perceptions may not provide valid group-level information.

While the intergroup perspective is compelling regarding the use of consensus data, a counterargument supporting the use of aggregated individual responses to represent units is available. For example, Schneider (1983) and Schneider and Reichers (1983) have noted that individuals in work groups, as a function of their interaction with each other, will come to share their views of the unit and its functioning. More specifically, Schneider (1983) presented the idea that through an attraction-selection-attrition cycle (ASA cycle), similar people tend to end up in similar units. Because they are similar to each other, they come to share each other's perceptions of their work setting. That is, being relatively similar, they naturally find it easy to interact with each other (similarity attracts, Byrne, 1971) and it is from this process of natural interaction that shared views of the world emerge.

Schneider's and Schneider and Reichers's views indicate that people in work units will tend to agree, not disagree, in their perceptions of unit functioning. The present research offered an opportunity to test the competing ideas coming from the intergroup perspective and the attraction-selection-attrition perspective. The procedures for collecting both kinds of data are presented next.

Method

Overview

Because the methods we used for collecting data are complex and two different samples have been studied, it is important to provide an overview first. In brief, the two samples were studied in the following manner: First, several interviews with subject-matter experts (SMEs) of the units to be studied were conducted; these are described more fully in chapter 1 by Schoorman and

Schneider. Second, on the basis of the interviews, items descriptive of the facilitators and inhibitors of unit effectiveness were written by the five different interviewers. Third, the items were evaluated, rewritten, sorted, and condensed into the Katz and Kahn subsystem framework. Fourth, representatives of intact work units individually completed a WFD and then, with the help of a facilitator, discussed each WFD item to achieve consensus. Concurrent with the WFD development and data collection, criterion data indicative of unit effectiveness were obtained.

The data analyses performed were of two kinds: internal analyses of the WFD and establishment of relationships between the WFD and the unit criterion data.

Conceptual issues associated with each phase of data collection and analysis are presented, as appropriate.

Sample 1

Sample 1 consists of twelve behavioral science, social science, and business departments from an Atlantic coast university. Individual interviews with a representative (SME) from each participating department (two-thirds of those contacted) were conducted to begin specification of the facilitators and inhibitors of classroom teaching effectiveness in their departments. In these interviews, the goal was the identification of the broadest range of facilitators and inhibitors of teaching effectiveness with no concern for the particular departments from which the information came.

Development of the WFD for Teaching Effectiveness. Each interviewer took copious notes and then converted those notes into items describing facilitators and inhibitors of departmental teaching effectiveness. The decision to use the group consensus procedure for collecting WFD data had an important impact on the step of converting the approximately three-hundred items into a useable WFD. That is, the consensus procedure severely limits the number of items that is practically possible to have the group rate. It is necessarily a time-consuming procedure. (N.B. Maier, 1983, cites length of time as a liability of group decision making.) An hour of each person's time (during normal working hours) was scheduled to collect consensus data. Despite this time limitation, a comprehensive diagnostic survey was desired. To meet these two criteria of survey development, short and comprehensive, multiple content-parallel items (as judged by the members of the research team) were condensed into a single terse item. Sample items illustrating this terseness include:

1. Classroom facilities (e.g., chairs, tables, desks, chalkboards) for teaching are in poor condition.

2. Faculty are given nonmonetary rewards (e.g., release time, public recognition) for good teaching.

Generic labels, such as "facilities" and "nonmonetary rewards," allowed us to capture a number of separate instances (parallel items) while limiting the total number of items in the diagnostic survey.

Generic labels, it turns out, also permit the survey items to cross samples. For example, the items in the survey for the telemarketing sample that parallel the two just mentioned are:

1. Workroom facilities (e.g., chairs, desk, headsets) are in poor condition.

2. [Employees] get nonmonetary rewards (e.g., public recognition, praise) for good performance.

Parenthetically, we included information specific to each kind of work unit to provide respondents with a familiar frame of reference for responding to the general diagnostic. This was done to capitalize on the Alderfer and Brown (1972) finding that survey items worded in the language of the system yield more valid data from respondents.

Thirty-five items emerged from the sorting and condensing process: 4 production items, 6 supportive items, 8 personnel-maintenance items, 5 equipment-maintenance items, 6 managerial items, and 6 adaptive items. (See table 4–1 for examples.)

The response format of the survey was a five-point frequency scale: (1) very infrequently, (2) infrequently, (3) sometimes, (4) frequently, and (5) very frequently.

Collection of the Group-Consensus Data. Once the survey was prepared, arrangements were made with three willing faculty in each department to collect the WFD data. Panel meetings were scheduled for 90 minutes (although an hour was usually sufficient time). A member of the research team attended these sessions to facilitate the consensus process.

Although collecting group-level data by our consensus procedure is conceptually appealing, the literature describing group and intergroup processes warns that both content (the composition of the group) and process (the style of interaction) variables can influence group-member behavior. Group-member composition, for example, may adversely affect the group's decision-making style. Thus, dominant or high-status individuals in the group may bias the consensus responses in their favor. In other words, lower-status individuals may *publicly* agree with their higher-status coworkers even though they actually disagree.

Groupthink (Janis, 1972), a group-level–process phenomenon, may also adversely affect the data collected by the consensus procedure. Group mem-

Table 4–1
Examples of Items on the Teaching-Facilitation Survey

Managerial subsystem items

  1. Faculty choose the courses they teach.
11. Faculty teach courses within their area of expertise.
30. Faculty teach three or more classes per semester. (reverse scored)

Personnel maintenance subsystem items

  2. Teaching ability is considered in the selection of new faculty.
14. Attempts to improve teaching performance (such as attending teaching workshops) go unnoticed by the department. (reverse scored)
28. This department offers programs (workshops, discussions, special colloquia, speakers) that help faculty improve their teaching.

Equipment maintenance subsystem items

  7. Audiovisual equipment breaks down during classes. (reverse scored)
25. The physical environment (lighting, ventilation, noise, temperature, cleanliness) of the teaching facilities is conducive to good teaching.
32. Laboratory facilities and equipment for teaching are well maintained.

Adaptive subsystem items

  5. The department collaborates with other departments in the development of new courses. (reverse scored)
24. Faculty lines are increased with increasing enrollments.
29. The curriculum is reviewed to keep it current.

Production subsystem items

  6. The size of the classes limits the use of certain teaching methods (discussion, group exercises, one-to-one interaction). (reverse scored)
10. There are unqualified students (those lacking the formal prerequisites and/or good language skills) in classes who inhibit teaching effectiveness. (reverse scored)
35. Research activities leave little time and/or energy for teaching. (reverse scored)

Supportive subsystem items

12. Clerical help is available for preparing (typing, duplicating) course materials (syllabi, examinations).
13. Faculty have the laboratory facilities and equipment they need for teaching.
18. Junior faculty have access to information (discussion with senior faculty, prepared lectures, course syllabi) that help them with their teaching.

bers may actually discourage internal dissent, particularly in front of the facilitator (who may be perceived by the group as an external threat). However, discussion of the dissenting opinions would provide a more accurate estimate of the group's responses. (N.B. The presence of the facilitator may also have the added effect of promoting a strong inclination to respond to the survey in a socially desirable fashion.)

One additional issue discussed in the intergroup literature is that of group representation (Miller and Rice, 1967). How do we know if unit representatives are actually representing their work unit or just themselves? When individuals are asked to represent their full work unit in the context of a subset of the full group, they may identify more strongly (that is, have stronger sentience) with the new functional group of representatives than the total work unit that they are intended to represent. Since they may temporarily be more identified with the functional group of representatives, they may misrepresent the total work unit in order to be in agreement with the functional group.

A number of precautions were taken in collecting the data to guard against these potential problems. First, care was taken to identify meaningful groups of people for the consensus process. Such variables as proximity, social contact, common fate, job title, and pay grade were considered when identifying groups. For example, we tried to choose people who shared similar status so that they would not (perhaps) feel inhibited about their responses in front of people of higher status. In this sample, we were also able to select group members who were especially sensitive to the criterion of interest. Faculty who were members of their department's teaching committee were asked to describe the conditions in their department that facilitate and/or inhibit teaching effectiveness. This group (teaching committee) within a group (faculty of a given department) shared a common interest in the role of teaching in academia and so perhaps could provide more informed, more accurate descriptions of the facilitating and/or inhibiting conditions that affect teaching effectiveness.

As a second precautionary measure, a member of the research team was present during the consensus procedure to facilitate the process. When group consensus was problematic, the facilitator encouraged *all* of the members both to discuss disagreements and to contribute their opinions to the discussion. By encouraging the sharing of any divergent opinions, the facilitator created a group climate, if you will, for dissent, thus reducing the potential for Groupthink to occur. In this way, relevant information and opinions from all participants were shared to resolve the disagreement and achieve consensus.

Written and oral instructions of the diagnostic survey served as a third precautionary measure to emphasize to members the need for their responses to represent those of their work unit rather than just themselves. The assembled individuals were instructed to act as representatives of their unit (department or sales unit) and to "describe how often each of these facilitating and inhibiting conditions happen in your [department or sales unit]." Their role as unit representative was emphasized orally as well.

At the group session, the diagnostic survey was distributed to each member. An introduction (including our objectives) and written instructions headed the survey. The group facilitator recited the instructions and emphasized each person's role as a department representative. The instructions were clear and concise:

> Directions: Indicate how often each of the following facilitating and inhibiting conditions occurs in your department by writing the appropriate scale number in the space provided.

An example followed these instructions. The participants were invited to ask questions. Then they completed the survey individually; it took them about 15 minutes to do so.

Sharing each person's responses and achieving group consensus followed the individual work. The faculty retained their surveys for reference; they were instructed to not change their responses to match the consensus responses. (Unfortunately, the faculty participants refused even bold requests to keep them from changing their responses so only consensus data could be analyzed for sample 1.)

The ground rules for achieving consensus were explained next. First, participants announced their survey responses in turn. Identical and adjacent responses (e.g., 2, 2, 2; 2, 3, 4; 3, 4, 4) were recorded as consensus (either the median or mode value in cases of adjacent responses) without discussion. When people differed by two or more scale points (e.g., 3, 5, 5; 1, 3, 5; 1, 2, 4), the facilitator encouraged them to discuss their responses. Typically, incidents relating to the item were shared by participants with each other. Occasionally, merely re-reading the item resolved the disagreement. In any case, discussion continued until everyone agreed to a response for the contested item. The facilitator of the consensus process recorded the consensus responses.

Criterion. Student evaluations of undergraduate classroom teaching were used as the criterion. At the end of each semester, the departments conduct these evaluations. The *Teaching Evaluation Questionnaire* contains forty items designed to evaluate courses. Twenty-nine items describe the characteristics of the instructor and eleven items assess the reactions and attitudes of the students to the course.

These data were obtained from the director of the teaching evaluation project and were already aggregated to the department level (thereby protecting the anonymity of the instructors). The two scales (instructor attributes and student reactions), at least when aggregated, are highly intercorrelated ($r = .88$) and so were combined into one summary estimate of the quality of teaching for each department.

Data Analysis. Data were analyzed to assess their reliability and validity. Two analyses were done. First, internal-consistency reliability estimates were calculated for each of the six subsystems and for the combined "system" scale. (Note: For sample 2, a discussion of issues surrounding the calculation of internal-consistency reliability is presented.) A second analysis, one assessing the validity of the six subsystems and the total system, was performed. For this analysis, Pearson product-moment correlations were computed between the subsystem scales (including the total system scale) and the student ratings.

Sample 2

WFD sample 2 participants were from twenty-three sales units (74 percent of all possible sales units) of a national financial-services telemarketing organization. The samples for analyses in this paper were 85 individual sales people, 23 sales units for internal analyses of the WFD, and 15 sales units for analyses of relationships between the WFD and the sales criterion.

For sample 2 WFD development, group interviews (rather than individual interviews as in sample 1) were used to generate facilitators and inhibitors. Again, the goal was specification of the broadest possible range of facilitators and inhibitors, this time of sales-unit effectiveness.

Development of the WFD of Sales-Unit Effectiveness. Seven group interviews were conducted with 4, 5, or 6 participants serving as SMEs. Interviews lasted about 2 hours and were typically very lively. Again, the interviewers took copious notes and all interviewers, combined, generated almost 400 facilitator and inhibitor items. After these items were clarified, sorted into the Katz and Kahn framework, and condensed into terse items, as described earlier, 40 items remained: 5 production items, 6 supportive items, 11 personnel-maintenance items, 5 equipment-maintenance items, 8 managerial items, and 5 adaptive items. (See table 4–2 for example items.) Twelve items appeared in both the teacher and salesperson versions of the survey: the majority of them ($N = 7$) were personnel-maintenance items. An identical response format was used in both work-facilitation surveys.

Collection of the Group-Consensus Data. Management arranged the twenty-three panel meetings in terms of who attended, when, and where. Only salespeople reporting to the same supervisor attended any one meeting. One hour was scheduled to collect the WFD data during normal working hours. As earlier, a member of the research team facilitated each meeting.

The panel meetings proceeded as earlier, with two exceptions. First, the facilitator emphasized the request that participants *not* change their responses to match the consensus responses. Once discussion of the items began, people were requested to lay their pencils down. The facilitator stressed the importance of their responses to the research effort.

Table 4-2
Examples of Telemarketing Sample Work-Facilitation Items

Supportive subsystem items

14. CRTs are unavailable when needed. (reverse-scored)
23. Supervisors do not have enough technical knowledge to answer questions. (reverse-scored)
30. Following training, employees are well prepared to do the job.

Equipment maintenance subsystem items

2. Manuals are adequate sources of relevant job information (organized, complete, and up-to-date).
10. The physical environment (e.g., noise, lighting, space, temperature, ventilation) is conducive to good performance.
27. It is difficult to get broken equipment repaired. (reverse-scored)

Production subsystem items

3. We have enough time to do our paperwork accurately.
21. Specific terms, policies, etc. are easy to explain to customers.
37. When a customer calls back, the original paperwork is used (even if the customer talks to a different employee.

Managerial subsystem items

13. Our supervisor lets employees know how they are doing on the job.
34. Our supervisor sets unrealistic goals for employees. (reverse-scored)
39. Sales employees are called upon to work the service gate (or vice versa). (reverse-scored)

Personnel maintenance subsystem items

16. Employee pay increases are based on work performance.
18. On-the-job training is unavailable for those employees who need it. (reverse-scored)
26. Our supervisor schedules enough employees to handle call volume.

Adaptive subsystem items

7. Staff meetings are held to discuss new job-relevant information.
15. Supervisors review practices and procedures to keep them current.
33. We are unaware of changes in company policies or procedures until after they go into effect. (reverse-scored)

The ground rules for achieving consensus were slightly changed. In four-person groups, adjacent responses that were evenly split (e.g., 2, 2, 3, 3) or sequential (e.g., 1, 2, 3, 4) were also discussed to arrive at the best response for consensus.

Criterion. Sales data, provided by management, were used as the criterion in this sample. The index used adjusts the monthly sales performance for each sales unit such that the opportunity to *make* sales is held constant: of the number of sales that *could* have been made to eligible applicants, how many sales *were* made? We refer to this index as SR (sales ratio).

The SRs, for two consecutive months were provided for fifteen sales units. Test-retest reliability of the SR was reasonable, $r_{tt} = .72$. These data were combined (the mean SR was calculated) into one summary performance statistic for data-analytic purposes.

Reliability Analyses of the WFD. Due to the collection of both individual and consensus data for sample 2, the reliability issues require extended treatment. First, the issue of the design of the WFD makes calculation of subsystem-scale internal-consistency reliability estimates somewhat problematic. That is, because of time limitations imposed on us by the consensus method, very terse yet inclusive items were written for each subsystem. In addition, as described by Katz and Kahn, each subsystem is, in fact, a menagerie of activities, again arguing against expecting internal-consistency reliability. In any case, the estimates of the internal-consistency reliability of the consensus data are tenuous given the small sample size ($N = 15$). Of course, internal-consistency reliability may not affect validity at all if the components are individually valid.

A second issue concerns the reliability of both the aggregated data and the consensus data. The James et al. (1984) procedure was used to calculate the interrater reliability of the aggregated individual responses.

Finally, we wanted to test the relationship between the consensus and the aggregated data. We chose to use a multimethod procedure to estimate the properties of these measures. Our two competing perspectives on this topic, the intergroup and the attraction-selection-attrition perspectives, suggest that either one or both of the procedures should yield useful data. A multimethod matrix (Campbell and Fiske, 1959) of the subsystems (the six Katz and Kahn subsystems) by methods (aggregated individual and consensus), it was thought, could offer additional insight into WFD measurement properties.

This solution to the reliability issue, however, fails to address a final question: should data be aggregated at all? To answer this question, the consensus data were not only correlated with aggregated individual responses but, in addition, the following calculations were made:

1. Consensus subsystem scale data were correlated with unaggregated individual responses to the WFD subsystem scale data by assigning relevant consensus scale data to each individual ($N = 85$ individuals).

2. Consensus *item* data were correlated with aggregated *item* data within each group ($N =$ forty items) and then the average of these correlations was calculated across groups.

Validity Analysis. Consensus subsystems scale data and aggregated individual subsytem scale data were correlated with the sales ratio.

Results

Results for the university sample are presented first, followed by the results for the financial-services telemarketing sample.

University Sample. Scale means, standard deviations, intercorrelations, and coefficients alpha are presented in table 4–3. The intercorrelations of the subsystem scales range from r = −.60 (managerial and adaptive subsystems) to r = .85 (supportive and equipment-maintenance subsystems). The middle 60 percent of these intercorrelations range from r = .03 (managerial and personnel-maintenance subsystems) to r = .31 (adaptive and personnel-maintenance subsystems), indicating that most of the subsystems are low to moderately correlated.

Table 4–4 presents the item–subsystem-scale correlations, item–validities, and subsystem-scale–validities. Also included is the correlation between the total-system scale and the quality-of-teaching criterion. All subsystem scales but the managerial subsystem were positively correlated with the criterion. However, only the correlation between the adaptive-subsystem scale and the criterion reached conventional levels of significance (r = .62, p < .01). As one would expect, most of the items in the managerial-subsystem

Table 4–3

Subsystem and Total System Scale Means, Standard Deviations, Intercorrelations, and Coefficients Alpha for University Sample (N = Twelve Departments)

Subsystem	Mean	S.D.	1	2	3	4	5	6	7
Managerial (1)	3.85	.54	(.67)						
Supportive (2)	3.23	.65	.13	(.72)					
Personnel maintenance (3)	2.33	.70	.03	.41	(.91)				
Equipment maintenance (4)	2.75	.82	.18	.85	.62	(.83)			
Production (5)	2.92	.47	−.14	.30	−.03	.12	(.32)		
Adaptive (6)	1.98	.51	−.60	.08	.31	.09	.26	(.50)	
Total system[a] (7)	3.36	.34	−.05	.73	.52	.78	.15	.07	(.63)

[a]Corrected subsystem–total-system correlations.

Note: Means based on 5-point frequency scale where 1 = very infrequently and 5 = very frequently.

Table 4–4
Item–Subsystem-Scale Correlations, Item Validities,
and Subsystem-Scale Validities for University Sample
(N = 12 Departments)

Item–Scale Correlation	Subsystem	Criterion
	Managerial	−.10
.58	V1	.15
.52	V11	−.26
.26	V17	−.09
.55	V23	−.12
	Supportive	.12
.35	V12	−.34
.53	V13	−.05
.57	V22	.24
.40	V27	.31
.55	V33	.19
	Personnel maintenance	.40*
.81	V2	.21
.76	V4	.39*
.66	V9	.21
.71	V14	.57**
.80	V16	.35
.59	V21	.31
.72	V28	.24
—	V31	.08
	Equipment maintenance	.21
.89	V3	.37
.34	V7	.31
.67	V19	.06
.62	V25	.11
.30	V32	.13
	Production	.14
.41	V6	.23
.25	V10	−.04
.00	V26	−.05
.38	V35	.12
	Adaptive	.62***
.08	V5	.10
.35	V20	.61***
.36	V24	.34
.49	V34	.52**
	Total system	.40*

*p < .10.
**p < .05.
***p < .01.

scale are negatively related to the criterion; also negatively correlated with the criterion were scattered items in the supportive-and production-subsystem scales. The adaptive-, personnel-, and equipment-maintenance–subsystem scales contain the items that are more highly (in some cases significantly) correlated with the criterion.

Financial-Services Telemarketing Sample. Results for this sample are presented in the following order:

1. Subsystem-scale means, standard deviations, internal-consistency reliability estimates, and intercorrelations of the data collected both individually and during the consensus procedure,
2. Within-group interrater reliability analysis of the data collected individually according to the technique advocated by James et al. (1984),
3. Similarity estimates of the (a) consensus-subsystem scales and the aggregated individual-subsystem scales, (b) consensus-item responses and the aggregated individual-item responses (calculated for each work unit and across work units), and (c) consensus- and individual-subsystem and total-system scales, and, finally,
4. Comparison of the predictive validities of the consensus data and the aggregated individual data.

Internal-Consistency Reliability Analysis. This analysis was conducted for the data collected from the participants both individually and during the consensus procedure. Table 4–5 presents the scale means, standard deviations, subsystem-scale–item intercorrelations, and subsystem-scale coefficients alpha of the data collected individually (unaggregated). Table 4–6 presents this same information for the data collected during the consensus procedure.

Tables 4–5 and 4–6 show the heterogeneous nature of the subsystem scales. As expected, coefficients alpha for both the individual and consensus data are generally low:

	Consensus	*Individual*
Managerial	.23	.37
Supportive	.43	.46
Adaptive	.50	.70
Production	.08	.17
Equipment maintenance	.64	.62
Personnel maintenance	.47	.48

although alpha tends to be a bit higher for the individual data than for the consensus data. This trend most likely is due to the larger N for the individual

Table 4–5
Subsystem-Scale Means, Standard Deviations, Intercorrelations, and Coefficients Alpha for the Unaggregated Individual Data for the Telemarketing Sample
(N = 85 Salespersons)

Subsystem	Mean	S.D.	1	2	3	4	5	6
Supportive (1)	3.66	.55	(.46)					
Equipment maintenance (2)	3.35	.64	.34	(.17)				
Production (3)	3.31	.55	.40	.20	(.37)			
Managerial (4)	3.88	.44	.57	.20	.35	(.37)		
Personnel maintenance (5)	3.39	.45	.22	.04	.38	.25	(.48)	
Adaptive (6)	2.95	.64	.53	.20	.46	.37	.35	(.70)

Means based on 5-point frequency scale where 1 = very infrequently and 5 = very frequently.

data. (N = 85 for the individual data; N = 15 for the consensus data.) Despite the low subsystem-scale coefficients alpha, the items were combined to estimate the degree of subsystem-related work facilitation. These subsystem scales were created with some hesitation. While this procedure is *conceptually* sound, the psychometric consequences were worrisome not only for conventional analyses but also for calculating within-unit interrater agreement.

Within-Group Interrater-Reliability Analysis. Within-group interrater reliability (IRR) was estimated using the technique advocated by James et al.

Table 4–6
Subsystem-Scale Means, Standard Deviations, Intercorrelations, and Coefficients Alpha of the Consensus Data for University Sample
(N = 12 Departments)

Subsystem	Mean	S.D.	1	2	3	4	5	6
Supportive (1)	3.70	.44	(.43)					
Equipment maintenance (2)	3.24	.55	.36	(.64)				
Production (3)	3.27	.44	.46	.15	(.08)			
Managerial (4)	3.99	.37	.50	.15	.37	(.23)		
Personnel maintenance (5)	3.40	.43	.61	.00	.50	.35	(.47)	
Adaptive (6)	2.87	.47	.72	.20	.60	.69	.55	(.50)

Note: Means based on 5-point frequency scale where 1 = very infrequently and 5 = very frequently.

(1984). The IRR analysis was done at the item level, not the scale level, since our subsystem scales lack one of their required "acceptable psychometric properties," internal consistency. In addition, we obtained judgments of work facilitation from only 3 ($N = 7$) or 4 ($N = 16$) raters per group, which is short of the 6 raters recommended by James et al. Results from the IRR analyses for 4 of the 16 four-member groups are presented in table 4–7. They are representative of the results obtained from all 23 groups.

The following conclusions appear warranted from viewing these data:

1. Interrater agreement on item responses across raters is generally satisfactory. That is, given that the data in table 4–7 are directly interpretable as indices of interrater reliability, the results are encouraging. We can only speculate about agreement had we had internally consistent *scale scores* to use as a basis for the calculation. Perhaps the average agreement provides a lower bound estimate.

2. There is considerable variability by both item and group in the level of interrater agreement. Thus, no consistent patterns emerged regarding some items revealing more agreement than others, and no group effect was observed with one or another group revealing more or less overall agreement. Again, perhaps the averages shown in table 4–7 are useful as a frame of reference.

Analyses of Similarity. Three analyses were done to assess the similarity of the responses obtained individually and by the consensus procedure. Two analyses involve the aggregated individual data and the consensus data. The third, more conservative, analysis involves the individual (unaggregated) data and the consensus data.

Table 4–7
**Results of the IRR Analysis for Four Representative Groups
from the Telemarketing Sample**

	Group			
Subsystem	*A*	*B*	*C*	*D*
Supportive				
V1	.91	.93	.72	.92
V14	.91	.53	.74	.74
V19	.91	.74	.81	.55
V23	.81	.91	.93	.91
V30	.18	1.00	1.00	.81
V35	.16	.63	.44	.91
	.65	.84	.77	.81

Table 4–7 Continued

	Group			
Subsystem	A	B	C	D
Equipment maintenance				
V2	—[a]	.93	.81	.25
V6	.53	1.00	1.00	.72
V10	.16	.72	xx[b]	.44
V27	.93	.74	.74	.37
V36	.37	.53	.74	.72
	.50	.78	.67	.42
Managerial				
V4	—[a]	.72	.53	.37
V9	.93	.55	.91	.91
V13	—[a]	.93	.44	.81
V17	.93	.74	.91	1.00
V20	xx[b]	.63	1.00	.93
V29	.93	1.00	.93	.53
V34	.93	.91	.74	.16
V39	.91	.74	.74	.93
	.77	.78	.78	.71
Production				
V3	.16	.74	.74	.74
V12	.81	.72	.93	.72
V21	.74	.93	.93	.37
V31	.93	.55	.53	.44
V37	.74	1.00	.37	xx
	.68	.79	.70	.45
Personnel maintenance				
V5	—[a]	.74	.81	.74
V8	.44	1.00	.81	.81
V16	1.00	.93	.63	.91
V18	.91	.44	.93	.55
V22	.53	.74	.72	—[a]
V24	.44	.53	.18	.16
V26	.93	1.00	.55	.91
V28	xx[b]	.93	1.00	.93
V32	.53	.74	.81	.44
V38	.91	.93	.93	.55
V40	.93	.92	.72	.93
	.66	.81	.74	.69
Adaptive				
V7	.93	.81	.74	.74
V11	.44	.74	.37	.37
V15	.63	.91	.81	.93
V25	.81	.81	.93	.93
V33	.81	.55	.81	.74
	.73	.76	.73	.74

[a]Data missing from at least one of the participants.

[b]An uninterpretable IRR estimate.

Table 4–8
Correlation Matrix of the Aggregated Individual-Subsystem and Total System Scales and the Consensus-Subsystem and Total System Scales for the Telemarketing Sample
(N = 23 Sales Units)

Consensus	Aggregated individual						
	1	2	3	4	5	6	7
Supportive (1)	.81	.43	.50	.63	.55	.73	—
Equipment maintenance (2)	.40	.92	.26	.33	.09	.41	—
Production (3)	.26	.17	.84	.48	.42	.54	—
Managerial (4)	.57	.19	.38	.80	.16	.46	—
Personnel maintenance (5)	.43	−.05	.36	.39	.87	.52	—
Adaptive (6)	.72	.21	.63	.73	.50	.85	—
Total system (7)	—	—	—	—	—	—	.95

Table 4–8 presents the intercorrelations of the aggregated-individual-subsystem and total-system scales with the consensus-subsystem and total-system scales in a multimethod matrix form. Corresponding subsystem scales (the convergent validity diagonal of the matrix) are highly correlated (range: r = .80 to r = .92), much more so than the correlations between differing subsystem scales (the heteromethod-heterotrait triangles). The highest correlation in the matrix (r = .95) is between the two total-system scales (the total-aggregated-individual and the total-consensus scales).

The second analysis involving the aggregated individual and consensus data was done at the item level. Within each group, the correlation between the aggregated individual responses and the consensus responses was calculated, essentially yielding each group's "profile" of similarity. Table 4–9 pre-

Table 4–9
Profile Analysis of the Aggregated Individual Level Item Data and the Consensus Level Item Data for Each Group in the Telemarketing Sample

Group	r	Group	r	Group	r	Group	r
A	.81	G	.84	L	.84	Q	.81
B	.89	H	.81	M	.85	R	.87
C	.89	I	.81	N	.81	S	.88
D	.88	J	.86	O	.78	T	.82
E	.72	K	.95	P	.75	U	.85
F	.90						

Overall r = .84

For this analysis the correlations represent covariation across items, not people.

sents the results for this analysis. Overall, the consensus and the aggregated individual data were quite similar (r = .84). Some groups' consensus responses were more similar to the aggregated individual responses (e.g., r = .95, r = .90) than other groups' (e.g., r = .72, r = .75).

The final analysis of similarity involves the individual data (unaggregated) and the consensus data. Thus, this analysis is a more conservative measure of similarity. It attempts to answer the question: if these data were obtained from only one person, how closely would the individual's responses match the group-consensus responses? Table 4–10 presents the correlations between the corresponding individual-subsystem scales and the consensus-subsystem scales (N = 85). Again, the correlations in the convergent validity diagonal are higher than the off-diagonal correlations, but they are much lower (range: r = .48 to r = .66) than those of table 4–8.

Analyses of Predictive Validity. Earlier analyses indicate that the aggregated individual data and the consensus data are similar. (See tables 4–8 and 4–9.) The last set of analyses involves both these sets of data and the criterion (mean telephone-sales performance or sales ratio). Table 4–11 presents the following information:

    item-subsystem scale correlations

    subsystem-item validities

    subsystem-scale validities

    total-system-scale validity

Table 4–10
Correlations Between Corresponding Unaggregated Individual-Subsystem Scales and Consensus-Subsystems Scales for the Telemarketing Sample (N = 85 Salespersons)

| | Unaggregated individual | | | | | |
Consensus	*1*	*2*	*3*	*4*	*5*	*6*
Supportive (1)	.51	.24	.16	.35	.28	.45
Equipment maintenance (2)	.28	.66	.09	.09	− .05	.12
Production (3)	.26	.11	.48	.19	.21	.36
Managerial (4)	.43	.12	.36	.61	.26	.52
Personnel maintenance (5)	.37	.12	.32	.10	.57	.30
Adaptive (6)	.54	.24	.43	.31	.35	.61

In this analysis, each individual is assigned the group consensus data for his or her sales unit.

for the aggregated individual data. Table 4–12 presents this same information for the consensus data. Our last table, table 4–13, highlights the validity data for the WFD. Table 4–13 reveals that for both procedures, the total system scores are significant ($r = .49$ and $r = .59$, $p < .05$). In addition, in the consensus mode, 3 of the 6 six subsystem scales are significantly correlated with sales (supportive, $r = .55$, $p < .05$; personnel maintenance, $r = .72$, $p < .01$; and adaptive, $r = .56$, $p < .05$). Validity of a comparable, but slightly lower level is also revealed for the aggregated data.

Discussion

There were a number of interrelated objectives for this chapter as part of the larger project also described in chapter 1 by Schoorman and Schneider and in chapter 7 by Schoorman et al. For this particular chapter, the goals were the following:

1. Develop a methodology for the design of a diagnostic procedure useful in operationalizing the facilitator/inhibitor perspective on unit effectiveness developed by Schoorman and Schneider.

2. Contrast the more common method of aggregating individual responses to represent unit data with a method using a group-consensus procedure.

3. Evaluate the measurement characteristics of these two alternative methodologies for assessing unit facilitators and inhibitors and demonstrate their respective validities vis-à-vis appropriate unit-level criteria of effectiveness.

In pursuit of these objectives, two samples (one, the departments from a university; the second, the sales units of a financial telemarketing organization) were studied. In both samples, a new procedure for the collection of unit data was tried. The consensus procedure used built on some assumptions from the intergroup-theory literature. These assumptions suggested that persons in a group in which perspectives can be shared might yield more valid data than the data typically obtained when individual members' responses are arithmetically aggregated.

To design the survey (the work-facilitation diagnostic), interviews were conducted in each organization as input for the development of survey items. The items generated from the interviews were subsequently sorted into the Katz and Kahn subsystem framework. The result of the sorting process was the WFD. It was administered to both samples individually and again in groups although a comparison of the two methods was only possible in the telemarketing-sales organization.

Table 4–11
Item–Subsystems-Scale Correlations, Item Validities, and Subsystem-Scale Validities for Aggregated Individual Data
(N = 15 Sales Units)

Item–Scale Correlations	Subsystem	Criterion
	Managerial	.44
.36	M4	.23
.31	M9	.10
−.06	M13	.19
−.00	M17	.23
.16	M20	−.33
.04	M29	−.08
.59	M34	.31
.10	M39	.56*
	Supportive	.38
.53	M1	.44
−.19	M14	.12
.10	M19	.22
.55	M23	.21
.16	M30	.15
.34	M35	−.01
	Personnel maintenance	.69**
−.03	M5	.32
.17	M8	−.03
−.05	M16	.43
.06	M18	.00
.47	M22	.28
.11	M24	.03
.11	M26	.43
.38	M28	.26
.21	M32	.42
.48	M38	.63**
.44	M40	.44
	Equipment maintenance	.01
.33	M2	−.08
.15	M6	−.12
.27	M10	−.10
.69	M27	.17
.52	M36	.08
	Production	.25
.02	M3	.27
.21	M12	.12
.03	M21	−.04
.07	M31	−.30
.03	M37	.64**
	Adaptive	.53*
.41	M7	.55*
.58	M11	.66**
.49	M15	.36
.48	M25	.03
.35	M33	.27
	Total system	.49*

*p < .05.

**p < .01.

Table 4–12
Item–Subsystem-Scale Correlations, Item Validities, and Subsystem-Scale
Validities for Consensus Data
(N = 15 Sales Units)

Item–Scale Correlations	Subsystem	Criterion
	Managerial	.32
.03	V4	.18
.53	V9	.00
.08	V13	.08
−.18	V17	−.01
.33	V20	−.30
.27	V29	−.21
.38	V34	.56*
−.27	V39	.51*
	Supportive	.55*
.13	V1	.56*
.11	V14	.22
.14	V19	.54*
.48	V23	.42
.08	V30	.20
.30	V35	.02
	Personnel maintenance	.72**
−.02	V5	.35
.37	V8	.18
−.04	V16	.20
.24	V18	.45*
.40	V22	.34
−.08	V24	.10
.23	V26	.41
.17	V28	.13
.39	V32	.31
.45	V38	.54*
.22	V40	.28
	Equipment maintenance	.11
.47	V2	.09
.11	V6	.28
.31	V10	−.05
.65	V27	.09
.51	V36	.08
	Production	.42
−.15	V3	.24
.29	V12	.28
.01	V21	.01
.20	V31	−.11
−.11	V37	.58*
	Adaptive	.56*
.27	V7	.60**
.31	V11	.35
.35	V15	.30
.28	V25	−.03
.17	V33	.23
	Total system	.59**

*p < .05.
**p < .01.

Table 4–13

Highlights of the Validity Data for the WFD: Telemarketing Sample
N = 15 Sales Units)

Subsystem	r For Aggregated Individual and Sales Data	r For Consensus and Sales Data
Managerial	.44	.32
Supportive	.38	.55*
Personnel maintenance	.69**	.72**
Equipment maintenance	.01	.11
Production	.25	.42
Adaptive	.53*	.56*
Total system	.49*	.59*

*p > .05.
**p > .01.

In both samples, some validity against appropriate criteria of effectiveness was demonstrated. For the university departments, the leading subsystem (Katz and Kahn, 1978) was the adaptive subsystem; it was the only one to correlate significantly with the teaching-effectiveness data (student evaluation of classes). For the telemarketing sample, improved validity was obtained. In that sample, three subsystems revealed significant relationships with unit sales performance and what can be considered leading subsystems: personnel-maintenance, supportive, and adaptive. In addition, an overall system-facilitation index was significantly related to sales.

Internal analyses of the WFD revealed some interesting data. These data were intriguing because the consensus procedure has, to our knowledge, never been used before to generate these kinds of diagnostic data. To evaluate the consensus procedure with more than criterion validity data (although that is not a bad start!), a number of analyses were conducted. These analyses suggested the following two conclusions:

1. Data collected from individuals within work units and then aggregated to produce unit-level data are highly correlated with the consensus data. In fact, in a multimethod analysis, good convergent and discriminant validity were revealed for both procedures as operationalizations of the Katz and Kahn subsystem framework.

This result suggests that previous criticisms of the aggregation procedure for the development of unit-level diagnostic data may have been overly severe. The debate over this issue has been underway since the 1970s (cf. Schneider, 1975), and more recent papers (cf. James, 1982) have been particularly critical of aggregation as a meaningful route to unit-level data. In fairness, it must be noted that with respect to validity, the consensus procedure is consistently superior, although not significantly so.

2. With diagnostics that are carefully designed to maintain respondent focus on the unit of analysis of interest, even single respondents may be useful for indexing unit functioning.

One analysis of the consensus data in the telemarketing sample examined the relationship between the consensus data for the sales units and the individual data for all of the people in those units. Operationally, this involved assigning appropriate unit consensus data to each salesperson. The resulting correlation is an index of the extent to which individual salespeople are likely to agree with a group of their cohorts. The resulting overall correlation was .62 and these unaggregated individual responses *also* revealed convergent and discriminant validity with the consensus data.

These findings, in combination, suggest that persons within work groups tend to see things fairly similarly to their peers. Thus, while some of the analyses reported here showed that on some items and in some groups there is nonagreement, the majority of the evidence developed here indicates that agreement, not disagreement or nonagreement, is the norm.

It seems safe to conclude that unit-level diagnostics of work facilitators and inhibitors, designed using procedures such as those we have outlined, can be reliable and valid in assessing unit functioning and unit effectiveness.

References

Alderfer, C. P., and Brown, L. D. (1972). Designing an "empathic questionnaire" for organizational research. *Journal of Psychology, 56,* 456–60.

Alderfer, C. P., Brown, L. D., Kaplan, R. E., and Smith, K. K. (1984). *Group relations and organizational diagnosis.* New York: Wiley.

Byrne, D. (1971). *The attraction paradigm.* New York: Academic Press.

Campbell, D. T., and Fiske, D. W. (1959). Convergent and discriminant validation by the multitrait–multimethod matrix. *Psychological Bulletin, 56,* 81–105.

James, L. R. (1982). Aggregation bias in estimates of perceptual agreement. *Journal of Applied Psychology, 67,* 219–29.

James, L. R., and Jones, A. P. (1974). Organizational climate: A review of theory and research. *Psychological Bulletin, 81,* 1096–112.

James, L. R., Demaree, R. G., and Wolf, G. (1984). Estimating within-group interrater reliability with and without response bias. *Journal of Applied Psychology, 69,* 85–98.

Janis, I. L. (1972). *Victims of groupthink.* Boston: Houghton Mifflin.

Jones, A. P., and James, L. R. (1979). Psychological climate: Dimensions and relationships of individual and aggregated work environment perceptions. *Organizational Behavior and Human Performance, 23,* 201–50.

Katz, D., and Kahn, R. L. (1978). *The social psychology of organizations.* New York: Wiley.

Maier, N. R. F. (1983). Assets and liabilities in group problem-solving: The need for an integrative function. In J. R. Hackman, E. E. Lawler, and L. W. Porter (eds.), *Perspectives on behavior in organizations,* 2nd ed. New York: McGraw-Hill.

Maruyama, M. (1978). Endogenous research and polyocular anthropology. In R. E. Holloman and S. A. Arutiunov (eds.), *Perspectives on ethnicity.* The Hague: Mouton.

Miller, E. J., and Rice, A. K. (1967). *Systems of organization.* London: Tavistock.

O'Connor, E. J., Peters, L. H., Eulberg, J. R., and Watson, T. W. (1984). Performance-relevant situational constraints: Identification, measurement, and influences on work outcomes. AFHRL-TR-83. Brooks Air Force Base, Tex.: Manpower and Personnel Division, Air Force Human Resources Laboratory.

Peters, L. H., O'Connor, E. J., and Rudolf, C. J. (1980). The behavioral and affective consequences of performance-relevant situational variables. *Organizational Behavior and Human Performance, 25,* 79–96.

Schneider, B. (1975). Organizational climates: An essay. *Personnel Psychology, 28,* 447–79.

Schneider, B. (1983). Work climates: An interactionist perspective. In N. W. Fermier and E. S. Geller (eds.), *Environmental psychology: Directions and perspectives.* New York: Praeger.

Schneider, B., and Reichers, A. (1983). On the etiology of climates. *Personnel Psychology, 36,* 19–39.

5
Measuring Work Obstacles: Procedures, Issues, and Implications

Lawrence H. Peters
Edward J. O'Connor

S everal years ago, we published a paper (Peters and O'Connor, 1980) in which we outlined a series of hypotheses regarding situational factors predicted to interfere with the translation of individual ability and motivation into effective performance. We labeled these factors situational constraints and suggested that serious attention be directed toward exploring their impact on performance, affective reactions, and turnover in work settings. Our efforts over the ensuing several years have been aimed at providing some of this attention.

We initiated a program of research that included both laboratory and field investigations. The lab studies involved the experimental manipulation of situational constraints in order to examine their hypothesized effects on both affective and performance outcomes. The field studies were designed to test many of these same, and other, propositions in actual organizational settings. The field work, however, did not involve experimental designs, but rather, correlational designs. We therefore needed to develop a methodology that could produce measures of meaningful situational constraint variance. It is the development of such measures that will be the focus of the present chapter.

In particular, we shall examine specific issues involved in the measurement of situational conditions that inhibit work performance. We shall organize our discussion of measurement issues from a construct validity perspective. Thus, we shall address (1) what to measure, (2) how to measure it, and (3) the demonstration of construct validity for those newly developed measures. In doing so, we shall attempt to highlight the issues and choice points we encountered and discuss their implications for future efforts to assess situational inhibiting conditions.

This chapter was based on and closely follows a chapter summarizing our research program on situational constraints. (See Peters et al., 1985.)

What to Measure

When we began our work on situational constraints, examples of constraining work factors came easily to mind. Thus, for example, faulty equipment, lack of available replacement parts, and inaccurate information all captured the notion of a situational constraint in the sense that persons who were both able and motivated should not produce as much output as their ability and motivation levels would suggest if needed machinery were faulty, needed replacement parts were unavailable, or needed information were inaccurate. Such examples clearly pointed to situational factors that seemed likely to act as impediments to effective performance.

As we considered other types of possible constraining work factors, however, the issue started to become clouded. The major issue centered around the meaning of the word *situation*. How broadly was this word to be applied and by what process did one pick among the many possible situational factors in order to identify those factors directly relevant to performance? It was at this point that we had to make early decisions regarding the conceptual nature of situational constraints.

Our thinking led us to define situational constraints as (1) inhibiting work factors (as opposed to the persons responsible for those work factors) that were (2) closely associated with the immediate work setting (as opposed to the broader organizational context). Since our interest was in explaining situational factors particularly relevant to individual performance, the focus on factors in the immediate work setting of the individual, regardless of who was responsible for their presence, seemed to fully capture the construct we initially set out to study. Thus, if people indicated that their performances were subpar because supervisors failed to provide needed information, we reasoned that it was the lack of needed information that was the constraint. In this manner, we focussed on the constraining "event" rather than on the "agent" who was responsible for that constraining event. This conceptualization assumes that performance is inhibited by the failure to obtain a needed task-relevant resource (e.g., faulty information, inadequate materials), regardless of who (e.g., supervisor, coworker, client) may be responsible for that inhibiting circumstance.

In like manner, we reasoned that the concept of a constraint needed to be closely tied to persons' assigned job duties. While not denying the importance of other sources of situational variance (e.g., organizational context), it is those factors in the immediate work setting that appeared to us to be the most likely candidates to have a *direct* impact on ability utilization. While organizational constraints might be identified (e.g., slow or inaccurate information systems, strict accounting regulations, hierarchical approval of key decisions), it is the impact of such organizational constraints at the level of the individual that best captures the notion we had in mind. Thus, for example, constraints on individual performance would exist only to the extent that the slow or inaccurate information system actually produced faulty or untimely information, the accounting system actually removed the flexibility associated with implementing a managerial program, or the hierarchical control actually created lengthy time delays.

This conceptualization formed the framework for our attempts to identify specific constraining work obstacles. To this end, we asked persons to reflect on and report specific instances at work in which subpar performance was due to one or more situational events in their immediate work setting. This method was consistent with that suggested by Schneider (1978) for identifying work factors that interfered with the translation of individual differences into performance. Procedurally, one starts with the behavior of interest (inhibited performance) and works backward to identify specific situational, as opposed to personal, factors that had an impact on that behavior.

This procedure was the basis for three separate taxonomic investigations. The first (Peters et al., 1980) involved sixty-two persons employed on a wide variety of managerial and nonmanagerial jobs in different organizations. The second study (O'Connor et al., 1984b) involved a large managerial sample from a national convenience store organization. The third study (O'Connor et al., 1984b) explored the taxonomic structure of constraining work factors within nonsupervisory enlisted positions in the U.S. Air Force.

In all cases, persons completed an open-ended questionnaire in which they were asked to identify one or two separate instances in which a specific situational factor was believed to be responsible for subpar performance. These written descriptions were then independently sorted into categories based on similarity of content. When disagreement occurred, the raters met and resolved the disagreement. Finally, both retranslation techniques and principal components analyses (see, for example, Eulberg et al., 1983) were utilized to confirm the adequacy of the obtained categories of situational constraints.

Results from these three studies are presented in appendix 5–A1. While the table shows that fewer categories of constraints were identified in the first (1980) study (nine constraint categories) than in the latter two studies nineteen supervisory and fourteen nonsupervisory constraint categories, respectively, these differences seem to reflect the small, diverse nature of the first sample as compared to the larger, more homogeneous samples utilized in the other investigations. This difference appears to have resulted in more general constraint categories in the Peters et al. (1980) study and more specific categories in the O'Connor et al. (1984a and 1984b) investigations. While differences are apparent, it is useful to note the high degree of similarity among these three induced-constraint category systems. The early, more general dimension space identified by Peters et al. (1980) appears fully represented by the more specific dimensions identified in our latter two taxonomic studies.

These findings, in conjunction with those from other taxonomic investigations (see Eulberg et al., 1984, for a discussion of these other investigations), suggest that there are eleven general constraint categories. These include the eight constraints reported in the Peters et al. (1980) investigation (i.e., job-related information, tools and equipment, materials and supplies, budgetary support, required services and help from others, task preparation, time availability, and work environment), and three additional constraint categories (scheduling of activities, transportation, and job-relevant authority) suggested from results based on other taxonomic studies. While all categories of situational constraints might not be equally applicable to all organizational settings and jobs, the eleven constraint categories identified do appear to represent a taxonomic system with sufficient generalizability to be applicable to a wide diversity of organizations and jobs. As such, it appears to provide a reasonable basis for the development of a general constraint questionnaire that could be appropriately administered within many work settings.

Measuring Constraints

At the outset of the measurement phase of our work, we considered a variety of alternative measurement strategies. These included both objective (e.g., frequency of machine downtime, time delay in receiving raw materials) and subjective (e.g., ratings of resource shortages) strategies. Our thinking suggested that it would be extremely difficult, time-inefficient, and costly to develop objective information regarding all possible constraints. We, therefore, examined alternative subjective approaches.[1] While several subjective sources of information about constraints can be identified (e.g., job incumbents, supervisors, specifically trained raters, task-design experts), we decided that the most appropriate source of information was the job incumbent. Our judgment was based on the simple fact that it is the job incumbent who interacts with various task demands and resources on a continuous basis, and thus, has first-hand information regarding the presence or absence of constraints and their severity. While the use of job incumbents poses particular problems from an ego-defensive (Vroom, 1964) and attributional perspective, job incumbents nonetheless have the most appropriate perspective for commenting on conditions that inhibit day-to-day performance on their jobs. We, thus, chose to measure situational constraints from the perceptions of job incumbents.

With this as a starting point, we implemented standard-scale development procedures, with corresponding psychometric checks of the resulting developmental versions of the scales. With few exceptions, the issues involved in developing a constraints measure were fairly straightforward and not noteworthy.

Prior to beginning work on scale development, however, a key issue involving the development of an overall constraints score had to be resolved. Our conceptual propositions involving situational constraints (Peters and O'Connor, 1980) suggested that it was *overall* job constraints that were important. Our goal, therefore, was to develop a measure that would both assess relevant constraint categories and result in an overall job-constraint score. The problem this presented results from the fact that not all jobs require persons to utilize the same resource mix in order to successfully accomplish their assigned work. Thus, for example, not every job has budget, tool, or transportation requirements. As a result, a general measure, one that assesses a fixed number of specific constraint dimensions, would likely include constraint dimensions that were irrelevant for some jobs. Such a measure, naturally, would have to allow respondents to indicate that some constraint categories are inappropriate.

In one sense, this does not pose a problem. Since we were concerned with obtaining an index of overall job constraints, we could compute such an index by summing the ratings from only relevant constraint dimensions, once all items were scored to reflect greater severity of constraints. Here, higher scores would reflect greater perceived overall constraints, no matter how many constraint dimensions were relevant. On the other hand, in samples including a diversity of jobs, the overall constraints score would be made up of linear combinations of different constraint dimensions, and an examination of specific constraints would necessarily include a large "missing-data" component. Indeed, the only way to have complete data on all dimensions and an overall constraint score based on a linear combination of the same constraint factors would be to specifically develop information about potential constraints operating within a very homgeneous job grouping.

Our field research on situational inhibitors involved two general phases of scale development. The first phase involved testing some of our initial ideas regarding the impact of situational constraints and was conducted in samples that included a wide diversity of jobs and/or organizations. (See, for example, O'Connor et al., 1982). Scales for this research were based on the initial eight constraint dimensions reported in Peters et al. (1980) and, due to the diversity of jobs included in these studies, were general in format. The second phase of this work involved in-depth exploration of the impact of constraints within specific field settings and, thus, involved the development of questionnaire content based on specific information obtained in those settings. Each type of instrument will be described shortly.

A semantic differential format, such as that exemplified in figure 5–1, was developed for each of the original eight constraint categories in the

Figure 5–1. Example of Some Items from a Situational Constraint Scale Using the Semantic Differential Format

INSTRUCTIONS: On the following pages, you will find a series of scales designed to assess your perceptions of various aspects of your work situation. For each item, you will find a series of adjective pairs separated by seven blank spaces. The adjective pairs were chosen to be "opposites" of each other. Your job is to *check one* of the seven blank spaces between each of the adjective pairs. For each adjective pair, please check one and only one of the blank spaces in order to *best describe* your work situation.

Consider the following example:

The FEEDBACK I receive about how well I do my job is:

UNIMPORTANT   ( ) ( ) ( ) ( ) ( ) ( ) (✔) IMPORTANT
ADEQUATE   ( ) (✔) ( ) ( ) ( ) ( ) ( ) INADEQUATE
NOT EASILY SECURED (✔) ( ) ( ) ( ) ( ) ( ) ( ) EASILY SECURED

The person making these responses would be indicating that having feedback was extremely important, but that the amount of feedback received was slightly less than adequate. Further, the last check mark would indicate that, on the job being described, feedback was extremely difficult to secure.

JOB-RELATED INFORMATION. Refers to the information (from supervisors, peers, subordinates, customers, company rules, policies and procedures, and so forth) needed to do the job assigned.

A. *To do my work, JOB-RELATED INFORMATION is:*

UNIMPORTANT   ( ) ( ) ( ) ( ) ( ) ( ) ( )   IMPORTANT
UNNECESSARY   ( ) ( ) ( ) ( ) ( ) ( ) ( )   NECESSARY

                   ⌐If BOTH of your responses to these items were to the left of the arrow, skip parts B and C and go directly to the next section of the questionnaire.

B. Availability: *JOB-RELATED INFORMATION needed to do my job is:*

UNAVAILABLE   ( ) ( ) ( ) ( ) ( ) ( ) ( ) AVAILABLE
NOT EASILY SECURED ( ) ( ) ( ) ( ) ( ) ( ) ( ) EASILY SECURED
OBTAINABLE   ( ) ( ) ( ) ( ) ( ) ( ) ( ) UNOBTAINABLE
ACCESSIBLE   ( ) ( ) ( ) ( ) ( ) ( ) ( ) INACCESSIBLE
HARD TO ACQUIRE   ( ) ( ) ( ) ( ) ( ) ( ) ( ) EASY TO ACQUIRE

C. Quality: *The QUALITY of the JOB-RELATED INFORMATION I receive is:*

SUFFICIENT   ( ) ( ) ( ) ( ) ( ) ( ) ( ) INSUFFICIENT
USELESS   ( ) ( ) ( ) ( ) ( ) ( ) ( ) USEFUL
HIGH   ( ) ( ) ( ) ( ) ( ) ( ) ( ) LOW
APPROPRIATE   ( ) ( ) ( ) ( ) ( ) ( ) ( ) INAPPROPRIATE
BAD   ( ) ( ) ( ) ( ) ( ) ( ) ( ) GOOD
ADEQUATE   ( ) ( ) ( ) ( ) ( ) ( ) ( ) INADEQUATE

O'Connor et al. (1982) study. This approach allows the investigator to assess the "availability" and "quality" of relevant resources. For each constraint category, persons responded by indicating the degree to which "availability" and "quality" were described by a series of adjective pairs chosen to be opposites of each other (e.g., useless–useful, appropriate–inappropriate). The initial questions regarding the relevance of each constraint category to the particular situation being investigated (Section A in figure 5–1) allowed the actual collection of constraint information (Sections B and C in figure 5–1) for only those dimensions that were applicable. This approach resulted in highly reliable measures (O'Connor et al., 1982; Pooyan et al., 1982).

More recent scale-development efforts (O'Connor et al., 1984a, 1984b) have asked respondents to indicate the extent to which specific statements regarding constraints accurately describe their work setting. This approach is exemplified in figure 5–2.

Item content for these scales was based on the critical incidents data from the open-ended questionnaires. All items were declarative statements describing a specific constraint. Respondents indicated the extent to which these statements accurately described their work setting on a five-point scale rang-

Figure 5–2. Example of Some Items from a Situational Constraint Scale Using the Graphic Rating Scale Format

not at all accurate	somewhat accurate	fairly accurate	very accurate	completely accurate	not applicable
1	2	3	4	5	NA

1. I often must work with and depend on others who are not well trained .... ____

2. I frequently cannot get necessary materials, supplies, and/or parts when I need them .... ____

3. I never have enough time to finish my duties without rushing .... ____

4. The information I receive is often incorrect when I receive it.. ____

5. I must follow specific policies, procedures, and instructions that I know to be wrong .... ____

6. I am not usually given enough training to handle new duties that are added to my job .... ____

ing from "not at all accurate" (1) to "very accurate" (5). A "does not apply" alternative was available for irrelevant items.

In both studies, preliminary versions of the constraints scales were developed. For this purpose, multiple items were written to assess each of the constraint dimensions identified during the taxonomic phases of these studies (as previously discussed). Internal-consistency reliability and principal-component analyses were then conducted to identify subsets of the original items that best reflected each specific constraint dimension. In all cases, results indicated highly reliable, homogeneous constraint scales.

Based on these procedures, it appeared that we were able to develop measures of situational constraints that could be meaningfully used in future research efforts. The results, to this point, suggested that situational constraints could be identified, empirically categorized in a meaningful manner, and reliably measured. The next step, that of providing information regarding the validity of these newly developed scales, suggested that our approach to measuring this source of situational variance might be somewhat deficient. It is to that topic we now turn.

Demonstrating Construct Validity

The scale-development procedures we implemented were in the context of other research aimed at testing conceptual propositions regarding the impact of situational constraints on work outcomes. The research conducted to test those hypotheses simultaneously provided results pertinent to the validity of our measures. To the extent that the data supported our original hypotheses, we would be able to conclude that our measures tapped relevant variance.

Results from four field investigations are pertinent. Two studies (O'Connor et al., 1982; Pooyan et al., 1982) examined the relationships between constraints as measured using the semantic differential format and both affective and performance outcomes. The other two investigations (O'Connor et al., 1984a, 1984b) examined the relationships between constraints as measured using the graphic rating scale format and a variety of affective, performance, and withdrawal outcomes.

With regard to the semantic differential format scales, the results consistently supported the proposition that constraints were negatively related to affective responses. In all cases, persons who reported higher levels of perceived situational constraints also reported greater dissatisfaction and frustration. The observed relationships between constraints and performance, however, were nonsignificant. It should be noted that these performance results were based on data from a mixed sample of managers and nonmanagers. It may well be that the aggregation of the performance ratings for persons employed on jobs as different as these was inadvisable.

The two investigations using the graphic rating scale format instrument also reported significant relationships between perceived constraints and affective reactions. In addition, the O'Connor et al. (1984b) study reported significant relationships between perceived constraints and both performance and turnover within a managerial sample from a national convenience store organization. The O'Connor et al. (1984a) study, however, failed to find significant associations between perceived constraints and either performance or intentions to reenlist within any of their seven Air Force samples.

Taken together, these findings offer mixed support for the validity of our measures of situational constraints. The evidence with regard to affective reactions suggests the validity of the measures for both rating formats. With regard to other outcomes, the evidence was spotty. Even when significant relationships with performance and turnover were observed (O'Connor, 1984b), those results were of limited magnitude. Since results involving performance are crucial to the determination of construct validity, we cannot conclude strong support for our measures. We, likewise, are not ready to reach the conclusion of limited validity either. Such a conclusion would require additional evidence that perceptual data regarding situational constraints were unrelated or weakly related to relevant measures of performance. The rest of this discussion, therefore, will be framed around issues associated with producing that evidence.

As just noted, only one field study (O'Connor et al., 1984b) produced results supporting the relationship between constraints and performance, and in that study, only 1 percent of the performance variance was explained. Peters et al. (1985) discussed the weak and nonsupportive results involving performance in terms of the low magnitude of constraints reported in the field settings investigated. In only one of the field investigations they reviewed (Phillips and Freedman, 1982) were reported constraint levels, on average, above the midpoint on the rating scales utilized. They went on to argue that since persons described their work settings as relatively free from situational constraints, it was not surprising that constraints have a limited impact on performance in those settings.

This explanation suggests that results from our field investigations to date should not have produced significant constraint–performance associations. Other field data, however, using different measures of constraints, have recently been reported in which perceptually measured constraints have been found to significantly relate to performance (Olson et al., 1984; Steel and Mento, 1986). Taken together, these findings and arguments suggest that conducting research aimed at producing evidence regarding the construct validity of constraint measures may not be the straightforward research problem it appears to be. Consistent with Cronbach and Meehl's (1955) discussion of nonsupportive findings in construct-validation research, we then examined the appropriateness of our design for testing hypotheses regarding the impact of constraints on performance.

The ideas presented next follow from our belief that our measures are valid. If this is true, and if the conceptual hypotheses are not in error, then we would be required to demonstrate that characteristics of the research or research setting explain the nonsupportive findings regarding performance (Cronbach and Meehl, 1955). Given that (1) laboratory evidence supports the conceptual constraint model (see Peters et al., 1985), (2) the current measures did bear consistent and appropriate relationships to relevant affective outcomes, and (3) our own and other field research (e.g., Olson et al., 1984) have produced significant perceived constraint–performance relationships, it would appear appropriate to examine the possibility that particular conditions in our field settings might have existed that reduced the impact of constraints on performance. The following discussion is directed toward that goal. It represents our speculations regarding broader situational factors that may both (1) act to prevent constraints from having their expected impact on performance in field settings and (2) have a more general, but direct, negative impact on performance in those work settings.

It should be recalled that we (Peters and O'Connor, 1980) defined a constraint as a situational factor that inhibits performance by preventing persons from fully utilizing their relevant abilities and motivation. The more severe the constraints, the greater their expected negative impact on performance. In similar work settings, this would imply that differences, across persons, in the severity of constraints would be related to differences in performance. It follows that in order to test this proposition in field settings, one would simply need to assess the systematic covariation in measured constraints and performance for a group of persons working in a setting for which a common measure of performance could be obtained. This research prescription, however, contains several assumptions about the setting chosen to conduct such an investigation, assumptions that we believe are critical to developing meaningful information regarding the construct validity of constraint measures.

It assumes (1) that persons are assigned tasks requiring the use of their abilities and motivation in order to produce effective performance, (2) that organizations are concerned about individual performance in the first place, (3) that persons cannot easily make excuses to justify their failure to meet meaningful performance standards, and (4) that resources are not so plentiful that their absence is improbable. If any of these four conditions were not fulfilled, apparent constraints would have only a minimal impact on performance (i.e., ability and motivation would not be hampered in an impactful way), and persons would be expected to indicate as much on perceptual measures. Each assumption will be discussed next.

Assumption 1: Persons are assigned to tasks that require the use of their abilities and motivation. Even if valid hiring practices are employed such that persons have the abilities that are useful in performing the various tasks assigned to them, it still does not guarantee that incumbents are required to use those abilities in order to be successful. If the job is one for which the formal minimum performance standards are moderate to high in difficulty, then abilities will need to be more fully utilized and persons will need to put forth effort to attain those performance standards. In such a situation, the probability of being successful is moderate at best; as a result, a lack of resources might be critical to successful performance. Here, constraints should have an impact and, as a result, be readily apparent to job incumbents.

If, on the other hand, persons are not required to perform their jobs particularly well (i.e., low formal performance standards exist), then most persons can be expected to meet those standards on a regular basis regardless of their abilities and effort. If most persons consistently do little more than meet those low standards, then small, and possibly moderate, resource shortages will not be particularly critical. Since less is expected of employees in such conditions, it would take an *extreme* resource shortage before any noticeable effect on performance were observed. Since only extreme resource shortages would actually impede performance, persons would not be expected to report mild, or possibly even moderate, levels of resource shortages as constraints. Thus, low performance standards should reduce the presence, recognition, and impact of constraints.

It is one thing to publicly state performance standards and quite another to consistently maintain them. Public statements of high performance standards would lose meaning unless they were actively maintained by management action aimed at enforcing those standards. (See Wilkins and Ouchi's [1983] discussion of the maintenance of performance standards in organizations.) If workers are never held to those standards by appropriate sanctions, then the lower bound of actual performance allowed before negative sanctions are applied becomes the "operational" minimum performance standard for those employees.

If employees are allowed "slippage" such that work failing to meet a deadline can be turned in late or less than adequate performance is actually accepted, then implicit rejection of public, formal standards will have been demonstrated. In effect, unless persons are made responsible for attaining specific, moderate-to-high performance standards, they are never held responsible for contributing meaningfully at work. If this is the case, there would be few constraints, because the low level of required performance is never really hampered. In effect, when we allow people to circumvent performance standards, any resource shortage would have to be very severe to truly have an observed adverse impact.

Assumption 2: Organizations value individual performance. We have traditionally assumed that effective individual performance is a valued outcome in organizations. This implies that the management of an organization sees its success tied closely to the success of its members. If that were not the case, then no real organizational pressures would exist to promote individual effectiveness, and substandard performance, although not desired, would be more likely to be tolerated. This condition might well lead to the evolution of low performance standards, as just described.

This rather heretical idea may actually represent an organizational reality that often goes unobserved. Such circumstances might exist in a profit-making organization that sees a large portion of its market and profits to result primarily from technological innovations. Since profits are thought to follow from the successful marketing of technologically innovative products, organizational decisionmakers may focus their attention in this area and, as a result, allow mediocrity in the performance of human resources to develop. Consider also a public organization that relies on state or federal legislatures to provide an ample budget. We can all think of programs that, because of their political popularity at a given point in time, were amply funded. Such programs often depend more on political events for their economic well-being than on the contributions of their members. In such instances, the key is to maintain the perception of appropriate behaviors for the organization's relevant internal or external constituencies (Gaertner and Ramnarayan, 1983). Finally, consider a military organization whose primary goal is a state of readiness in the event that it is called on to carry out a military operation. Such an organization needs only to demonstrate that it is prepared to fulfill its mission in times of emergency as opposed to actually having to fulfill that mission efficiently and effectively every day. Indeed, one cannot, on a daily basis, fight a war that is not in progress!

In such settings, where high levels of individual contributions are not seen as integral to the current health and survival of the organization, only lip service to individual effectiveness might be expected, with corresponding greater tolerance for substandard, mediocre performance. Under these conditions, the *necessity* of focussing attention on individual performance is reduced. When this occurs, the conditions that foster "slippage" in performance standards exist, and (just like the situation in which actual performance standards are low) only severe resource shortages will both be recognized and have a negative impact as constraints.

Assumption 3: Persons cannot easily make excuses to justify their failure to meet high performance standards and still be given high performance ratings. There are times that persons can really be hampered by constraints. Machines do break down, supplies are sometimes unavailable, required help occasionally is delayed, and information can be unclear. Anecdotal accounts of failures to perform tasks due to such constraints testify to their impact in ways that create consensual validation for their existence. The very fact that we share this consensual meaning with others, however, suggests that we may be prepared and even primed to accept constraint explanations to justify inadequate performance.

Not only can people identify appropriate external factors to explain their inability to fulfill performance expectations, but sometimes they may point to such circumstances even when they are not true obstacles. Kelley (1972), in discussing the discounting principle from attribution theory, has argued that any single cause will be increasingly discounted as a sufficient explanation for an event as the number of other possible causes for that event increases. Consistent with this argument, to the extent that employees can convince others that the presence of constraints makes meeting performance standards beyond their control, they can reduce their own felt responsibility and blameworthiness in the matter. In this sense, constraints may provide a post hoc justification for explaining performance that does not meet standards (or that failed to take advantage of existing work opportunities). Persons who do not meet work expectations may, therefore, use the presence of constraints to try to convince others (and themselves) that justifiable reasons beyond their control existed that make it appropriate to dismiss the occurrence of subpar performance, therefore making them less blameworthy. Evidence by Wood and Mitchell (1981) suggests that this may be an effective strategy for employees who are more interested in minimizing punitive responses rather than in maximizing personal and organizational performances.

To the extent that pointing to constraints is legitimized within an organizational setting, it creates a "culture of justification." It not only legitimizes after-the-fact justifications for failure to meet performance standards, but, more generally, it legitimizes an alternative to being effective within that setting. Such organizational settings not only relieve persons from personal responsibility, as previously discussed, but actually create a culture where verbal behavior can be exchanged for performance-related behavior.

Under such conditions, the perceptual measurement of constraints confounds variance due to situational factors with variance due to justificatory biases. The more dominant and widespread that culture of justification, (1) the more likely justificatory biases will be expressed in varying degrees by workers responding to perceptual constraint measures and (2) given that this confound is likely to differentially exist in responses across individuals, the less likely it is that those perceptual measures will relate to performance.

Assumption 4: Resources are not so plentiful that their absence is improbable. Even if persons are assigned to jobs for which high performance standards are stated and maintained and even if their attainment is valued, the organizational conditions surrounding work may still be such that it is improbable that impactful constraints would exist. Such would be the case if excess resources or slack were present to guard against crises or provide a cushion for adapting to internal or external changes (Bourgeois, 1981). While plentiful resources would not guarantee high levels of performance, they effectively remove the situational obstacles to effective performance. One would expect, therefore, to find low levels of perceived constraints when high levels of slack have been effectively built into an organization or work setting. Under such conditions, people would realize that their performance would not be negatively affected by the level of resources actually available and, therefore, not consider the available resources to be severe obstacles to effective performance. Variance in reported resources in such a setting might exist, but it should not be expected to relate to performance since, regardless of the existence of such variance, the needed resources are available to all or most persons within that setting.

This discussion suggests that the successful validation of measures developed to assess situational constraints may depend on the presence of other factors related more directly to performance. Unless we set work standards that engage persons' abilities and motivation, we expect persons to be fully responsible for attaining those standards, we value high levels of individual contributions, and we make it difficult for persons to justify failure to attain those performance standards, constraints should not have an adverse effect on performance outcomes. By extension, this argument points to organizational conditions that do not promote effective individual performance in general, and as a consequence, should blur relationships between individual performance and relevant individual and situational variables.

When individual effectiveness is devalued in the manner described, the variance in observed performance should be less precisely understood and, as a result, it should become more difficult to have a meaningful impact on performance levels. By contrast, in organizations in which high standards are set and actively enforced, the performance variance should be more strongly determined by factors theoretically expected to affect performance (e.g., ability, motivation, and constraints). Since doing well is expected of people in these organizational settings, factors affecting how well people do become important. As a result, these factors should more readily be observed to demonstrate their theoretically predicted relationships when made the subject of field investigations.

The purpose of this discussion is to emphasize that the demonstration of construct validity for measures of situational constraints (or for any variable hypothesized to partially determine performance) is not always a straightforward research problem. We, therefore, suggest that such attempts should be viewed within a broader, organizational conceptual framework focussing careful attention on developing a relevant sampling plan for construct validation research involving the prediction of performance. This argument implies that the observation of supportive construct validity evidence for measures of situational constraints may require the same conditions that promote individual effectiveness. Future field research aimed at providing construct validity evidence for measures of constraints (or, more generally, at investigating relationships involving performance) therefore should sample organizations that promote individual effectiveness in order to obtain individual performance variance that most strongly favors the observation of significant and meaningful associations with performance.

Conclusion

This discussion reflects our belief that the impact of individual differences in both talent and access to resources on performance is lessened to the extent that the work setting does not require their use for the attainment of meaningful and challenging performance outcomes. In a sense, we are suggesting that the likelihood of observing significant results in all field research aimed at predicting performance may depend on conditions currently unspecified. Thus, we are hypothesizing the construct of "performance tension" as a necessary condition for the prediction of performance variance from relevant individual and situational factors.

Performance tension might be produced in a variety of ways, all of which would act to compel job incumbents to strive for and not be satisfied with less than truly effective levels of performance. Thus, high performance standards, superiors who are not easily compromised to accept less than effective performance, zero-sum competition, acculturation pressures to develop and maintain personal standards of effectiveness, and the like all would result in tension placed on job incumbents to utilize their talents and needed resources. Under such conditions, a lack of either talent or resources would be expected to have a noticeable effect on performance outcomes. While similar levels of performance tension might be produced in a variety of different ways, the presence of such tension always results from either the purposeful actions of those who are charged with fully utilizing an organization's human resources or the determination to succeed seen in internally motivated employees.

By implication, this line of thinking suggests that one's sampling plan for construct validation studies must go beyond identifying variance along relevant variables. Indeed, simply having variance in talent or variance in access to resources will matter little unless persons are expected to perform highly enough to make demands on that talent and be prevented from meeting those standards by resource shortages. From this perspective, construct validation research takes on additional requirements suggesting that the success of individual level-of-analysis research may strongly depend on the specific work unit studied. Such an interaction-based prediction may not only help explain the poor showing of much individual level-of-analysis field research aimed at predicting performance, such as that reported in this chapter, but, in addition, is suggestive of useful future paths to explore.

Note

1. While more difficult to produce for all possible constraint categories, objective measures, where readily obtainable, have great potential utility as a check on the perceptual measurement strategy. In this regard, one could assess the extent to which subjective measures of particular constraints mirror "objective" indices of that same constraint category. Thus, for example, archival records of machine downtime could be compared with subjective ratings for this constraint category. Convergence between these two measurement strategies would suggest that perceptual measures are capable of capturing appropriate variance in work settings, thus supporting a necessary assumption of the perceptual measurement strategy.

References

Bourgeois, L. J., III. (1981). On the measurement of organizational slack. *Academy of Management Review, 6,* 29–39.

Cronbach, L. J., and Meehl, P. E. (1955). Construct validity in psychological research. *Psychological Bulletin, 52,* 281–302.

Eulberg, J. R., O'Connor, E. J., Peters, L. H., and Watson, T. W. (1983). Measuring performance constraints in Air Force work environments. *Proceedings of the 1983 annual meetings of the American Institute for Decision Sciences.*

Eulberg, J. R., O'Connor, E. J., Peters, L. H., and Watson, T. W. (1984). Performance constraints: A selective review of relevant literature. *Psychological Documents.*

Gaertner, G. H., and Ramnarayan, S. (1983). Organizational effectiveness: An alternative perspective. *Academy of Management Review, 8,* 97–107.

Jones, E. E., and Nisbett, R. E. (1971). *The actor and the observer: Divergent perceptions of the causes of behavior.* Morristown, N.J.: General Learning Press.

Kelley, H. H. (1972). Attribution in social interaction. In E. E. Jones et al. (eds.), *Attribution: Perceiving the causes of behavior.* Morristown, N.J.: General Learning Press, pp. 1–26.

O'Connor, E. J., Peters, L. H., Eulberg, J. R., and Watson, T. W. (1984a). Situational constraints in Air Force work settings: Effects on performance, affective reactions and reenlistment plans. Paper presented at the Annual Meeting of the Academy of Management, Boston.

O'Connor, E. J., Peters, L. H., Pooyan, A., Weekley, J., Frank, B., and Erenkrantz, B. (1984b). Situational constraint effects on performance, affective reactions and turnover: A field replication and extension. *Journal of Applied Psychology, 64,* 663–72.

O'Connor, E. J., Peters, L. H., Rudolf, C. J. and Pooyan, A. (1982). Situational constraints and employee affective reactions: A field replication. *Group and Organization Studies, 7,* 418–28.

Olson, D. M., Borman, W. C., Roberson, L., and Rose, S. R. (1984). Relationship between scales on an Army work environment questionnaire and measures of performance. Paper presented at the 92nd Annual Meeting of the American Psychological Association, Toronto.

Peters, L. H., and O'Connor, E. J. (1980). Situational constraints and work outcomes: The influences of a frequently overlooked construct. *Academy of Management Review, 5,* 391–97.

Peters, L. H., O'Connor, E. J., and Eulberg, J. R. (1985). Situational constraints: Sources, consequences, and future considerations. In K. M. Rowland and G. R. Ferris (eds.), *Research in personnel and human resources management,* vol. 3. Greenwich, Conn.: JAI Press, pp. 79–113.

Peters, L. H., O'Connor, E. J., and Rudolf, C. J. (1980). The behavioral and affective consequences of performance-relevant situational variables. *Organizational Behavior and Human Performance, 25,* 79–96.

Phillips, J. S., and Freedman, S. M. (1982). Situational constraints, task characteristics, and affective task reactions. Paper presented at the 42nd Annual Meeting of the Academy of Management, New York.

Pooyan, A., O'Connor, E. J., Peters, L. H., Quick, J. C., Jones, N. D., and Kulisch, A. (1982). Supervisory/subordinate differences in perceptions of performance constraints: Barriers are in the eye of the beholder. *Proceedings of the annual convention of the Southwest Academy of Management,* 170–74.

Schneider, B. (1978). Person-situation selection: A review of some ability-situation interaction research. *Personnel Psychology, 31,* 281–97.

Steel, R. P., and Mento, A. J. (1986). Opportunity knocks: The impact of situational constraints on relationships between job performance criteria. *Organizational Behavior and Human Decision Processes, 37,* 254–65.

Vroom, V. (1964). *Work and motivation.* New York: Wiley.

Wilkins, A. L., and Ouchi, W. G. (1983). Efficient cultures: Exploring the relationship between culture and organizational performance. *Administrative Science Quarterly, 28,* 468–81.

Wood, R. E., and Mitchell, T. R. (1981). Manager behavior in a social context: The impact of impression management on attribution and disciplinary actions. *Organizational Behavior and Human Performance, 28,* 346–78.

Appendix 5A–1
Categories of Situational Constraints

Category Names and Definitions	Peters et al. (1980)	O'Connor et al. (1984b)	O'Connor et al. (1984a)
1. *Job-related information:* The information (from various sources) needed to do the job assigned	Job-related information	Job-related information Knowledge of company policies and procedures	Job-related information Policies and procedures
2. *Tools and equipment:* The specific tools, equipment, and machinery needed to do the job	Tools and equipment	Inadequate equipment	Tools and equipment
3. *Materials and supplies:* The materials and supplies needed to do the job assigned	Materials and supplies	Insufficient materials and supplies Inadequate amounts of merchandise Excess inventory Wrong inventory	Materials and supplies Forms
4. *Budgetary support:* Financial resources and budgetary support needed to do the job assigned	Budgetary support	Budgetary support	
5. *Required services and help from others:* The services and help from others needed to do the job assigned	Required services and help from others	Shortage of help Unkept appointments Inadequate help from construction department	Cooperation from others Personnel
6. *Task preparation:* Preparation through education, training, and experience	Task preparation	Insufficient training	Training

(*continued*)

Category Names and Definitions	Peters et al. (1980)	O'Connor et al. (1984b)	O'Connor et al. (1984a)
7. *Time availablity:* Availability of time to do job assigned taking into consideration time limits, interruptions, unnecessary meetings, non–job related distractions, etc.	Time availability Work overload	Inadequate response time Frequent long and inappropriate meetings Excessive paperwork	Time Red tape
8. *Work environment:* Physical aspects that affect ability to do the job assigned	Work environment	Inappropriate workspace	Physical working conditions
9. *Scheduling of activities:* The arrangement of work schedule for best utilization of resources		Unscheduled activities	Planning and scheduling of activities
10. *Transportation:* Transportation needed to get to and complete the job			Transportation
11. *Job-relevant authority:* The authority needed to do the job assigned		Authority to enforce company standards Bypassed authority	Job-relevant authority

6
An Aggregation Problem
and Organizational Effectiveness

Karlene H. Roberts
Stephen B. Sloane

Our mandate is to discuss the problem of organizational measurement and how this can influence research concerned with organizational effectiveness. We shall concentrate on one aspect of measurement: the problem of aggregation.

We shall use our experience aboard the aircraft carrier *U.S.S. Carl Vinson* to provide examples for our analysis of why system linkages cannot be ignored if veridical pictures of organizational effectiveness are to be obtained. In a very general sense, this is the problem of choosing appropriate levels of analysis to guide our explanation. It is also the problem of moving across levels of analysis in explanation. We argue here that a neglected aspect of aggregation is concern with the linkages that actually tie subparts together to form whole systems. Without concern for this issue, description and explanation of organizational processes are incomplete.

First, we shall examine the state of the art of aggregation methodology. Then, we shall add to the aggregate literature the problem of specifying conceptual linkages among components of organizations, both within and across levels of analysis. We propose that both practical organizational design and theoretical research design are sensitive to the linkage problem. Our example illustrates this.

Major Aggregation Issues—A 1978 Perspective

We begin here by reviewing the major aggregation issues we saw in 1978. Roberts et al. (1978) discussed six major aggregation issues: conceptual aggregation, aggregation over samples, aggregation over time, aggregation over measurements, aggregation in data analysis, and aggregation of data and interpretations.

Conceptual Aggregation. Conceptual or theoretical aggregation refers to the discipline-oriented paradigms guiding our theory and research development.

It is linked to the levels of analysis associated with the various disciplines that "do" organizational science. If a paradigm used to explain a phenomenon emphasizes conceptualization and measurement at the organization level, it often either tucks individuals into the organization through some organizational construct or it misses them all together. If a paradigm emphasizes individuals, it often forgets the organizations in which they live and work. Thus, a potential problem in conceptualization drawn from one level is that it misses all the other aggregate levels and fails to reveal the full truth in research designed from the conceptualization.

Aggregation over Samples. Units of theory appropriate to a problem should clearly direct the level of analysis at which data should be collected. While this is straightforward enough, we have in our field many examples of inferences made about one level of analysis based on data from a different level. The most obvious example of this is the ecological correlation (Robinson, 1950) in which correlated group scores are used to indicate something about individuals. We know that the relationship between correlations of individual scores and correlations of their group aggregates is far from perfect.

Aggregation over Time. Time aggregates provide possibly the most important aggregation problem for organizational researchers. When time intervals are considered at all in data collection, they are usually chosen for convenience rather than for any other reason. In most sciences, events and processes have natural, knowable time cycles. In the organizational sciences, it is often difficult to specify what these time cycles might be. In obviously seasonal industries, time cycles are easier to incorporate into theorizing, but for many interesting questions, it is not easy to select appropriate time cycles. For example, what is the half-life of a career? Does it vary by industry, regional area in which the career is being played out, and so on?

Aggregation over Measurements. Three measurement-aggregation issues bear discussion. The first has to do with summary variables. Many variables we use, including age, are summaries of numerous things. We usually fail to address questions of variable composition relevant to organizations. The second measurement-aggregation problem is closely related to the first. Some variables are not easily attached to particular units of analysis. These variables often reflect both things people do and aspects of their organization and are, thus, interactional variables. Clarifying the degree to which variables are interactional helps in theory building and it also helps in selecting appropriate data-analytic strategies. The third measurement-aggregation problem arises from the fact that some variables are causally interactive or reciprocal. For example, organizational variables such as structure and function can influence each other. Causal interaction and reciprocation among variables is usually ignored in model building in favor of unidirectional causality or avoiding the issue all together.

Aggregation in Data Analysis. Aggregation in data analysis is the most commonly addressed aggregation problem. The way data are grouped affect the estimated parameters. The most commonly studied effect of aggregation is change in correlation and regression coefficients following a shift in level of aggregation.

Aggregation of Data and Interpretations. Aggregation problems in interpretation usually occur because of what went on before. The absence of composition theories contributes to interpretational aggregation problems. The most commonly discussed interpretational aggregation problems are the fallacy of the wrong level and the ecological fallacy.

> The "fallacy of the wrong level" consists not in making inferences from one level of analysis to another, but in making direct *translation of properties or relations* from one level to another, that is, making too simple inferences. The fallacy can be committed working downward, by projecting from groups or categories to individuals, or upwards, by projecting from individuals to higher units. . . . The ecological fallacy in general consists in this: "*properties found to be correlated at the higher level are assumed correlated, i.e., found within the same unit, at the lower level.*" (Galtung, 1967, pp. 45–46)

Progress in Addressing These and Other Aggregation Issues

Since the early 1980s, scholars have addressed aggregation issues more vehemently than they have in the past. (See, for example, Glick, 1985; Glick and Roberts, 1984; Mossholder and Bedeian, 1983.) They have also become more adroit at giving them lip service and then scurrying on to do the same kinds of research they did in the past.

In the gains column, there is at least one textbook for courses on multilevel analysis (Boyd and Iversen, 1979). While an explosion of research that simultaneously considers more than one level of analysis and addresses various aggregation issues that influence interpretations of results is nowhere apparent, some small beginnings have appeared. If we use as our standard the fact that only a few years ago virtually no attention was given in research to integrating knowledge from different levels of analysis, nor was attention devoted to designing studies that simultaneously provided information from different levels, things look a little better today.

As evidence of this, a cursory examination was done of a recent issue of the *Journal of Applied Psychology* (JAP). *JAP* was chosen because, as we all know, it is the bastion of micro analytic, small studies, whose strength is in their statistical rigor. One might expect other journals in our field, more eclectic and less constraining as they are, to be more likely repositories of studies that address the difficult problems involved when one goes across levels of analysis in conceptualization, measurement, data analysis, interpretation, and so on.

Even *JAP* offers some evidence of increased awareness of these issues. Of the twenty-two studies in the February 1985 publication, three consider simultaneously more than one level of analysis, and one is concerned with group composition. Group composition research, in and of itself, has to consider many of the factors we have only alluded to here. That work always has at least implicitly dealt with aggregation problems, but often not in very sophisticated ways.

Unfortunately, while organization researchers may be growing from an embryonic to an infant state with regard to the commonly discussed aggregation problems, a specification problem they never consider is linkage within and across levels of analysis. This seems to us to be yet another form of aggregation that can be added to those forms more commonly discussed in the organizational literature. In organizational-effectiveness research, failure to be concerned with any of these aggregation issues can lead to serious misinterpretation. Alternatively, attention to these issues will result in better conceptualization of what constitutes effectiveness and what facilitates and inhibits it.

A Pervasive Aggregation Problem

All organizations are hierarchically ordered; consequently, linkages are pervasive to all organizations. In fact, all natural systems seem to be hierarchically ordered. It is not at all strange that human-made social systems follow the same rules.

Clearly, organizations are not solely the high-level systems and functions sometimes attributed to them by the public and researchers nor the lower-level people and processes found in them. They are some combination of these. At a system level of hierarchy, we have entire organizations that we describe using relatively vague and ambiguous constructs (compared to those we use to describe the lower-level components). We then construct a series of whole-part relationships using our knowledge of various organizational levels. What strike us as real or natural categorical differentiations among hierarchical levels arise from the decomposability properties of the system (Simon, 1969; Brownowski, 1970). In natural systems, low-level properties give the impression of having fewer components necessary to the survival of the system than do higher-level properties, and they have fewer attributes than higher-level properties. Thus, our descriptions of them are clearer and crisper than our descriptions of higher-level properties. Since organizations are comprised of interdependent hierarchical orderings, the science of organizations should reflect this. It is almost prevented from doing so by the way science itself is structured:

> Scientific knowledge exhibits a curiously laminated quality. This is not to say that scientific explanations cannot extend across hierarchical levels because they may, at least in certain instances. And it is just these level-connecting or bridging explanations which make reductionism work. For example, the chemical bond (e.g., the covalent bond) has a satisfactory physical explanation, and quantum mechanics accounts for a number of other chemical properties as well. . . . Most scientific theories seem to have the property of accounting for things at one or two adjoining levels, and of being largely "horizontal" affairs. . . . Systematic "vertical" explanations of significant range are uncommon. (Blois, 1983, p. 34)

The fact that science itself as well as organizations are hierarchically linked is often overlooked. For both the physical and social scientists, there are two kinds of propositions: those that deal with wholes and those that deal with units that make up the wholes. Linking the two is more comfortable for the physical scientist than for the social scientist. The propositions of thermodynamics that aggregate properties of matter in order to explain the behavior of matter have been reduced to propositions of statistical mechanics. Boyle's thermodynamic law explains the aggregate behavior of gas in an enclosed space. (At a constant temperature, pressure and volume vary inversely). Gibbs could not observe directly the behavior of atoms and molecules. Yet he was able to reduce thermodynamics to statistical mechanics when he demonstrated that the aggregate relationship of variables explained by Boyle could be deduced from his own individualistic or disaggregated propositions that dealt with the behavior of molecules. Gibbs showed how one named science (thermodynamics) could be deduced from another (mechanical statistics). In this way, aggregated and disaggregated propositions are linked, and the physical scientist has little trouble understanding or accepting this (Homans, 1967). At least some "vertical" explanations exist, along with horizontal explanations.

Social scientists are more protective of their own named science or of their chosen paradigms or research programs. This reflects more than just stubborn parochialism. There are few organizational science propositions that are sufficiently powerful to qualify as "iron laws." (Physics envy is a social-science occupational hazard.) The more general propositions of social science tend to be valid in one set of circumstances, but not in others (Homans, 1967). Paradoxically, organizational science is disorganized.

Most of the valid propositions of social science in general and in organization science in particular are about human behavior, a domain that disaggregates social systems. Many aggregated propositions can be deduced from what we know about human behavior. However, aggregated propositions fail to be explicit about the deductive linkages between what is proposed to be true at one (aggregate) level and what is known to be true at another, which is the hierarchical aspect of the linkage problem.

While the situation is understandable for organizational as well as other sciences, it is nevertheless potentially misleading because even if our explanations of organizational phenomena include most of the relevant properties from the several levels of organizational functioning, they usually miss entirely considering the linkages among properties at the same level (within level linkages) and always miss considering the linkages among properties across levels. Thus, the linkage problem becomes paramount if we are to fully understand organizational functions. Without attending to the linkage glue that ties organizations together, one can have less than a complete view of what facilitates or inhibits effectiveness. It is improbable, too, that one can fully explicate the effectiveness construct.

How Organizational Science Deals with the Linkage Problem

Two attempts to deal with linkages come to mind from organizational research—neither of them satisfactory to our task of tying organizations together.

In the small-group literature, there has always been the notion that the whole of the people in the group is greater than or at least something other than the sum of the parts. That notion has been demonstrated repeatedly, but what the actual linkage is that is greater than or different from the sum of the parts remains somewhat elusive. Some may call it differential abilities (e.g., Hill, 1982); others, cohesiveness (e.g., Lott and Lott, 1965); still others, diffusion of responsibility (e.g., Wallach et al., 1964); and so it goes. The small-group literature usually focuses on linkages that we would call "within-level" as opposed to "cross-level." Thus, it is deficient for our purposes by remaining at a single level of analysis and, consequently, failing to consider some of the kinds of linkages that may determine the outcomes of behaviors at various organizational levels.

The organizational network literature, too, investigates linkages. It usually identifies them and then asks about the communication in them, frequently focussing on the nature of its content, its frequency, and importance

(Roberts and O'Reilly, 1978; Lincoln, 1982; Tichy, 1981). This literature is static in that it does not often consider the fact that linkages change over time, and it is relatively insensitive to the cross-level view of the problem. The only exception to this insensitivity is observations of superior–subordinate communication. Research is typically concerned with communication linkages among individuals or groups, but is rarely concerned with the nature of communication from a significant person to a group (or vice versa), how linkages change in response to some environmental change, how individuals fit into groups, and so on. The literature is also limited to the communication content of linkages. In fact, linkages are often something other than communication. The network approach can and has been used to capture organizational characteristics from the patterning of individual linkages. And network analysis provides a series of compositional rules linking individual responses to organizational characteristics. In sum, some areas of organizational research deal with linkages, and within-level linkages are better dealt with than cross-level linkages.

While even the small-group and communication research areas fail to help us develop ways to deal adequately with linkages, the problem is compounded when we look at statistical models for handling cross-level organizational analyses. Mossholder and Bedeian (1983) argue that appropriate statistical models for cross-level organizational research are regression and ANACOVA models. A problem is immediately apparent. Here we use the regression model to provide the example.

$$Y_{ij} = B_1X_{ij} + B_2X_j + e_{ij} \text{ where}$$
$$(i = 1,2, \ldots k; j = 1,2, \ldots m)$$

Regression models consider the simultaneous impact on some variable, Y, of individuals B_1X_{ij} and groups B_2X_j, but fail to consider the linkages among them. The example is simple in that it only includes individuals and groups. In any complex organization, interactions are considerably more complicated than just those by individuals and groups. Individuals simultaneously interact with one another to produce materials that groups then interact about. Groups provide inputs and extract outputs from organizational systems and so on. Thus, three or more levels of analysis may be appropriate. Further, linkages and interactions are changed by changing goals of organizations, changing constraints from environments, and so on.

Then, too, the content of linkages is not always communication. Linkages in organizations are often in the form of economic resources, logistical–spatial exchanges, authority (which might be broken down further to consider status differences, allocation of decision premises, legitimacy, power, and so forth), and functional linkages. Many organizations are arranged in ways that call out their functional logic. The many kinds of linkages may have no common measure. Thus, it is impossible to find a common metric across them.

In light of all this, perhaps it goes without saying that the reason linkages among organizational units have not drawn attention from organizational researchers is that they are too difficult to identify and measure in field settings. Our colleagues might caution us to do the "doable" first. We certainly agree with this position. In fact, we fail to specify completely organizational processes in our research virtually all of the time. And it usually may not even make too much difference to research interpretations that we leave out of our equations linkages among organizational units.

One can imagine, for example, that if we want to develop models of organizational commitment, the linkage of the individual to the organization is inherent in the problem and need not be further specified. While it might be useful to specify the kinds of linkages operating in the organization and how they operate at something other than the individual level, we might be able to live with models that ignore this issue and still develop fairly good policy about how to encourage organizational commitment.

We argue, however, that with regard to certain research issues (such as those concerned with organizational subunit interdependence or other issues in which linkage specification is called out by the nature of the problem), ignoring linkages will result in incomplete specification or misspecification. In addition, if it is not true that linkages should be attended to in all kinds of organizations, there is a class of organizations that are so dependent for reaching their goals on linkages that develop across subparts that failing to consider these linkages will probably result in models of processes in these organizations that fail to map reality and can lead to erroneous policy decisions.

Dubin (1976) notes that the theoretical contribution of any scientific endeavor depends on the correct specification of the domain of the central construct. If that domain is incompletely specified, the result is likely to be a flurry of redefinition as researchers respond to misspecification by attempting to patch holes in the original arguments. This suggests that to the extent possible, we should completely specify variable sets, linkages among them, and so on in the service of developing more complete theories that are less subject to holes and the ensuing frazzled activity to fill them.

An Organizational Setting in Which Linkages Cannot Be Ignored

For some time now, an interdisciplinary group of scholars, primarily at the University of California, Berkeley, has been interested in problems of managing extremely complex systems. By extremely complex systems, we mean those systems in which, while the probability of error may be low, the consequences of error are unacceptable to the organization or to a larger society. Such systems include but are not limited to the Three Mile Island nuclear power plant, the Union Carbide chemical manufacturing plant at Bhopol, NASA's space shuttle *Challenger,* and the Soviet's nuclear power plant at Chernobyl.

The intellectual heritage for this work is provided by Charles Perrow's work and can be read in his book, *Normal Accidents* (1984). Perrow is interested in the same phenomenon as we are. He asks the question, "What kinds of systems are inherently prone to catastrophic accidents regardless of the proficiency of their operators?" His conclusion is that these systems are characterized by complexity and tight coupling. Coupling has in it suggestions of linkages, though the term does not differentiate between vertical and horizontal links nor does it address the issue of the content of the linkages.

For Perrow, the essence of complexity is the inability of decisionmakers to discern cause-and-effect networks that comprise the system. Coupling deals with the connections among various parts of the whole system. Tight coupling results when an event in one part of the system inevitably affects other parts of the system. Perrow gives us two ways to classify organizations into a typology: by complexity and by coupling. However, he goes no further either by way of increasing our understanding of the kinds of organizations we are interested in here or by way of learning to cope with the problem he identified. Perrow is interested in system-level qualities (complexity/coupling) and does not attempt to link these to unit or component qualities.

Thus, we have the kind of hierarchically defined organizations we described, organizations that might best be thought about as extremely complex and variously tightly and loosely coupled. A large number of variables oscillate simultaneously. Decisionmakers in such situations do not pay attention to all of the variables presented them. They appear to generally "scan" the situation alert to variables that begin to oscillate away from some acceptable standard. There is an "envelope of acceptable" variable behavior and when a variable begins to come close to the edge of its envelope, the decisionmaker turns attention to it. Even a very few variables in such systems can produce a large number of possible outcomes. From a practical standpoint, extreme complexity may mean wide ranges for the values of each variable or rapid change in variables.

This describes part of the problematic situation. More of the situation is brought into focus when we realize that when a decisionmaker corrects one variable, others are influenced, often in unpredictable ways. As long as the system operates in a steady state, things work nicely. But because of this situation, variables do oscillate out of their envelopes, things become unravelled in a hurry, and catastrophes occur because variables that are expected to be tightly coupled come uncoupled or variables that are not expected to be coupled become coupled, leading to extreme ineffectiveness. Again, vertical versus horizontal linkages are not differentiated, a point that is acceptable until we burrow further into systems and subsystems.

If the technology and structure of extremely complex systems are laid out as we have stated (that is, in hierarchically defined manners that encompass large numbers of simultaneously oscillating and connected variables), then the psychosocial subsystems used to operate these technical-physical organizations must mirror them in complexity. One of these social systems is the decision-making subsystem of the organization.

In the decision-making subsystem, one important linkage is the logic of the functional organization, another is communication, and a third is authority. (Certainly, many more important linkages are at work, but for simplicity's sake, here we limit our discussion to these three.) If we fail to factor those linkages into decision-making models, particularly those designed to describe extremely complex systems, we could easily make inferences from research findings that imply social-engineering policies for decision-making situations that will lead to faulty decisions and raise the probability of catastrophe, the ultimate in organizational ineffectiveness.

With these thoughts in mind, our research group became committed to a course of action designed to give us deep conceptual understanding of extremely complex organizations. Particularly since we are more interested in success than failure, we looked for a set of organizations that appeared to us to have the properties of extremely complex organizations (that is, they are organizations in which the probability of error is low, but the consequences can be very high). We also looked for a set of these kinds of organizations that appeared to operate near optimal effectiveness. We want to learn how to do it right, not how to do it wrong.

The organizations we selected for observation are Pacific Gas and Electric Company's part of the Western States Electrical Switching Grid and its nuclear power plant, the Federal Aviation Administration's proposed new $3 billion air-traffic–control system, and the nuclear aircraft carriers *U.S.S. Carl Vinson* and *U.S.S. Enterprise.* Here we use *Carl Vinson* to describe some of the details of an extremely complex organization of the kind we are interested in and to provide a decision-making example that must include decision linkages if we are to fully understand how effective decisions are made.

An Extremely Complex Organization

To understand decision making aboard *Carl Vinson,* it is first necessary to provide a brief description of the vessel's overall characteristics. *U.S.S. Carl Vinson* (hereafter *CVN-70*) is like a city, for when deployed, it has a population of six thousand people. This particular city has an airport on the roof.

The accuracy required to land at this airport far exceeds that required for landing at commercial airports. Here, a plane approaches the ship at around 140 knots and must land to be arrested by one of four deck wires designed for that purpose. There is little room for error. The purposes of the system as a whole are to project sea-based power ashore (bomb things) and to effect control of the sea (sink ships and shoot down enemy planes and missiles). *CVN-70* moves through the water using steam generated by two nuclear reactors.

This system can commit errors that result in catastrophe in various ways. Nuclear power plant accidents are a possibility, as are accidents involving aircraft, aircraft fuel, or weapons. More generally, the ship is part of a national security system where errors can result in unintended military confrontations that can be disastrous. The consequences of failing to be victorious in sea battles can also have catastrophic impact on society at large.

The number and technical intensity of operational, logistic, and administrative functions that must be performed by the ship in order to accomplish its missions result in extreme complexity. It is not possible for any of the ship's decision-making officers to fully understand the entire process. This is one reason computers are in aircraft and aboard the ship. This is explicit recognition that tools are needed to help decisionmakers understand what is going on. Furthermore, most parts and subsystems are tightly coupled. Aircraft, for example, cannot safely land aboard ship unless hundreds of people who work with flight-deck equipment carry out their functions perfectly, in a tight synchrony. The flight deck cannot do its part unless the radar air-traffic–control system (CATCC) does its part in tight coordination with the flight deck and other parts of the ship.

If the reactor and engineering personnel cannot run the power plant of the ship free of error, the ship cannot position itself to use aircraft in any way. For one bomb to drop on one target, thousands of actions must be completed and coordinated. These actions span a spectrum of technical intensity ranging from feeding the crew to maintaining state-of-the-art electronics equipment. The job of protecting the ship from airborne, surface, or submarine attack is even more complex.

Here are some statistics about the ship that should support our argument for its magnitude. Commissioned in 1982, *CVN-70* carries approximately 90 airplanes and 9 squadrons, and displaces approximately 95,000 tons of water. By early 1986, it had arrested 46,000 aircraft. *CVN-70* carries a variety of aircraft representing an assortment of technologies: the A7-Corsair (a light-attack aircraft), A-6 Intruder (medium-level bomber), EA-6B Prowler (electronic-warfare aircraft), F-14 Tomcat (fighter aircraft), E-2 Hawkeye (airborne early-warning defensive aircraft), S-3 Viking (antisubmarine aircraft), and SH-3H Sea King helicopter (antisubmarine aircraft).

CVN-70 has two nuclear generators providing power sufficient to run the ship for 13 years on a single load of fuel. It travels at approximately 30 knots and its flight deck is about the length of four football fields. This allows pilots to land in the space of less than one football field on a deck that is simultaneously moving forward while pitching and rolling. The rest of the length of the field may be required for a pilot to take off in the event that the plane's hook misses the wire. Additional flight-deck space is used to catapult planes off the ship, park planes, move planes from point to point, and move planes from hangar to flight deck on elevators.

A Decision Example

Night flight operations and flight operations in poor visibility or low ceilings are a normal part of carrier operation. Here we describe the decision environments of three units that are simultaneously active and interactive in night and bad-weather flight operations: the bridge, the air-traffic–control center, and the primary flight-control center or the tower. This is a situation in which three distinct cultures interact in a contingency that requires perfect synergism. If this is not present, effectiveness will not be achieved.

The bridge's primary responsibility during this evolution is to turn the ship into the wind and sail it at an appropriate speed to catapult and recover aircraft. This fundamental job is done within the web of numerous other jobs, such as avoiding other ships, and communicating with other members of the formation. The language and interaction among people is quite formal and procedures are standardized, as they are everywhere on the ship. The captain presides over this activity and the navigator is ready to step in and take the captain's place at a moment's notice. The situation on the bridge is quiet and dignified during normal operations. The ship must be maneuvered so the vector sum of the true wind and the wind caused by the ship's movement equals the desired wind over the deck, both with respect to direction (down the angle) and with respect to required speed for takeoffs and landings. As the saying goes, "Constant vigilance is the price of good navigation." Comradery prevails, but is implicit and quiet.

The air-traffic–control center's primary responsibility is to control aircraft around the ship and implement decisions made in air operations that concern the big picture. The big picture has to do with the status of airplanes. A configuration might take the following form: there are thirty-six aircraft aloft, two need refueling, and one has failed to catch the deck wire—or has boltered (failed to trap)—and must be restacked, so to speak. That is, the plane failed to catch one of the arresting wires, was waved off, and now has to be replaced in the line of incoming aircraft. No two problems in configuration are ever the same. CATCC also establishes the intervals from "push-to-ramp" time or the time from leaving the stack to trapping aboard the ship.

It is important to shorten these intervals as much as possible in order to allow the flight deck to trap planes quickly in succession.

The crew in CATCC work in a fairly relaxed manner, at least on an evening of normal flight operations with no emergencies. The air-traffic controllers have time to think, jokes are mild, conversation is easy going; if one makes a mistake, the time interval before the impact of that mistake will be felt is often sufficient to correct the mistake. What the air-traffic controllers do is tied to the ship's overall operation managed on the bridge. What the bridge does ties to what the tower is able to do by way of bringing the planes in quickly and safely. In fact, at one time, this ship sailed 15 knots astern to recover its aircraft, a symphony that was, no doubt, carefully orchestrated by the bridge, tower, and CATCC.

Tower personnel are neither formal nor laid back. They are refreshingly stripped of all hypocrisy and direct their attentions to getting aircraft on and off the ship safely and quickly. This group of people is in direct visual contact with its task environment (which is not true of the CATCC crew). They take their responsibilities seriously and have cool confidence. There is no doubt who is in charge. The air officer commander on aircraft carriers is called "airboss" and the mood is somewhat like that of an old Jesse James movie where everyone defers to Jesse and Jesse plays it cool. These folks are much closer to both the technology and the people they control than are any of the other groups. They have instant information about both the planes and the specific air crews they work with, and they know the limitations of both of these. In addition to their work with the air crews, the people in the tower control a vast number of flight and hangar deck operations, operations too numerous for us to go into here.

On this night, a number of interlinked decisions have to be made. Here, we have an example of just some of the interaction that takes place, linking the ship's three components of concern. Prior to trapping his first plane of the evening, the airboss calls from the tower to the bridge to ask how long a wait it would be until the ship came around into the wind. He is responded to by the navigator, "I've been waitin' for you guys all night. Now you wait for me," as he maneuvers this giant into position to take on the aircraft. At sea, *CVN-70* maneuvers with the ease of a sports car. In port or close to other vessels, it is a behemoth. Later on, as landings take place uneventfully, and an occasional plane misses or has a technique wave off and must be restacked, the airboss is challenged by CATCC about why he had not gotten a plane down that had boltered repeatedly. He responds to CATCC, "I don't land 'em. I just provide the real estate."

During this operation, in CATCC, air-traffic controllers feel a pride in that they have moved the push-to-ramp time to exactly where they desire it to be, when suddenly the airboss shuts down all air operations because of a wire problem on the deck. Decisions unfold and everyone waits for the situation to be corrected. Close to the end of the operation the airboss says, "One error never occurs. Things ALWAYS happen in sequence, and they just tumble in on you." And they tumble in across the bridge, tower, and CATCC in our story, which necessarily leaves out what is happening simultaneously in the ship's fourteen other departments (e.g., reactor, engineering).

Within this already very complicated circumstance, let us consider a situation in which an aircraft reports a malfunction and a decision has to be made about what to do. Carriers fly a number of kinds of aircraft during any particular air operation, complicating the matter, in that the aircraft technologies are somewhat different from one another. To add to this, the deck technologies used to trap various aircraft are different and must be adjusted to the specific incoming aircraft. Most simply put, given a reported aircraft malfunction, the decision alternatives (from most risky to least risky from the standpoint of the ship) are to bring the plane on board under the assumption that the airplane indicators of a problem are incorrect, raise the barricade and bring the aircraft on board, or fuel the aircraft and send it to a land base (BINGO the aircraft).

When this happens, the tower personnel think about the nature of the aircraft and exactly what to advise the pilot to do in the short term. At the same time, the carrier air group commander (the only person on the ship with experience in all of its aircraft), located with aircraft squadron commanders in CATCC, quickly discusses the matter with the squadron commander, and the bridge stands by. Ultimately, the decision about what to do is the captain's. The carrier air group commander (CAG) makes a recommendation that is sent simultaneously to the bridge and tower. The bridge may or may not accept the recommendation.

On this particular night, an EA6-B radios the ship that its cockpit indicators show an unsafe landing gear. A decision has to be made about what to do with the plane. In the process leading to the decision, the functional logic of the ship first comes into play. The tower takes its functional lead and orders the plane to fly over the ship so a visual assessment can be made. The assessment is inconclusive and the information is relayed simultaneously to the bridge and CAG that no decision can be reached based on a flyover. Simultaneously, the CAG consults with the squadron commanding officer about the probable nature of the problem. Attention shifts to the CAG and his squadron commanders who assess what they know about the probable state of the aircraft. Simultaneously, the bridge enters with the functional linkage of informing everyone of the status of the ship.

Communication linkages operate simultaneously with functional linkages. However, because of the impossibility of finding common metrics for communication and functional linkages, they must be described relatively separately of the functional linkages. A challenge in describing the communication linkages is to assess their meaning. (The nature of the conduits can be left to the information science people.) From the tower, the communication to the bridge and CATCC is short and to the point, with equivocal meaning. "We don't know whether there is a real landing gear problem." The nature of the communication from CATCC back to the bridge and tower is that regardless of the possible nature of the problem, the landing conditions on board and at land-based fields dictate that the best action is to divert the aircraft to a shore landing field (BINGO). That communication contains precise meaning. The bridge is silent on the matter. And that communication, too, has precise meaning. In this situation, all three cultures have learned that if the captain does not interfere, the recommendation of the CAG is to be accepted, and bridge, tower, and CATCC are to move to fuel the plane from an airborne tanker and send it to a land base. What remains is for air operations to identify the appropriate land base, arrange for the tanking, and bid the aircraft on its way.

The authority linkages here are fairly obvious. For various reasons, the tower commander must await word from CAG about the appropriate action. One reason is that legitimate authority (French and Raven, 1959) belong with CAG since he (not any player in the tower) legitimately "owns" the aircraft in his role as air wing commander. However, if CAG's recommendation is overridden by the bridge, that order is accepted. Again, authority for the safety and operation of the ship ultimately resides on the bridge, which is legitimate and, moreover, is where the bigger picture is always in view and expertise for that larger picture is supposed to reside.

In summary, we here provided a picture of some of the many kinds of activities that go on simultaneously on the bridge, in the tower, and in CATCC during a normal night's flight operations aboard an aircraft carrier. We then extrapolated from this general description one kind of decision. Finally, we attempted briefly to show the simultaneous operations of three kinds of linkages (function, communication, and authority) involved in that one decision. Imagine the number and kinds of linkages operating simultaneously across the entire decision milieus of these three units in our extremely complex organization!

Our final task is to suggest what can happen if these linkages are neglected in describing the appropriate decision activities for a situation such as this. A simple illustration of this is to show what can happen to change the decision when a linkage is activated or deactivated for some reason. A common reason for activating or deactivating linkages is change in environmental constraints of one sort or another. For purposes of illustration, we will assume that when these constraints change, the changes will be perceived and interpreted similarly by all players (and we know that in real life, this is not true).

Let us say that a BINGO field was not available, as happens frequently for *CVN-70*. If that is true, a vast amount of expertise and information used to make the decision rests in the hands of the tower personnel. In fact, the alternative decisions are reduced from three to two (attempt a normal landing or raise the barricade), and the tower is not only a major participant in the decision making but also a primary implementer of the decision. CATCC is a supplement to the tower in that it attempts to arrange all other airborne aircraft in order to facilitate the job of bringing the potentially hobbled aircraft down. Any decision-making model that does not consider the deactivation of functional, authoritative, and communication linkages will misinterpret the desired inputs from the various units, and it might well make the wrong predictions about which linkages should be left open. Any decision-making model that does not differentiate vertical and horizontal coupling is likely to suggest inappropriate policy. It will grossly misspecify the desired coupling among the three units, leading to gross ineffectiveness on the part of the organization.

As another example, imagine that the aircraft is armed. At this point, the authority systems take over in determining the decision, and the bridge becomes a major player. Regardless of the assessment of the aircraft's possible problems made by the tower or CATCC, and even if a decision is made that the overall best strategy is to beach the aircraft, the captain will do everything possible to trap it on board. The captain is a very important part of the decision milieu, and the authority linkages may override the communication and functional linkages to get the plane on board. Again, a misspecification either of the nature of the linkages or of when they are brought into play may lead to incorrect description of decision-making processes or prescriptions about how to facilitate them through closing down certain linkages and letting others bear full weight in the situation.

In these decision situations, the mechanistically designed organization that is consistent with its functional logic is in a state of redesign (Weick, 1977) as the same contingencies are met by units that are linked together in multiple ways. Our major point is that to ignore these linkages in research on extremely complex organizations misses the points of full specification of organizational properties and of full knowledge of vertical and horizontal linkages that tie the system together. Inferences and prescriptions from research that fail to consider these linkages may result in real surprises for these kinds of organizations. Surprises, by definition, are components of ineffectiveness.

The Organization Member as Organization Scientist: How to Tease Out Linkage Aggregations

We believe the best methodologies for understanding complex organizations are hidden among the mazes that outline the design and decision-making skills of expert practitioners. As organizations become more complex, it becomes *more* difficult for organization scientists or for members of organizations to distinguish between methods of discovery that result in intended achievement and those that result in error. Therefore, attention must be turned to what expert operators in these organizations do.

Successful experts at chess or at medical diagnosis, for example, cannot explain why they do what they do because their expertise is dependent upon a process of intuition that maps the transition from novice to expert capability (Dreyfus and Dreyfus, 1986). The unintended consequences of Three Mile Island and Bhopol have been explained in terms of the narrow specifics of operator error or faulty safety devices. At best, even experts do not understand all the implications of the technical and psychosocial subsystems at their disposal (Perrow, 1984). They, therefore, cannot explain errors as operator failures if the part that failed was unknown to the operator.

Do the members of organizations hold the key that will unlock the secrets of research methodology? Or is this key the exclusive property of the organization scientist? Is there a conceptual difference between the methodology of the scientist and that of the practitioner? It seems to us that there is a paradox here that may inform us. Participants instinctively and intuitively *experience* a methodology—in our example, the methodology of decision making about complex events involving complex technologies. However, they do not know how to, or do not want to, explain this methodology.

Since organizational scientists do not live in the world of extremely complex organized systems, they usually must forgo immersion in the whole experience over extended periods of time. We, therefore, cannot expect them to develop instinct and intuition for the whole process or for a method that can lead to an understanding of the whole as do the expert operators of such systems. Most scientists compensate for this disadvantage by concentrating specialized skills and attention on a narrow range of what is a broad interdisciplinary problem, the specification of how these systems operate. Conceptual integration that ties together the parts without leaving holes in the whole is filed in the "too-difficult" basket. Most of us disaggregate the problem of understanding complex systems and methods. We develop methods designed to understand only the parts. In short, the practitioner understands the gestalt, but cannot explain it (Dreyfus and Dreyfus, 1986). The scientist usually explains parts, but does not understand the whole. If this paradox is at all valid, the scientist must learn how to understand the methodology of the organization—the methodology that organizational experts invoke every day to run their organization.

Organization scientists strive to explain, predict, and even prescribe by applying some form of scientific method. We deduce hypotheses and test these in the field, or we infer hypotheses from our observations and handling of data. It has been suggested (Landau and Stout, 1979) that the subjects of our observations (the members of organizations) do exactly the same sort of thing, i.e. they design organizations as hypotheses.

Similarly, Pfeffer (1982) discusses organizations as paradigms. As used in science (Kuhn, 1970), a paradigm is a system of shared understanding and exemplars that emerge in science as guides to research and understanding. A paradigm is a way of doing things and a way of looking at the world. "A paradigm is a technology, including the beliefs about cause–effect relations and standards of practice and behavior as well as specific examples of these, that constitute how an organization goes about doing things" (Pfeffer, 1982, pp. 227–28).

Participants at or near the top of a hierarchy, at the strategic level, design structures intended to tie together individuals, groups, and organizations to aggregate technical, psychosocial, and managerial subsystems and environmental suprasystems. The purpose of such structure building or aggregation of parts is to deduce an organized human system that will satisfy the specification of a dependent variable expressed in some form of the concept of "effectiveness." It is in this sense that design strategies are hypothesized (Landau and Stout, 1979).

At lower tactical or technical levels, groups and individuals may perceive errors (surprises) that result from hierarchically imposed structural strategies. These may be faults in the specification of the technical subsystem (e.g., task rules or procedures), elements that fail to satisfy the needs of the psychosocial subsystem (e.g., worker dissatisfaction or lack of group cohesiveness), disconnects in the linkages needed to satisfy the requirements of interdependence within and among working groups and between the organized system and its task environment (e.g., inadequate information flow, infomation overload, or parochial norms), or any other conditions that "surprise" the structure. When this happens, a process of self-design (Weick, 1977) can modify structure by changing the rules of the game and/or by respecifying the way the concept "effectiveness" is made operational.

A first attempt at bringing linkages into the organizational picture might be to examine interdependencies in organizations as their participants design and change them. The best available theoretical notion about interdependence is the Guttman-type scale developed by Thompson (1967). When a part of an organization renders a discrete contribution to the whole, there is *pooled* interdependence. *Sequential* interdependence occurs when units both make contribution to the whole and are sustained by the whole, and when their direct interdependence can be specified. That is, unit A must act properly before unit B can act, and unless unit B acts, A cannot solve its problems. Finally, *reciprocal* interdependence exists when the outputs from each unit become the inputs for the others. "Under conditions of reciprocal interdependence, each unit involved is penetrated by the other" (Thompson, 1967, p. 55). The conditions of a Guttman scale are met because all organizations have pooled interdependence; more complicated organizations have sequential as well as pooled; and the most complex have reciprocal, sequential, and pooled interdependence.

We propose that organizational researchers attempt to extend or further develop notions of interdependence as linkages among organizational units. Notions of interdependence offer a way to consider simultaneously horizontal and vertical linkages. In focussing on interdependence, researchers will have to struggle with the problem of linkage content, wherein there is no common metric across a variety of kinds of content (e.g., information, authority, power). To make this extension, researchers and practitioners should work closely together to peel back the layers of organizational design, redesign, and management, as reflected not just in static components, but in dynamic components with multiple linkages, and known only to expert organizational operators.

We finally propose that at least in complex organizations in which the failure stakes are high, not to consider linkages among units and people in research will result in misspecification errors that will contribute to the probability of organizational error. Organizational error is the opposite side of the effectiveness coin.

References

Blois, M. S. (1983). Conceptual issues in computer diagnosis and the hierarchical nature of medical knowledge. *Journal of Medicine and Philosophy, 8,* 29–50.

Boyd, L., and Iversen, G. (1979). *Conceptual analyses: Concepts and statistical techniques.* Belmont, Calif.: Wadsworth.

Brownowski, J. (1970). New concepts in the evolution of complexity. In J. Brownowski (ed.), *A sense of the future.* Cambridge, Mass.: MIT Press.

Dreyfus, H., and Dreyfus, S. (1986). *Mind over machine: The power of human intuition and expertise in the era of the computer.* New York: Macmillan/Free Press.

Dubin, R. (1976). Theory building in applied areas. In M. D. Dunnette (ed.), *Handbook of industrial and organizational psychology.* Chicago: Rand McNally.

French, J. R. P., and Raven, B. H. (1959). The bases of social power. In D. Cartwright (ed.), *Studies in social power.* Ann Arbor: University of Michigan Press.

Galtung, J. (1967). *Theory and methods of social research.* New York: Columbia University Press.

Glick, W. H. (1985). Conceptualizing and measuring organizational and psychological climate: Pitfalls in multi-level research. *Academy of Management Review, 10,* 601–16.

Glick, W. H., and Roberts, K. H. (1984). Hypothesized interdependence, assumed independence. *Academy of Management Review, 9,* 722–35.

Hill, G. (1982). Group versus individual performance: Are N + 1 heads better than one. *Psychological Bulletin, 91,* 517–39.

Homans, G. C. (1967). *The nature of social science.* New York: Harcourt, Brace & World.

Kuhn, T. S. (1970). *The structure of scientific revolutions,* 2nd ed. Chicago: University of Chicago Press.

Landau, M., and Stout, R., Jr. (1979). To manage is not to control or the fallacy of type two errors. *Public Administration Review,* March-April.

Lincoln, J. R. (1982). Intra- and inter-organizational networks. In S. Bacharach (ed.), *Research in the sociology of organizations,* vol. 1. Greenwich, Conn.: JAI Press, p. 38.

Lott, A. J., and Lott, B. E. (1965). Group cohesiveness as interpersonal attraction: A review of relationships with antecedent and consequent variables. *Psychological Bulletin, 64,* 259–309.

Mossholder, K. W., and Bedeian, A. C. (1983). Cross-level inference and organizational research: Perspectives on interpretation and application. *Academy of Management Review, 8,* 547–58.

Perrow, C. (1984). *Normal accidents.* New York: Basic Books.

Pfeffer, J. (1982). *Organizations and organization theory.* Boston: Pitman.

Roberts, K. H., Hulin, C. L., and Rousseau, D. M. (1978). *Developing an interdisciplinary science of organizations.* San Francisco: Jossey-Bass.

Roberts, K. H., and O'Reilly, C. A. (1978). Organizations as communication structures: An empirical approach. *Human Communication Research, 4,* 283–93.

Robinson, W. S. (1950). Ecological correlations and the behavior of individuals. *American Sociological Review, 15,* 351–57.

Simon, H. A. (1969). *The science of the artificial.* Cambridge, Mass.: MIT Press.

Thompson, J. D. (1967). *Organizations in action.* New York; McGraw-Hill.

Tichy, N. M. (1981). Networks in organizations. In P. C. Nystrom and W. H. Starbuck (eds.), *Handbook of organizations design,* vol. 2. London: Oxford University Press, pp. 225–49.

Wallach, M. A., Kogan, N., and Bem, D. J. (1964). Diffusion of responsibility and level of risk taking in groups. *Journal of Abnormal and Social Psychology, 68,* 263–74.

Waltz, K. (1979). *Theory of international politics.* Reading, Mass.: Addison-Wesley.

Weick, K. E. (1977). Organization design: Organizations as self-designing systems. *Organizational Dynamics, 6,* 30–46.

Part III
Management Issues

This part addresses the question: can facilitation be managed to increase effectiveness? In chapter 7, Schoorman et al., present some evidence to suggest that the management (nonpersonal) and leadership (interpersonal) of facilitation will be very difficult to differentiate and that neither is as strongly related to work facilitation as they appear to be. In chapter 8, Moses and Lyness suggest some reasons why the management of effectiveness may be difficult both to do and to assess. They build their argument around the construct of ambiguity, arguing that as the pace of change increases in organizations, managers have less information available as a basis for decision making. They present, in addition, the interesting idea that organizations, themselves, are characterized by differing levels of ambiguity. Finally, Kaplan presents a rich picture of the job of the general manager in chapter 9. Through in-depth observation and interviewing, he isolates some key issues with which the general manager must struggle in order to facilitate an organization's effectiveness.

7

Facilitating Work Effectiveness through Leadership and Management

F. David Schoorman
Daniel Schechter
Anne Moeller
Benjamin Schneider

I n this chapter, we first argue for the idea that both leadership behaviors (defined as the interpersonal facets of management) and management behaviors (defined as the other functions of management) are important for understanding work-unit effectiveness. While this is a seemingly logical idea, we note that the largest proportion of the research by behavioral scientists on the topic of management has really focussed almost exclusively on the leadership component (Campbell et al., 1970). Brief overviews of the leadership and management literatures are presented, followed by a research framework for studying the roles of both in creating the kinds of work conditions that facilitate unit effectiveness. Finally, results testing the framework are presented.

Managing for Work Effectiveness

It could be argued that behavioral and social scientists have not been as helpful as they could be with respect to understanding what differentiates more from less successful organizations. A case can be made that psychologists in particular have not grappled well with the very great diversity of issues that obviously need to be considered in understanding even one organization. So, for example, psychologists' concern for individual variables such as ability or motivation, studied from an individual differences perspective, surely fails to yield insight into organizational functioning (Schneider, 1985).

Some psychologists, or scholars of at least a psychological persuasion, have been able to run counter to this trend. Such researchers as Katz and Kahn (1978) with their systems perspective on organizations, Argyris (1957 and subsequent works) with his long-term concern about how managers think and behave in their organizations, and more recent efforts in the quality of work-life/organization-development/sociotechnical-systems perspectives on organizations (e.g., Beer, 1980) have begun to conceptualize the great range of chores that require accomplishment for an organization to be effective. Some recent efforts in summarizing research following on these more macro conceptualizations of organizations suggest that interventions based on them can yield some dramatic improvements in productivity (Nicholas, 1982).

Perhaps the nub of the issue regarding the impact of behavioral and social science perspectives on organizations is demonstrating some relationship between the variables studied and organizational productivity (Schneider, 1985). To be more explicit, the preoccupation of researchers with the topic of leadership in organizations cannot be criticized as irrelevant to important organizational outcomes, but the focus on leadership to the exclusion of research on the full range of managerial behavior is a critical oversight (Campbell et al., 1970). A focus on leadership ignores the noninterpersonally oriented classical managerial functions such as planning, organizing, and setting goals and it leaves behavioral scientists with a slim arsenal of approaches when asked to intervene in the area of managerial practices.

Assuming that with proper recruiting, selection, and training techniques, the organization can be staffed with potentially competent individuals, it is a matter of internal organizational practices and conditions whether those individuals actually perform up to their full potential. This is the message that McGregor (1960) and Argyris (1957) proposed long ago. They advocated the idea that the basic job of management is to remove the constraints to effectiveness that keep individual potential from being realized. When looked at in this way, a question for a behavioral and social science approach to understanding organizational functioning becomes: what is it that managers actually do to facilitate the effectiveness of competent employees?

It is in attempting to answer this question that some researchers (Mintzberg, 1973; Dowell and Wexley, 1978; Tornow and Pinto, 1976; Yukl and Nemeroff, 1979) recently have approached the issue of assessing the role of management behaviors in understanding unit and organizational effectiveness.

These researchers have treated leadership as only one of the roles that a manager must perform. While the sheer volume of research on leadership dictates that special attention be given to this role in any analysis of managerial behavior, the field's preoccupation with the leadership construct has caused an incongruity between that research and organizational reality. In other words, because leaderhsip is only one of the functions of management, a focus only on leadership leads to a narrow focus when the reality is that breadth of inclusiveness is demanded for understanding organizations. It can be argued that this failure to capture all of the roles of managers in leadership research is what led Stogdill (1974) to the conclusion that "the endless accumulation of research has yielded very little cumulative knowledge." Parenthetically, it is interesting to realize that Stogdill failed to index the word *management* in his 1974 *Handbook* (although Bass rectified this in his 1981 revision).

What Is Leadership?

Leadership has been defined in many ways over the years. Effective leadership refers to influencing individuals to do things they might not otherwise do in the absence of the leadership attempt (Stogdill, 1974); leadership is the extent to which an individual in face-to-face interaction can influence others to resolve problems without arousing hostility (Moses and Ritchie, 1976); leadership is the style with which managers carry out their work (Gannon, 1982); and leadership is the use of noncoercive influence to direct and coordinate the activities of the members of an organized group toward the accomplishment of group objectives and goals (Jago, 1979).

The common thread in these definitions is that leadership is an interpersonal influence process that occurs through mostly face-to-face interaction (either implicitly or explicitly stated), with the basis of influence being persuasion rather than coercion. While some of this "leaderhsip" certainly occurs in organizations, the amount of this engaged in by managers varies across positions, levels, and organizations; and whatever the amount exhibited, it definitely does not encompass the full range of managerial behavior. While management works toward facilitating effectiveness through any variety of rules, practices, and procedures (e.g., providing proper equipment and support staff, keeping distractions to a minimum in the work environment), leadership attacks the same problem of effectiveness only through influencing employees to work toward organizational goals. If we accept Mintzberg's (1973) classification of managerial work, there are actually ten roles performed, only one of which is "leadership."

It has been argued that leadership is very rare in organizations because most "leadership" situations in organizations do not involve face-to-face interactions between the leader and follower (Dubin, 1979). The image conjured up by Dubin's argument is that of the CEO who "leads" a company without ever interacting with most of the employees (followers). The person at the top may be called the "leader," but simply calling the person that does not mean this top official leads every subordinate. The "leader" may stand for certain values, beliefs, and norms that become the dominant ones in the organization, but there are behavioral ways to explain why these get passed on without involving the concept of leadership.

The leader at the top, in a behavioral sense, really only leads those who have regular access and contact with him or her. The fact that the norms and beliefs resulting from that leadership contact get passed down through the organization was demonstrated long ago by Fleishman (1953) as well as many other researchers in the area of organizational climate and culture (cf. Schein, 1985.) That the literature suggests that not only the content of leader beliefs and values, but also the actual style of leadership get transmitted is what Fleishman termed the "climate effect." Thus, while on the surface there is the appearance of "noninteractive leadership" occurring in organizations, what is really occurring are many similar superior–subordinate interactions throughout the organization. The real leaders behaviorally are the superiors that actually interact with the subordinates, while those at the top are "leaders" only for their immediate subordinates.

In summary, what we know about leadership is that it is an interpersonal, noncoercive, influence process that exists at all levels of organizations, but is only one of the many roles a manager plays. Generically speaking, the CEO at the top of an organization is said to be leading all of the organization's employees, while in fact what appears to be happening is that successive superior–subordinate pairs model the interpersonal nature of CEO–subordinate relationships.

What is not at all clear from the literature on leadership is the relationships between leadership behaviors and other management roles, between leadership behaviors and work unit or organizational effectiveness, and between leadership behaviors and other important productivity outcomes such as turnover, absenteeism, and quality.

The reason this is not clear is the implicit assumption made by early leadership researchers that they were capturing what managers do in their measures. Sashkin and Garland (1979), Argyris (1979), and Yukl and Nemeroff (1979), for example, have noted how the Leadership Behavior Description Questionnaire (LBDQ) has dominated studies of leadership, but that the LBDQ has no conceptual or empirical logic. It has no conceptual logic because it is tied to no definition of leadership and it has no empirical logic because it fails to map onto any of the analyses of what managers do. It would appear to be necessary to integrate the study of leadership and the study of management.

What Is Management?

This realization has seemingly caught on among behavioral science researchers in recent years. The need to study what managers actually do in organizations began to be pushed as early as 1970 when Campbell et al. resurfaced Hemphill's (1959) job-analysis technique for describing the activities of management and decried the lack of follow-up research. Since then, there have been several attempts to classify managerial behavior in organizations: Tornow and Pinto (1978) extending Hemphill's (1959) work with the managers in one company, Mintzberg (1973) attempting to classify the activities of chief executive officers across several companies, and Yukl and Van Fleet (1982) using a critical-incidents technique to construct a measure of the dimensions of managerial behavior.

A focus on what managers actually do necessarily moves the field further away from the previous sole emphasis on the leadership of individuals and groups. As a result of this new emphasis on the phenomenon as it really occurs in organizations, the relative importance of leadership and its influence on productivity has been questioned. Kerr and Jermier (1978), for example, have identified "substitutes" for leadership in terms of subordinate, task, and organizational characteristics that may affect subordinates without any interpersonal contact. The substitutes can be considered to be the result of effective *managerial* practices, practices not related to interpersonal issues.

In summary, what we know about managerial behavior is that it is a multifaceted endeavor involving as many as seventeen different kinds of activities, one of which may be leadership kinds of activities. The nonleadership kinds of managerial behaviors have not been studied by many people and almost no studies exist relating what managers do to the effectiveness of the units they manage (Campbell et al., 1970). Thus, while a literature on what managers do is beginning to grow, and some analyses exist showing how managers spend their time, the relationship between these studies and productivity or effectiveness is yet to be established. Figure 7–1 reflects the research framework just discussed.

A Conceptual Model of Manager Behaviors

The preceding discussion indicates that the studies of leadership have, in effect, been studies of a subset of what managers do. The subset is characterized as including only interpersonal behaviors directed at subordinates. In order to expand the scope of research to include those nonleadership behaviors that managers also engage in, we needed a conceptual framework within which the full spectrum of managerial behaviors could be represented. Implicit in the generally accepted definition of leadership are two dimensions, both related to the object or focus of the behavior, that specify the boundaries of the concept. These dimensions are (1) whether the behavior is internal (directed within the system) or external (directed outside the system) and (2) whether the behavior is interpersonal (directed at people) or noninterpersonal (directed at objects).

Internal versus External Focus. The issue of whether the behavior of the manager is directed internally or externally has been prominent in studies of managerial behavior. Mintzberg (1973) reports that CEOs spend as much time

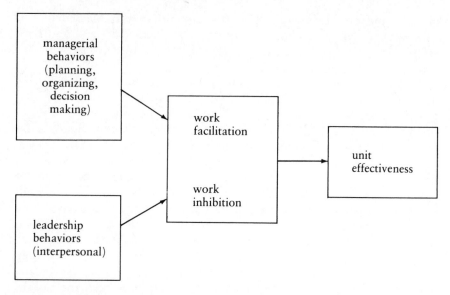

Source: Adapted from Schneider and Schoorman (1982).

Figure 7–1. A Conceptualization of Management, Leadership, and Work Facilitation

(one-third to one-half) dealing with people outside the organization as they do with subordinates. Not only is the absolute amount of time spent substantial, but in relative terms, the time spent internally versus externally appears to be approximately equal, which lends empirical support to the utility of this conceptual distinction. Schoorman (1981) emphasized this distinction between internal and external behaviors in a study of university department heads.

Interviews with department heads revealed two externally focussed roles, an entrepreneur role and a negotiator role, that were critical aspects of the job. The entrepreneur role included contacts with strategic external organizations (such as funding agencies, private corporations, alumni groups, and state legislatures) that provided resources for the department. The negotiator role involved interactions with the university administration, regulatory agencies, and professional organizations to advocate the work of the department, protect faculty from external criticism, and lobby for favorable treatment. Schoorman's (1981) data provide strong support for the position that externally focussed behaviors are a significant component of department-head behaviors.

In the present research, the behaviors of the manager of the system are classified as being internally or externally directed. It is important to recall that following the Katz and Kahn systems model as outlined in chapter 1 by Schoorman and Schneider, the level of analysis or system boundaries are carefully specified in each of the samples. Internal behaviors, therefore, are behaviors directed within the system, and external behaviors are those directed outside the system.

Interpersonal versus Noninterpersonal Focus. The second dimension implicit in the definition of leadership is the conceptually orthogonal issue of whether or not the behavior is directed at people. In order to better articulate this dimension, we adopted the classification scheme for task statements proposed by Fine and Wiley (1974). This scheme codes tasks as involving either people, data, or things. In the context of the present analysis, this coding scheme (people, data, things) succesfully separated the interpersonal from the noninterpersonal behaviors in a conceptually meaningful manner.

The two dimensions just presented yield a 2 × 3 matrix within which all manager behaviors may be coded (figure 7–2). An important characteristic of this matrix is that one of the cells, internal-people, represents all of the behaviors that are usually classified as leadership. All five other cells represent various aspects of management behaviors. This is completely consistent with our earlier arguments (supported by the literature) that leadership is only a small component of what managers do.

The Present Research

Based on the research literature reviewed and the conceptual model developed in this chapter, a study was conducted to test the propositions of the conceptual model that are illustrated in figure 7–1.

	people	data	things
internal	leadership	management	management
external	management	management	management

Figure 7–2. Classification of Tasks in Leadership and Management Activities

1. Leadership and management behaviors will directly result in a higher level of work facilitation in organizational work units.
2. Leadership and management behaviors will indirectly affect unit effectiveness.
3. Leadership and management behaviors will be compensatory in that higher levels of management behaviors will reduce the need for leadership.

Having developed and justified a model that includes six unique components of a manager's job, we must note that some adjustments were made to the present model in the test of the model described in the following sections. Unlike the internal-external dimension, the people-data-things dimension is greatly affected by the type of system being studied. For example, in service organizations, the relative frequency of behaviors in each of the categories is very different than in traditional production organizations. This is related to the issue of how tangible a product the system is creating. Organizations creating tangible products tend to have more activities related to things. Since the sample of systems we studied represented a service organization creating an intangible product, the vast majority of the behaviors of the managers fell into the category of people. The data category contained many fewer behaviors and the things category was extremely small. Based on this preliminary finding, the data and things categories were combined in the analyses that follow. While this was clearly not the most optimal strategy for testing the model, it seemed to be the most prudent one for conceptual and statistical reasons.

Method

Sample. Thirty-one salesperson supervisors from a financial-services telemarketing organization completed a task-analysis survey describing their job as a first-level manager. Sufficient information was obtained to match each supervisor's task-analysis responses with the work-facilitation responses obtained from subordinates in the sales unit. Work-facilitation data were collected in fifteen sales units using the group-consensus procedure described by Moeller et al. in chapter 4. Criterion data were obtained for each of the units. Analyses were conducted at the unit level for units in which we had collected the work-facilitation data, so $N = 15$ for all analyses.

Procedure

Development of the Supervisory-Task–Analysis Survey. Semistructured group interviews were conducted with 6 groups of 3 subject-matter experts (supervisors) each. The interviews took 2 hours to complete and yielded the information used to design the task-anslysis survey. All supervisors and all salespersons had been previously informed about the project detailed in chapter 4.

During these interviews, we obtained as much information as we could about the job: the "key results" (or major goals) of the job; the tasks necessary to accomplish these key results; the knowledge, skills, and abilities required to do the job, and so forth. Copious notes were taken to record the information given during the interviews.

One product of the interviews was a list of 111 statements describing the tasks that the supervisors do on their job. In order to test the model presented earlier, these task statements were sorted into the four categories shown in figure 7–2:

1. Tasks internal to the system, involving people,
2. Tasks internal to the system, involving data or things,
3. Tasks external to the system, involving people,
4. Tasks external to the system, involving data or things.

The first category (internal people) operationalizes the activities of leadership as defined earlier. Fifty-five task statements were included in this category. The remaining three categories (internal data/things, external people, and external data/things) define three broad sets of management tasks. These categories contain nineteen, twelve, and twenty-three task statements, respectively. Table 7–1 presents samples of the task statements that were used, sorted into the four categories. As can be seen in table 7–1, leadership is operationalized with tasks that are immediately interpersonal in nature, while the management behaviors concern persons outside the work unit or dealing with data and things.

Table 7–1
Examples of Tasks by Leadership and Management Subclassification

Leadership (internal, people)

Tells sales representatives about changes to keep them up to date.

Assists sales representatives in resolving conflicts to maintain a cohesive working section.

Management (external, people)

Talks with other unit supervisors about problems and issues to work out recommendations for change for management.

Management (internal, data/things)

Reviews sales-level information to plan for assignments of sales representatives.

Management (external, data/things)

Prepares sales reports on section performance as an information service to management.

Two sets of ratings were obtained from supervisors for all task statements: ratings of importance and ratings of time spent on each task. The latter data are reported here. For respondents, time spent was defined as "the amount of time, relative to other tasks, that is spent on each of the tasks listed." The rating scale for time spent had six scale points:

1. No time spent
2. Very little time spent compared to other tasks
3. Somewhat less time spent compared to other tasks
4. Same amount of time spent compared to other tasks
5. More time spent compared to other tasks
6. A great deal more time spent compared to other tasks

Criteria. Two sets of data served as the outcomes of managerial behavior: (1) the work-facilitation data collected from the supervisor's subordinates and (2) the telephone-sales ratio of the work unit.

Briefly, work-facilitation survey data were collected from eighteen groups of subordinates via a consensus procedure. These data were organized into six subsystem (Katz and Kahn, 1978) categories: the supportive, production, adaptive, managerial, personnel-maintenance, and equipment-maintenance subsystems. (See Chapter 1 and Chapter 4.)

Telephone-sales ratio (SR) was also used as a criterion. It is a summary statistic describing the monthly sales performance for each unit. (SR is an average of the data collected for two consecutive months.) Management provided this information for the fifteen sales unit (see Chapter 4).

Data Analysis. Three sets of data analyses were performed to explore the hypothesized relationships among the variables of interest. First, the supervisory-task–analysis time-spent data were analyzed, including scale means, standard deviations, and internal-consistency reliability estimates for the leadership-behavior and three management-behavior scales. Second, analyses of construct validity were conducted by examining the intercorrelations among the leadership and management scales.

Finally, the criterion-related validities of the one leadership-behavior and three management-behavior scales were estimated. For this analysis, Pearson product moment correlations were calculated among the various supervisor-behavior scales and the two criteria (sales-unit work facilitation, and sales-unit effectiveness).

Results

The three sets of data analyses described earlier are presented in turn: (1) internal-consistency reliability analysis of the supervisory-task–analysis data,

(2) leadership- and management-behavior–scales intercorrelations, and (3) criterion-related validities of the leadership- and management-behavior scales, with the work-facilitation–subsystem scales and the telephone-sales ratio (SR).

Supervisor-Behavior Scales. The term *supervisor-behavior scales* is used in this chapter to refer to the leadership and management scales as a group. Table 7–2 presents the scale means, standard deviations, intercorrelations, and internal-consistency reliability estimates for the leadership-behavior scale and the three management-behavior scales. The table shows that the mean for the leadership-behavior scale is greater than the means for the management scales. This finding indicates that supervisors spend relatively more time doing leadership tasks than management tasks.

These supervisor-behavior scales are all highly correlated. Supervisors who report spending relatively more time doing leadership tasks also report spending relatively more time doing management tasks than other supervisors.

Criterion-Related Validity: Work Facilitation. Table 7–3 presents the correlations between the four supervisor-behavior scales and the work-facilitation subsystems. The results are quite unexpected. For two of the work-facilitation dimensions (managerial and adaptive), the supervisor-behavior scales are modestly correlated with work facilitation. These correlations reach statistical significance for the three "management" scales with facilitation in the managerial subsystem. However, each of these correlations in both subsystems is in the opposite direction to that which was predicted. Specifically, the results indicate that the more time supervisors spent on leadership and management behaviors, the *less* work facilitation existed in the work unit. While the correlations in the other subsystems are very close to zero,

Table 7–2
Means, Standard Deviations, Intercorrelations, and Internal-Consistency Reliability Estimates for Supervisor-Behavior Scales

			Scale			
	Mean	*S.D.*	*(1)*	*(2)*	*(3)*	*(4)*
Internal people (1)	3.11	.66	(.93)			
Internal data/things (2)	2.92	.75	.87	(.81)		
External people (3)	2.78	.83	.82	.85	(.77)	
External data/things (4)	2.62	.84	.76	.85	.88	(.86)

Note: Internal-consistency reliability estimates are in parentheses.

Table 7–3

Intercorrelations of Supervisor-Behavior and Work-Facilitation Subsystem Scales

	Supervisor Behavioral Scales			
Subsystem Scale	Internal People	Internal Data/Things	External People	External Data/Things
Supportive	.11	−.06	−.05	.04
Production	.30	.01	.01	−.10
Managerial	−.21	−.43*	−.45*	−.45*
Equipment maintenance	.01	−.02	−.01	−.09
Personnel maintenance	.24	.05	−.06	−.15
Adaptive	−.08	−.29	−.35	−.24

*p < .05.

the systematic pattern of inverse correlations for the managerial and adaptive subsystems are cause for concern. Is it possible that leadership and management activities create inhibiting working conditions? An alternative explanation that is consistent with the results is that the hypothesized causal direction was in error. Perhaps the lack of facilitating conditions in a work unit dictates where a supervisor will expend effort and time in terms of leadership and management behaviors. This explanation will be elaborated on in the discussion.

Criterion-Related Validity: Sales Ratio. Table 7–4 shows the correlations between the supervisor-behavior scales and the sales-ratio scores for all work units. In contrast to the data on work facilitation, these correlations are uniformly positive (as predicted). The correlations for the two "internally" focussed scales are moderately high. In fact, later analyses with an increased sample ($N = 20$) of sales units revealed that both the internal/people scale ($r = .39$, $p < .05$) and internal/data-things scale ($r = .38$, $p < .05$) were statistically significant. These data suggest that there is a direct relationship between supervisor behavior and the unit effectiveness, rather than an indirect one as proposed earlier.

Table 7–4

Correlations between the Four Supervisor-Behavior Scales and Sales-Ratio Data

Internal people	.32
Internal data/things	.25
External people	.13
External data/things	.04

Discussion

The focus of this chapter was on examining the relationship between supervisor behavior and work facilitation. Supervisor behaviors were presumed to not have a direct effect on unit effectiveness, but, rather, an indirect effect through work facilitation. The results of this analysis were contrary to expectations in a number of respects. First, the operationalization of supervisor behaviors into leadership and management scales was not successful in that the four scales were highly intercorrelated, indicating that supervisors who engage in one type of activity were likely to engage in each of the other activities as well. Second, the measures of leadership and management were generally unrelated to work facilitation. In the two subsystems where a modest correlation was observed, they were in the opposite direction to that predicted. That is, when supervisors spent more time on leadership and management behaviors, there was *less* work facilitation. Finally, in spite of the lack of relationship between supervisor behavior and work facilitation, the direct relationship between supervisor behavior and unit effectiveness was consistently positive and reached statistical significance in an expanded sample ($N = 20$). An examination of the joint effects of supervisor behavior and work facilitation on unit effectiveness in a multiple regression analysis yielded a statistically significant ($r = .56$, $p < .05$) result. This analysis suggests that supervisor behaviors and work facilitation have independent direct effects on unit effectiveness.

The Supervisor-Behavior–Work-Facilitation Relationship. The results seem to indicate that when supervisor behaviors are high, work facilitation is low but unit effectiveness is high. One possible explanation for these results is that the causal direction in the relationship between supervisor behavior and work facilitation is the opposite of that which was expected. It is plausible that supervisors devote greater amounts of time and energy when they perceive lower levels of work facilitation. Thus, one possible causal model suggested by the data is that work facilitation and supervisor behavior are independent but complementary antecedents of unit effectiveness. Supervisors may deliberately choose to compensate for lack of work facilitation by engaging in leadership and management behaviors.

An alternate explanation for the observed relationship would focus on the sources of data on each variable. One is reminded of the observation that supervisors appraise subordinate performance, but subordinates report that their performance is never appraised. Interestingly, it is precisely on these kinds of items where the negative correlation exists between what supervisors say they do and subordinates reports that it does not get accomplished.

Perhaps there is an additional methodological issue that can explain this and it concerns the different perspectives from which superior and subordinate view each other and the work situation. In the climate literature, for example, it has been shown in a number of papers that people at different levels in an organization see the organization in generally uncorrelated ways (Powell and Butterfield, 1978). Some have interpreted this finding as if it is a negative aspect of climate research. They do this under the assumption that everyone in an organization should agree on the characteristics of their work situation. However, since managers and subordinates really function in different kinds of work situations, nonagreement in perceptions is to be expected, not decried.

This kind of finding suggests that perhaps the best source of data with regard to the relationship between work facilitation and managerial behavior is the subordinate who is influenced by both. In the present research, we attempted to have the data come from two different sources so that response–response contamination would not be an issue. This may have been a strategic error for two reasons. First, Yukl (personal communication, 1985) reports that assessments of managerial behavior from the perspective of the behaving manager are seriously flawed in terms of both reliability and validity. Of course, leadership data have consistently been collected from subordinates and not from the leaders themselves. Second, in retrospect, it turns out that it is possible to collect both sets of data from subordinates without having response bias. This can happen precisely because of our innovation for the collection of work-facilitation data, namely the consensus procedure.

Thus, in future research, it should be possible to use some of the subordinates in a work unit as the source for the work-facilitation data and other subordinates as the source for the supervisor-behavior data. Both sets of subordinates could use the consensus procedure, the work unit could still be the unit of analysis, and there would be no response–response contamination to contend with in the analyses. Logic suggests that if there really is a relationship between what supervisors do and the conditions under which subordinates work, it can best be discovered through this methodology.

The Supervisor-Behavior–Unit-Effectiveness Relationship. The proposed model presented earlier in this chapter predicted that leadership and management activities would have an impact on unit effectiveness by increasing work facilitation. The results suggest that supervisor behavior may have a direct effect on unit effectiveness that is independent of the effect of work facilitation. If future research confirms this pattern of relationships, it will leave unanswered the primary question of this study: what are the antecedents of work facilitation? If future research also supports the view that work facilitation is an antecedent of supervisor behavior, we may have learned something very interesting about leadership and management. It certainly is plausible, however, that over time, work facilitation and supervisor behavior are reciprocally related and that leadership and management behaviors may indeed influence work facilitation at a later point in time.

Management as a Substitute for Leadership. One of the propositions of this chapter was that, to the extent that good management existed, leadership would be less important. Unfortunately, the operationalization of the leadership and management scales failed to differentiate between leadership and management, making it impossible to adequately test this hypothesis. The use of task statements from a job analysis of supervisors as the source of leadership and management data must be reexamined in light of this evidence. The assumption on which this choice was made was that responses to task statements would represent more specific activities and would be more likely to differentiate between leadership and management than more generic "off-the-shelf" leadership and management measures. Perhaps a compromise between the specificity of the task statements and a more general measure may be appropriate in future research. For example, clusters of task statements may be written as a single more general item reflecting a more complete behavior of the supervisor.

Conclusion. The results of this analysis do not support the proposed model of the impact of leadership and management on work facilitation. However, the data suggest that supervisor behavior may have a direct effect on unit effectiveness and that the lack of work facilitation may contribute to an increase in leadership and management activities. The measurement of supervisor behavior needs further development in order to differentiate between leadership and management activities.

References

Argyris, C. (1957). *Personality and organization.* New York: Harper.

Argyris, C. (1979). How normal science methodology makes leadership research less additive and less applicable. In J. G. Hunt and L. L. Larson (eds.), *Crosscurrents in leadership.* Carbondale: Southern Illinois University Press, pp. 47–63.

Bass, B. M. (1981). *Stogdill's handbook of leadership,* rev. ed. New York: Free Press.

Beer, M. (1980). *Organization change and development: A systems view.* Santa Monica, Ca: Goodyear.

Campbell, J. P., Dunnette, M. D., Lawler, E. E., III, and Weick, K. W., Jr. (1970). *Managerial behavior, performance and effectiveness.* New York: McGraw-Hill.

Dowell, B. E., and Wexley, K. N. (1978). Development of a work behavior taxonomy for first line supervisors. *Journal of Applied Psychology, 63,* 563–72.

Dubin, R. (1979). Metaphors of leadership: An overview. In J. G. Hunt and L. L. Larson (eds.), *Crosscurrents in leadership*. Carbondale: Southern Illinois University Press.

Fine, S. A., and Wiley, W. W. (1974). An introduction to functional job analysis. In E. A. Fleishman and A. R. Bass (eds.), *Studies in personnel and industrial psychology*, 3rd ed.) Homewood, Il.: Dorsey.

Fleishman, E. A. (1953). Leadership climate, human relations training, and supervisory behavior. *Personnel Psychology, 6*, 205–22.

Gannon, M. J. (1982). *Management: An integrated framework*, 2nd ed. Boston: Little, Brown.

Goldstein, I. L. (1986). *Training in organizations; Needs assessment, development and evaluation*, 2nd ed. Monterey, Calif.: Brooks-Cole.

Hemphill, J. K. (1959). Job descriptions for executives. *Harvard Business Review, 37*, 55–67.

Jacobs, T. (1970). *Leadership and exchange in formal organizations*. Human Resources Research Organization.

Jago, A. R. (1979). Leadership: Perspectives in theory and research. Paper presented at the TIMS International Conference, Honolulu, Hawaii.

Katz, D., and Kahn, R. L. (1978). *The social psychology of organizations*, 2nd ed. New York: John Wiley & Sons.

Kerr, S., and Jermier, J. M. (1978). Substitutes for leadership: Their meaning and measurement. *Organizational Behavior and Human Performance, 22*, 375–403.

Mahoney, T. A., Jerdee, T. H., and Carroll, S. J. (1965). The job(s) of management. *Industrial Relations*, February, 97–110.

McGregor, D. M. (1960). *The human side of enterprise*. New York: McGraw-Hill.

Mintzberg, H. (1973). *The nature of managerial work*. New York: Harper & Row.

Moses, J. L., and Ritchie, R. J. (1976). Supervisory relationships training: A behavioral evaluation of a behavior modeling program. *Personnel Psychology, 29*, 337–43.

Nicholas, J. M. (1982). The comparative impact of organization development interventions on hard criteria measures. *Academy of Management Review, 7*, 531–42.

Powell, G. N., and Butterfield, D. A. (1978). The case for subsystem climates in organizations. *Academy of Management Review, 3*, 151–57.

Sashkin, M., and Garland, H. (1979). Laboratory and field research: Integrating divergent streams. In J. G. Hunt and L. L. Larson (eds.), *Crosscurrents in leadership*. Carbondale: Southern Illinois University Press.

Schein, E. A. (1985). *Organizational culture and leadership*. San Francisco: Jossey-Bass.

Schneider, B. (1985). Organizational behavior. *Annual Review of Psychology, 36*, 573–611.

Schoorman, F. D. (1981). *The impact of leadership role behavior on the performance of professionals as subordinates: A study of university department heads*. Unpublished doctoral dissertation. Pittsburgh: Carnegie-Mellon University.

Stogdill, R. M. (1974). *Handbook of leadership: A survey of theory and research*. New York: Free Press.

Tornow, W., and Pinto, P. (1978). The development of a managerial job taxonomy: A system for describing, classifying and evaluating executive positions. *Journal of Applied Psychology, 61,* 410–18.

Yukl, G. A., and Nemeroff, W. F. (1979). Identification and measurement of specific categories of leadership behavior: A progress report. In J. G. Hunt and L. L. Larson (eds.), *Crosscurrents in leadership.* Carbondale: Southern Illinois University Press, pp. 164–200.

Yukl, G., and Van Fleet, D. D. (1982). Cross-situational, multi-method research on military leader effectiveness. *Organizational Behavior and Human Performance, 30,* 87–108.

8
Individual and Organizational Responses to Ambiguity

Joseph L. Moses
Karen S. Lyness

One of the givens of managerial and organizational life is change and its consequences: ambiguity, uncertainty, complexity, and turbulence. No description of the contemporary manager's world appears complete without one or more of these words.

While managers and organizations have always had to contend with a certain level of change, today's managers face even greater challenges. In the past, both the rate and direction of change were relatively steady and predictable. Managers had time to prepare and execute appropriate responses, and they could extrapolate from past experience.

On the other hand, many contemporary managers face changes that are much less predictable and can occur at a dizzying rate. Less time is available for response, and the interrelatedness of events results in complex series of consequences and implications, following even seemingly simple decisions. Fluid organizational structures and the difficulties of goal and problem definition also contribute to the ambiguity confronting managers.

Ambiguity thus emerges as a key theme for both managers and organizations, leading to several important questions: How do people and organizations adapt to a more ambiguous world? What behavioral styles inhibit or facilitate responses to uncertainty? What might we recommend to managers and organizations grappling with these issues?

We began our research on this topic as our organization, AT&T, experienced massive organizational change as a result of the divestiture of the Bell System. Much of our thinking and early data collection concerning ambiguity and its effect on managerial behavior preceded the Divestiture period. Thus, we were able to compare this base-line period of individual and organizational responses with later responses to the phenomenal ambiguities associated with the largest corporate reorganization in history.

We initially focussed on the individual as our major unit of analysis and then gradually expanded our thinking to examine organizational responses as well. As we shared our findings with others, it became apparent that much of our work at AT&T was generalizable to other individuals and organizations as they experience change and its consequences.

This chapter summarizes our research on the topic of ambiguity as it affects individual and organizational behavior. It rests on two primary assumptions:

1. Ambiguity and complexity are here to stay.
2. Managers and organizations that can respond effectively to ambiguous environments will be best positioned to succeed in the future.

Ambiguity and Managerial Behavior

Ambiguity has become a fact of organizational life due to the ever-increasing complexity and rapid pace of the business environment and society at large. For example, global competition for customers and resources increases the pressure and demands facing managers. Sophisticated market research segmentation of consumers and business customers leads to ever-increasing diversity of product and service offerings. In other instances, technological advances provide the impetus for change. Deregulation also has led to increased competition for new markets. Simultaneously, boundaries between traditionally distinct industries, such as banks and brokerage firms, are eroding. These changes appear to be driven by an effort to be more responsive to customers' needs as well as an attempt to adapt to the environmental uncertainty experienced by each industry as it responds to an increasingly complex world.

Organizations attempt to adapt to changing and uncertain environments through internal changes and reorganizations, mergers and acquisitions, or divestitures of entire units. All of this results in tremendous ambiguity for managers as working relationships are altered and responsibilities become less clearly defined.

In other settings where the organization itself is fairly stable, managers may wrestle with particular problems or decisions that are ambiguous. For example, managers often face complex decisions where time is limited and the available information is inadequate, inconsistent, or unreliable. Other types of ambiguity arise when managers confront ill-defined problems or goals, uncontrollable factors, or insufficient feedback or when they must proceed without past experience, precedent, or structure to guide them.

Many theorists have identified ambiguity as a critical aspect of organizational environments. We have, with the collaboration of Sheldon Zedeck and Susan Jackson, reviewed the literature and developed an integrative conceptual model to represent key categories of variables related to ambiguity in organizations. Based on this model, we defined ambiguity as "a global characteristic of the situation that is determined by the summation and interaction of the specific components of the immediate work context, members of the organization and the external environment" (Lyness et al., 1985).

The components of this definition are illustrated in the preceding examples of ambiguity confronting contemporary managers. Ambiguous problems and ill-defined goals are examples of ambiguity in the immediate work context. Role ambiguity due to structural changes is an example of ambiguity resulting from interaction with members of the organization. Finally, global competition and erosion of boundaries between industries are examples of environmental ambiguity that can impact managers in an organization. The ambiguity facing a particular manager can arise from any or all of these sources.

On a more personal note, managers may also experience ambiguity not only in their work, but also in their careers. As organizational structures become more fluid in response to changing environments, it is often unrealistic for managers to depend on upper management or even an immediate supervisor to design an optimal career path. Instead, managers must assume more responsibility for their own career development, often without adequate information or instruction. Organizational incumbents may have difficulty predicting where future opportunities will lie as companies reorganize and old networks become less reliable. Also, there is uncertainty associated with future employment prospects as organizational force reductions and layoffs are coupled with recruitment of recent graduates with different types of skills.

As industrial psychologists in a corporate management research unit, we were struck with the importance of understanding how managers approach ambiguity as a key to predicting effectiveness in the work environment. As noted, we began studying ambiguity and managerial behavior over six years ago, long before the divestiture of the Bell System. However, we were able to collect data and refine our thinking as both researchers and subjects during this period of tremendous change and ambiguity.

Our research indicated that when ambiguity is present, some fundamental changes occur in the nature of the situation a manager confronts. For one thing, skills and approaches that work well in more traditional, structured work environments may be less effective in ambiguous settings. In many cases, managers may not have been trained to deal effectively with ambiguity since this is not the type of knowledge that can be easily articulated or generalized from one situation to another. As a result, ambiguous problems may not be addressed or may be so fragmented that attention is focussed only on their more manageable aspects, with major issues left unresolved.

In addition to pointing up skill or knowledge deficits, ambiguity may give rise to complex emotions that either facilitate or inhibit effective performance. For example, some people are energized and stimulated by ambiguous situations that they perceive as challenges or opportunities to be creative. Thus, their positive reaction to ambiguity could facilitate their effectiveness in this type of situation. In sharp contrast, other people are uncomfortable in ambiguous situations, which they perceive as threatening or sources of pressure. Their lack of comfort and negative emotional reaction to the ambiguity can actually inhibit their utilization of the skills that they possess, although these skills might be effective in other, less ambiguous settings.

Research Objectives

Having recognized the importance of understanding how managers respond to ambiguous situations, we set out to learn more about the area. A review of the published literature (Lyness et al., 1985) revealed that while many writers suggest that ambiguity is an important situational characteristic, little agreement exists about how to define or operationalize the word. The many meanings attributed to *ambiguity* and its organizational corollary, *uncertainty*, result in an imprecise use of the concept. However, despite the lack of specific answers, the literature helped to confirm our belief that ambiguity is an important and pervasive aspect of managerial work.

Due to the complexity of the topic and seeming lack of agreement among others about how to approach it, we decided to begin our research with fairly broad objectives. Specifically, we wanted to (1) gain a better understanding of the concept of ambiguity and its effect on managerial behavior, (2) study the types of ambiguous situations managers experience, and (3) identify ways in which we could help managers cope more effectively with ambiguity.

The Interview Study

In order to learn first-hand about managers' experiences with ambiguity, we conducted a series of in-depth interviews (Moses and Lyness, 1983). We interviewed over forty managers from a variety of organizations. These organizations were chosen from a broad spectrum of industries, including computer services, international banking, retailing, manufacturing, investment, advertising, and education. The interviewees were identified by in-house contacts as people who experienced considerable ambiguity in their jobs. In most cases, the respondents were senior managers in policy-making positions. Respondents were drawn from many functional areas.

The managers were interviewed in their work settings. Most interviews lasted approximately 2 hours. A semistructured format was followed after pretesting indicated that a more stuctured format tended to narrow the range of responses. We asked each manager for a definition of ambiguity and the characteristics associated with ambiguous situations, as well as specific examples of ambiguous situations.

We also asked the managers for critical incidents of effective and ineffective behavior in ambiguous situations. The respondents were asked to describe exactly why the situation was perceived as ambiguous, what they did in behavioral terms, why this was effective or ineffective in the situation, what factors facilitated or inhibited effective behavior in the situation, and so on. They were encouraged to explain what seems to make the difference between effective and ineffective behavior in ambiguous situations.

We were impressed with the level of candor and insight among our respondents. The ambiguous situations they described tended to be important situations that they had thought about a great deal. They provided rich behavioral data that we used to generate a frame of reference by identifying the main themes that emerged.

We can briefly summarize some of the findings from these interviews as follows:

1. Ambiguity is an important and pervasive part of the manager's job. As one respondent put it, "It is important that people are willing to accept ambiguous situations as normal. . . . Ambiguity simply *is,* it is not a negative thing."

2. Ambiguity is a highly individualized perception. Situations that are very ambiguous for one manager might be much less so for another. Ambiguous situations were seen as uncertain or unpredictable, lacking clarity or definition, or novel. One manager summed it up by saying, "You don't know what to do."

3. Ambiguity tends to be stressful. It can be viewed as positive, negative, or both, depending on the manager. As a positive stressor, an ambiguous situation may be seen as a challenge or opportunity that serves to energize the manager and bring forth the manager's best efforts. As a negative stressor, an ambiguous situation may be seen as a threat or pressure that inhibits effective performance. Often there were mixed feelings, as when a senior executive explained, "I age with every ambiguous situation, but if my job didn't have these types of challenges, I couldn't survive."

4. Several key determinants were identified that differentiate managers who are effective in ambiguous situations from managers who experience difficulty.

Thus, there appears to be general agreement that many senior managers experience considerable ambiguity in their jobs and that it permeates most of the significant problems or decisions they face. Yet, ambiguity remains an elusive area to study and understand since it means different things to different managers. Ambiguity can arise from many sources and can be experienced in different ways by different managers. Also, managers differ in both their emotional reactions and behavioral responses to ambiguity.

The Assessment Research

The interview study provided us with a frame of reference and led to the quadrant model of coping styles, which we shall describe in the next section. In addition, we learned a great deal about how managers respond to different types of ambiguous situations through our ongoing assessment center research.

For many years, we have been directing AT&T's Advanced Management Assessment Program. This program is designed to evaluate senior-level management potential in promising middle managers (Moses, 1984). Based on our ambiguity interview findings as well as other research concerning contemporary management behavior at AT&T, we reformulated several parts of this program to assess participants' characteristic strategies for coping with ambiguity.

As described in more detail elsewhere (Lyness and Moses, 1983), we incorporated a multimethod approach to measure managerial behavior in ambiguous situations. New measures and techniques were developed for the assessment process that reflected the various types of ambiguity that managers encounter. Our ambiguity measures included group and individual simulation exercises, clinical interviews, projective instruments, personality inventories, biographical and other background data, as well as modifications of contemporary paper-and-pencil tolerance-of-ambiguity instruments. The development of these measures permitted us to operationalize many of our ideas about the diverse types of ambiguity confronting managers. Analyses of the resulting data permitted us to differentiate among the managers with respect to their abilities, personalities, motivational characteristics, and work and life experiences, as these relate to performance in ambiguous situations. We were able to differentiate among key behavioral styles and could reliably classify managers according to our model.

Coping with Ambiguity: The Quadrant Model

Our interview-and-assessment research suggested that no single characteristic determines whether or not a manager will be effective in ambiguous settings. This is, in part, due to the unique nature of ambiguity for each individual.

However, we identified two underlying factors that resulted in four distinct coping strategies that managers use.

The two key factors that have a significant impact on coping style are (1) the manager's level of the *skills* needed to respond appropriately in an ambiguous situation and (2) the manager's level of *comfort* with the ambiguity. As might be expected, managers differ greatly on both of these dimensions.

The problem is heightened by the fact that the necessary skills vary from one ambiguous situation to the next. For example, managers who are perceptive, flexible, and capable of effective interaction are able to respond to ambiguous interpersonal problems more effectively than managers who lack these skills. On the other hand, a different set of skills are needed in situations where the ambiguity results from incomplete, inconsistent, or contradictory information. Here, analytical, data-gathering, and problem-solving skills may be most critical. Thus, possessing the appropriate managerial skills is one of the key determinants of effectiveness in ambiguous situations. However, simply possessing these skills is not enough.

Managers also differ in their degree of comfort with ambiguity, which is the other key determinant of effectiveness in ambiguous situations. Some are quite upset by uncertainty and work very hard to control, manage, or eliminate it from their lives. Other managers acknowledge ambiguity as a part of the managerial turf, and they respond in a more relaxed, accepting manner. Still other managers actively seek out ambiguous situations because they enjoy the challenge and opportunities.

Figure 8–1 presents the coping styles that result from high and low levels of managerial skills and comfort with ambiguity. We labeled the styles adaptive, stylized, unconcerned, and overwhelmed. As will be explained later in the chapter, these styles can be used to describe individuals as well as organizations. We shall first describe each of the four quadrants in our model as it applies to individual managers.

Adaptive managers have both the managerial skills and the comfort level to deal effectively with a wide range of ambiguous situations. They recognize and accept ambiguity and adapt their approach to the situation at hand. Adaptive managers maintain a broad perspective, are sensitive to feedback, and can use both intuition and logic in solving problems. Not only do they respond well in ambiguous situations, but adaptive managers may actually seek out these challenges because of the latitude and opportunities they provide due to the lack of preexisting boundaries and limitations.

Stylized managers have the potential to handle ambiguous situations well, but often they do not. They have the managerial skills needed to take appropriate action, but their lack of comfort inhibits their effectiveness in ambiguous situations. In fact, they are so uncomfortable that they focus their efforts on managing or reducing the ambiguity, often with disastrous results.

comfortable with ambiguity?

	yes	no
yes	I adaptive	II stylized
no	III unconcerned	IV overwhelmed

requisite
abilities
present?

Figure 8–1. Styles of Coping with Ambiguity

We call them stylized because they tend to rely on habitual, standard responses, particularly if these have worked well in the past. These managers also like to create or follow rules, procedures, and precedent because these provide a structure for their approach. When confronted with an ambiguous situation, they seek structure, resulting in actions designed to minimize ambiguity rather than deal with the real issues presented.

Unconcerned managers are not bothered by ambiguity. In fact, they give the appearance of being unconcerned about most problems and may trivialize their importance. Although these managers may be comfortable with ambiguity, they lack the skills needed for effective responses. Their lack of inhibition is typically compounded by an inflated self-image and insensitivity to feedback, particularly when it is negative. Unconcerned managers are quick to take action in ambiguous settings, with little reality testing about the appropriateness of their actions. They may appear confident, self-assured, and in control when they confront ambiguous situations. However, unconcerned managers can be unpredictable or even problematic from an organizational perspective. Since they are so action-oriented and outwardly confident, they may persuade others who are less comfortable with ambiguity to follow their early lead.

Overwhelmed managers have considerable difficulty in ambiguous situations since they lack the necessary skills and are extremely uncomfortable with ambiguity. They are often hesitant to take action in ambiguous situations, and they may deny or fail to understand the critical aspects of the problem or situation. Often they focus on an insignificant part of the problem and "work it to death," while avoiding the more complex issues. Although these managers are overwhelmed in ambiguous situations, they may be much more effective in structured, familiar environments if they can utilize procedures or past experience to guide their actions.

The quadrant model is useful for describing different coping styles that managers use in ambiguous situations. It is important to keep in mind, however, that both comfort and managerial skills are continuous dimensions rather than discrete categories. Also, while it is usually possible to identify a dominant or characteristic style, many managers use different approaches in different situations.

We have found that most people tend to manifest a preferred style and can be reliably classified based on the data collected in the assessment process. A small percentage of individuals are hard to classify, but the majority show a consistent preference for one quadrant. We have also found that when managers are exposed to these concepts, they usually report little difficulty in placing themselves in one of the quadrants.

The identification of relatively stable coping styles was an important step in understanding how managers respond to ambiguity. This in turn led to exploration of how these styles are developed and whether it is possible to influence the process through appropriate organizational strategies.

Development of Characteristic Coping Styles

There are many determinants of a manager's coping style when the person is confronted with ambiguity. In fact, there appear to be specific critical periods that play a key role in the development of these coping styles. These include early childhood, early job experiences, and periods of critical change. During early childhood, for example, values concerning achievement, goal setting, level of aspiration, and comfort with uncertainty are established. Early job experiences during a manager's formative years in business are also critical. Imitation of bosses and other influential managers, as well as formal and informal socialization processes, all have a critical influence on new managers entering an organization. Early job experiences, coupled with exposure to an effective role model, are important determinants of later behavioral style. The experience of going through a major change or period of uncertainty can also affect a manager's coping style. It is during these intense periods that managers can feel most threatened, isolated, or stimulated by the rapid change or uncertainty they face.

Helping Managers Cope

Our research concerning the development of one's coping style is still in a formative stage. Understanding how coping styles emerge and the extent to which they can be modified is a complex undertaking and all the answers are not yet known. It is important to learn more about how styles develop in order to design intervention strategies to help managers modify inappropriate coping behaviors. We have stressed, however, that a generic training or development strategy designed to assist all managers in coping with ambiguity is unlikely to be effective.

Instead, different strategies should be used for managers with different coping styles. For example, stylized managers need to learn to become more comfortable with ambiguity and try alternative approaches. These strategies would be highly inappropriate with unconcerned managers who are already too comfortable and need, instead, to learn to be more controlled and sensitive to feedback. Similarly, approaches used to control the free-wheeling style of the unconcerned manager would send the wrong message to the stylized manager.

A better understanding of the key developmental periods should lead to innovative approaches that will help managers deal with these transitions and the associated ambiguity. Also, an individual diagnosis of a manager's characteristic style can lead to specific developmental or placement recommendations.

Organizational Responses to Ambiguity

In addition to examining the determinants of an individual manager's coping style, the manager's behavior can be better understood if it is examined within a specific organizational context. Just as our quadrant model of coping styles can be used to describe individual behavior, it can also be used to describe organizational behavior. There tend to be similarities among managers from the same organization, suggesting that there are learned organizational norms concerning how to approach ambiguous situations.

There are many factors that may influence an organization's style. These include the size of the organization and its history, its stage in its corporate life cycle, the extent of industry regulation, and the nature of its markets, technology, and competition.

Different types of coping strategies may be exhibited during the evolution and growth of an organization as it passes through various stages in its life cycle. For example, young, entrepreneurial, state-of-the-art, high technology industries may be more likely to recruit, select, and develop managers who have both the abilities and comfort level to effectively handle ambiguity, resulting in an open, adaptive organizational style. In contrast, a larger, well-established, bureaucratic organization with highly developed procedures may be more likely to utilize the stylized or overwhelmed strategies in dealing with ambiguity. It is thus possible to classify organizations using our quandrant model, as described next.

Adaptive organizations are characterized by a sense of energy and commitment. They tend to be innovative, forward-looking companies that are very sensitive to important developments outside the organization. Complex issues tend to be addressed, new ideas are rewarded, and frequently there is a short response time between ideas and action. Ambiguous issues are not ignored, and people at all levels in the organization often participate in problem definition and idea generation through informal communication systems. Adaptive organizations convey a sense of excitement and discovery. They effectively adapt to their environment and often emerge as market leaders.

Stylized organizations are somewhat older and have developed rules and procedures for most contingencies. Strong hierarchical power structures are in place, and the communication flow is primarily vertical. Problems are usually identified and defined by the senior management group and then delegated. Ambiguous issues may be initially ignored and complexities segmented into more solvable pieces. Thus, stylized organizations may excel at short-term firefighting, but be ill-equipped for grappling with longer-range issues in a dynamic environment. Once these organizations have articulated financial or business objectives, the objectives tend to drive performance, with little flexibility to meet unanticipated contingencies. Stylized organizations tend to be most successful in environments where change is gradual and predictable.

Unconcerned organizations are often in a state of flux as a result of reorganizations, mergers, and other realignments. These come about as the organization attempts to deal with change through structural modifications, which often have some unanticipated consequences. Managers work at a demanding pace and activity levels are high. Unconcerned organizations tend to focus on short-term problems and managers are frequently driven to meet unrealistic time deadlines. Risk taking and competition are encouraged, although the focus may be more internal than external. Rather than trying to develop their own management talent, these organizations are quick to recruit from the outside or turn to outside consultants for advice on major decisions. There may be loyalty to a particular organizational unit, but rarely to the entire organization.

Overwhelmed organizations are often large, bureaucratic, and uncoordinated. Managers try to protect their own "turf" rather than view issues from an organizational perspective. Often they direct their efforts toward discussion rather than action. These organizations are also very resistant to change and may be slow to take advantage of technological innovations. They are usually successful only when they have historically dominated a particular market. Overwhelmed organizations are prime candidates for failure, however, when change is needed and they are too encumbered by policies and practices to adapt to the realities of the market place. In addition to market-driven organizations, many public or civil service organizations may exhibit overwhelmed behaviors, particularly when they are viewed as "institutions" rather than as organizations that need to compete for their continued success.

Why Organizational Coping Styles Persist

Once established, many powerful processes serve to reinforce and perpetuate the style of an organization. These processes include the selection, socialization, reward structure, and culture of the organization, all of which help to shape managerial behavior. Selection practices are often designed to identify people similar to organizational incumbents. Also, self-selection among potential applicants may further narrow the range and serve to perpetuate the status quo (Schneider, 1987). Socialization practices expose new employees to organizational norms and values, and help shape behavior in accepted directions. Reward systems further reinforce accepted behaviors. When all of these systems embody and reinforce the same corporate values, they become a very powerful influence on managerial behavior. In fact, organizational theorists, such as Lorsch (1985) and Sapienza (1985), suggest that cultural values even affect perceptions of environmental events. Thus, the managers in a particular organization tend to "see" things in a particular way, which in turn affects the range of options they consider as well as subsequent actions.

As an example of how these forces may operate in a dysfunctional manner, consider the case of a stylized organization that attracts individuals who have the potential to become stylized managers. The organization's selection and staffing systems would also reward stylized behaviors. This works well as long as the organization is in an environment where change is gradual and predictable, markets are established, and so on. Unfortunately, in many organizations, stylized managers reach the top just when a changing environment requires adaptive managers. Not only can the mismatch be problematic, but there is a strong likelihood that most adaptive managers will either have left the organization or learned to adapt by developing a stylized approach.

Influence of Organizational Coping Styles
on Staffing Practices

There are also characteristic recruiting and staffing practices exhibited by each of the four organization types. Since adaptive and stylized organizations tend to be successful, they are able to recruit and retain talented managers. Both reward for performance and promote from within. However, there are some important differences in how these two types of organizations approach staffing decisions.

Adaptive organizations recognize and reward people for what they know rather than for who they know. The composition of work teams or task forces is determined by problem content rather than organizational structure. Stylized organizations, on the other hand, rely on status and level as the major considerations when forming task forces. While accomplishment is emphasized in adaptive organizations, stylized organizations tend to emphasize advancement as the prime motivator. An unfortunate consequence of the overemphasis on advancement in stylized organizations is that fear of failure may inhibit risk taking or innovation.

Unconcerned organizations are less concerned with failure as long as they have a few successes. However, they tend to staff key management functions from outside the organization rather than by promoting from within. Since outsiders may be chosen for their expertise in a narrow specialty, managers who lack generic management skills may be placed in key positions. Also, the emphasis on outside recruiting may result in insufficient attention to internal management development as well as diminished motivation among the insiders. This reinforces loyalty to the immediate boss, with little transference to the organization as a whole.

Overwhelmed organizations also promote from within, but tend to base promotion decisions on seniority or organizational knowledge rather than competence or skills. These organizations may be perceived by the general public as employers of last resort; consequently, they do not attract or retain many high potential managers. Security is likely to be more of a motivator in these organizations than either accomplishment or advancement.

Facilitators and Inhibitors of Effectiveness

We have used our quadrant model to examine both individual and organizational responses to ambiguity. The model also provides a useful framework to examine potential facilitators and inhibitors of effectiveness at several different levels of analysis. These include the effectiveness of an individual manager confronting ambiguity, the effectiveness of an organization in an ambiguous environment, and the effectiveness of an individual manager within a particular organizational context.

First, at the individual level of analysis, both a manager's skills and comfort level can serve to facilitate or inhibit effectiveness in ambiguous situations. Adaptive managers would be expected to respond effectively across a broad range of ambiguous situations. In fact, they may be stimulated by the ambiguity so that it actually facilitates their performance.

In contrast, stylized managers may be much less effective when ambiguity is present. They have the necessary management skills, but are so uncomfortable with ambiguity that they direct their energy toward removing it rather than addressing other salient aspects of the situation. Thus, the stylized approach inhibits their effectiveness in ambiguous situations. Managers in the unconcerned and overwhelmed categories tend to be undermined by their lack of appropriate skills, and they have much less potential for effective performance when ambiguity is present.

Second, at the organizational level of analysis, skills and comfort level can facilitate or inhibit an organization's effectiveness when ambiguity is present. For example, adaptive organizations would be expected to enjoy a competitive advantage by responding effectively in ambiguous environments. In contrast to the outward orientation of adaptive organizations, stylized organizations in ambiguous environments would probably focus more internally, with renewed emphasis on methods and procedures to increase their managers' comfort level. Unconcerned organizations would probably respond irrationally, while overwhelmed organizations would be least likely to respond at all.

The third and most complex connection between these approaches and effectiveness concerns the relationship of the individual manager to the organizational setting. Although practices such as selection, socialization, and reward structures all operate to make individuals congruent with their organization, it is possible that they are not. When the individual and organizational styles are incongruent, the dominant organizational style can be viewed as a facilitator or inhibitor of the individual's effectiveness. For example, an adaptive manager hired into a very stylized organization might actually be less effective than the person would be in a less constraining context. On the other hand, a stylized manager who joins an adaptive organization might actually become more effective by learning more flexible approaches and being rewarded and encouraged for these attempts. A less optimistic scenario would occur for managers so stylized that they could not be induced to venture into trying new approaches. For this type of manager, an adaptive organization might be quite threatening due to the lack of structure, causing the person to become even more stylized and thus not fit in or meet performance expectations.

A more complex situation occurs when an unconcerned manager joins a stylized organization, and there are many possible scenarios that could result. This manager may not be able to meet the stylized organization's performance standards or may be viewed as risky or untrustworthy by upper management, leading to dismissal or voluntary exit. Another possibility is that the unconcerned manager might acquire a power base due to not sharing the other managers' reluctance to take action in ambiguous situations. This could lead to unfortunate consequences if no controls or feedback mechanisms were established to counter the unconcerned manager's whims. On the other hand, it is possible that this manager could serve as a useful catalyst for bringing about a more proactive approach.

While we have only discussed the quadrant model at the individual and organizational levels of analysis, it could also be used to describe the style of particular organizational units. While the units within an organization would be expected to resemble each other, there might be notable differences. For example, certain functional areas that are driven by methods and procedures (e.g., accounting, engineering) might be uncomfortable with ambiguity and favor approaches that try to structure it. However, other functional areas, with an orientation toward the external environment (e.g., marketing) might have a higher comfort level due to the ambiguity inherent in more fluid boundary positions.

Understanding different coping styles within organizational units can be useful in conflict resolution and team building. For example, traditional conflicts between marketing/sales and engineering/production may be due, at least in part, to the differences in how they approach ambiguity and change. This perspective may lead to a more constructive approach to building trust and cooperation rather than confrontations based on organizational stereotypes.

If specific organizational units differ in their approaches to ambiguity, then managers would be exposed to different organizational styles if they transfer from one group to another. Whether the group style facilitates or inhibits the manager's effectiveness would depend upon the congruity of styles and their impact on each other, as we discussed concerning the organizational level of analysis.

A similar congruity issue arises when a manager's style differs from that of the boss. For example, an adaptive manager's effectiveness might be hampered by reporting to a stylized or overwhelmed boss. In many respects, this may be the most serious mismatch of coping styles. The creativity, risk taking, and flexible approach of an adaptive manager would be seriously inhibited, especially if such a manager worked for a stylized boss and the dominant organizational behavior were stylized as well. If this continued, the adaptive manager might be faced with two unpleasant choices—either adapt to the boss and environment by becoming more stylized or leave the organization.

Conclusions

We began this chapter by suggesting that the future will be more complex and ambiguous for most people and organizations. We have presented a quadrant model with four distinct coping styles used by individuals and organizations in ambiguous environments. Charcteristic coping styles are determined by comfort with ambiguity and possession of the skills needed for effectiveness. In contrast to previous approaches limited to tolerance versus intolerance of ambiguity, we have identified four distinct coping styles. Of these, only the adaptive style, resulting from the optimal combination of appropriate skills and comfort with ambiguity, consistently leads to effective responses.

Our research efforts continue, with particular emphasis on identifying effective interventions at both the individual and organizational levels. However, we can summarize some key findings to date as follows:

1. Individual and organizational coping styles in ambiguous situations are identifiable, discrete, and predictable. These coping styles are not simply labels. They have a major impact on a wide variety of emotions and behaviors at the individual level as well as on practices and strategies at the organizational level.

2. Intervention strategies—whether at the individual, unit, or organizational level—need to begin with diagnosis of the dominant or characteristic coping style prior to initiating any action.

3. Understanding why individuals and organizations develop a characteristic coping style is a key determinant in developing intervention, socialization, and staffing practices that can help both individuals and organizations successfully adapt to the future.

By identifying characteristic individual and organizational coping styles, we can make better selection and placement decisions. Not every manager needs to cope with high levels of ambiguity on a daily basis. However, most will need to deal with more rather than less ambiguity in the future. This suggests the need for additional research on developmental strategies and organizational interventions to foster more effective coping styles. Attention to these issues should play an important part in helping to maximize individual and organizational effectiveness.

References

Lorsch, J. W. (1985). Strategic myopia: Culture as an invisible barrier to change. In R. H. Kilmann, M. J. Saxton, and R. Serpa (eds.), *Gaining control of the corporate culture*. San Francisco: Jossey-Bass.

Lyness, K. S., and Moses, J. L. (1983). Measurement strategies for studying ambiguity and managerial behavior. Presentation at Ninety-first Convention of the American Psychological Association, Anaheim, Calif.

Lyness, K. S., Zedeck, S., Jackson, S., and Moses, J. L. (1985). Ambiguity: A review and conceptual framework. AT&T Technical Report.

Moses, J. L. (1984). Using clinical methods in a high level management assessment center. Presentation at the Sixth Annual Symposium on Applied Behavioral Science, Blacksburg, Va.

Moses, J. L., and Lyness, K. S. (1983). A conceptual model for studying ambiguity and managerial behavior. Presentation at Ninety-first Convention of the American Psychological Association, Anaheim, Calif.

Sapienza, A. M. (1985). Believing is seeing: How culture influences the decisions top managers make. In R. H. Kilmann, M. J. Saxton, and R. Serpa (eds.), *Gaining control of the corporate culture*. San Francisco: Jossey-Bass.

Schneider, B. (1987). The people make the place. *Personnel Psychology, 40,* 437–53.

9

The Warp and Woof
of the General Manager's Job

Robert E. Kaplan

> Being a mayor is like walking on a moving belt while juggling. Right off you've got to walk pretty fast to stay even. After you've been in office a short time people start throwing wads of paper at you. So now you've got to walk, juggle, and duck too. Then the belt starts to move faster, and people start to throw wooden blocks at you. About the time you're running like mad, juggling, and ducking stones, someone sets one end of the belt on fire. Now if you can keep the things you are juggling in the air, stay on the belt, put out the fire, and not get seriously injured, you've found the secret to the job. You have managed to put it all together into something that works.
> —the former mayor of Dallas
> as quoted in Kotter and Lawrence (1974)

> A common thing is for the weaver to cover a coarse warpe with a fine woofe. The warpe being spon hard and small, and the woofe soft and round to cover the warpe from sight.
> —J. May, 1613

The premise of this chapter is that individuals in executive roles can greatly help or hinder an organization's efforts to position itself effectively in the world. The chapter zeroes in on one such executive role, the general manager's job, that makes a big difference to the effectiveness of the organization for which the general manager is responsible.

In many organizations, the position of general manager (GM) is the first point, looking up the hierarchy, at which the several functions of the organization come together. Although it is at the lowest level of the executive echelons, the position sits high in the organization and is potentially of great consequence. It may be the most important role below the CEO.

Several people in addition to me conducted the study reported in this chapter: Theresa Amabile, Stan Gryskiewicz, Bill Drath, Joan Kofodimos, Russ Moxley, and Leonard Sayles. For their review of an earlier draft, I would like to thank Michael Lombardo, Russ Moxley, Leonard Sayles, and Alice Warren. Special thanks to Bill Drath and Joan Kofodimos for helping me structure the chapter and to "B. C.," the organization that commissioned the study.

What does it take to be an effective general manager? To answer this question, the chapter draws from a study by my colleagues and me as well as from other research (e.g., Kotter, 1982a; Gabarro, 1985). The bulk of the material in this report comes from our study with other research spliced in when appropriate.

In laying out what makes for general-manager effectiveness, the report examines two aspects of the job. The first aspect consists of the requirements of the job that remain constant across situations. These are core attributes that one would find in the GM job wherever one came across it. The second aspect is the *variation* in the job and those factors that account for variation in the job across situations. Thus, based on our study, the first section offers generalizations about the general manager's job and next section examines it in its particularistic glory in one corporation. Having established the basic requirements and the factors that give the job variation, the chapter moves to a third section that considers the configuration of effectiveness measurements. The fourth section addresses the process by which the job is actually defined and redefined, again taking examples from the corporation in which the study was done.

Constants in the General Manager's Job

Everyone knows that general managers are in charge of a full range of functions in an organization; that they manage the managers in charge of those functions. Recent research, including long interviews we conducted with eleven general managers, gets us below this superficial definition to some of the underlying complexity. Following is a list of several critical requirements of the general manager's job, including the needs to function both strategically and tactically, to think multidimensionally, to build and make use of large networks of contacts, to manage organizations of large scope and scale, and to occupy an elevated position with its visibility and trappings. These constants are akin to the series of yarns, usually colorless, strung lengthwise in a loom—the starting point for weaving fabric.

Operate Strategically

Since the middle to late 1970s, *strategy* has been the watchword of senior managers, a watchword only recently joined by vision. Strategy has to do with setting long-term direction, keeping one's eye on the big picture, doing the right things, and not just doing things right (Bennis, 1982). It has to do with looking for openings and positioning one's organization to move through them. It has equally to do with "closings"—recognizing diminishing opportunities and taking steps to cut back or exit altogether. It tends to have a flavor of innovation and new departures, rather than maintaining the status quo.

One of the general managers we interviewed was responsible for a business—one of many under his jurisdiction—that had gone from making $20 million in profit to losing money three years later, primarily because of Japanese competition and because quality "went to hell." Sentiment around the corporation was to get out of the business, but this GM made a judgment that the business could be salvaged. That was the strategic decision. Next came the attempt to implement the strategy. First, he licked the quality problem. Then, he went to a lot of trouble to persuade top management to file a dumping suit. One fellow GM resisted because the Japanese company in question was a customer of one of his divisions. The corporation won the suit, and a 35 percent duty was placed on the Japanese product. That duty allowed the corporation to raise its price without sacrificing marketability. The product generated $15 million in profit the following year.

Other examples of the strategic decisions that GMs make include whether to take a product into a new market based on a new application; whether to market a product as the company's own brand or to market it through rebrander-distributors; whether to enter a consumer market when the company's strength is in industrial marketing; in which countries to create a local manufacturing presence; and whether to build an R&D capability in a new business or to gain it through an acquisition.

Strategies sometimes get handed down to the GM. Examples include a top management decision to play down commodity products in favor of high-value-added specialty products or a decision to pursue an aggressive growth strategy based on a big R&D effort in a certain business. Sometimes the GM inherits a strategy—for example, to gain market share in a particular business. In these cases, the GM's effort goes into implementation. At other times, the GM develops the strategy through a process of consulting subordinates and peers and selling superiors. This is especially true of GMs who preside over many different product lines, each one of which must be continually evaluated as a candidate for expansion, contraction, or redirection. The challenge in developing strategy is assessing the future; projections are necessarily based on soft data. One GM, who described himself as the chief planner for his business units, said he relished the planning at this level—"developing all the scenarios, anticipating competitors' responses, reading the situation."

Implementation is a matter of making the strategic idea operational by finding vehicles for moving the business in the desired direction. GMs launch major projects. They also practice an admirable opportunism by taking advantage of impromptu daily events to push long-term agendas (Kotter, 1982b). One GM put it simply: "I define the direction and then translate it to others and keep the strategy going." He said he had daily interactions on strategic direction. Another listed several steps he takes to push a strategy, in this case that of becoming the absolute market leader in one area:

1. Ask yourself: is the strategy right?
2. Maintain clarity of purpose and long-term orientation.
3. Spend time communicating internally and externally in the industry.
4. Fend off criticism. (The strategy is a gamble.)
5. Review progress at least quarterly and specific tactical approaches twice a year.
6. Every year, bring the executive committee up to speed. Reinforce their commitment.

What is difficult about strategy, whether framing or implementing it, is that it is not a unidimensional goal or objective, but a direction rooted in a complicated series of interrelated factors.

Other relevant data from our study comes from our interviews with the eleven general managers and with fourteen other executives who worked closely with or had themselves been general managers. We asked each respondent to relate, from his experience, a brief example of an effective GM and an ineffective GM. Our content analysis of the responses appears in table 9–1. Of twenty-one people cited as effective general managers, six were seen as having what amounts to strategic ability. Of sixteen cited as ineffective, four were seen as lacking this ability—as having a short-term focus or being a "crisis manager." Also relevant is the ability to convey strategy once it is framed, to excite people's imaginations. Five of the effective GMs were credited with communication skills; three of the ineffective ones were faulted for lacking these skills.

Operate Tactically

Accompanying the need to take the long view and to manipulate basic parameters is the continual press for action (Kotter, 1982b, McCall and Kaplan, 1984). At the opening of this chapter, the vivid description by the ex-mayor of Dallas made this point amply. The long days of general managers are filled with a procession, not always orderly, of items requiring their attention. Some of these items are fairly routine and require only the action orientation that any line manager brings to the job. Others are particularly thorny. Here is a sampling of the midrange problems that, on a typical day, crossed the desks of the GMs we interviewed:

> Getting rid of seventy-five rail cars that everyone dealing with a shutdown forgot about, leading to a cash drain of $2.5 million.

Table 9–1
Analysis of Short Descriptions of Effective GMs and Ineffective GMs

	Effective GMs (n = 21)	Ineffective GMs (n = 16)
1. Strategy	Six mentioned as having vision, thinking long-term, setting direction.	Four mentioned as having short-term focus, being a crisis manager.
2. Communication	Five mentioned as being a good communicator, communicating well with other groups.	Three mentioned as being noncommunicative and cloistered, having poor communication skills.
3. Business knowledge	Six mentioned as having a deep-rooted understanding of the business understanding other functions, taking a broad view.	Three mentioned as not being close to the business, not trying to understand the business.
4. Learning	Four mentioned as being curious, not resisting change, being a quick study.	None mentioned.
5. Influence	Ten mentioned (in a positive vein) as getting support, knowing how to sell, getting people on board, motivating people. Two others mentioned (in a negative vein) as kicking ass, being domineering.	Three mentioned as being dictatorial; not assertive.
6. Relationships	Seven mentioned (in positive vein) as being good interpersonally, being a good listener, having good people skills.	Five mentioned as having an inability to deal with people, not talking to people or interacting enough.
7. Delegation	Six mentioned as being a good delegator.	Six mentioned as being a poor delegator, being too detail-oriented, dealing too often with inconsequential detail, nitpicking, being a doer and not a delegator.
8. Priorities	Four mentioned as knowing where to spend time, being able to prioritize.	Two mentioned as being unable to set priorities.
9. Integrity	Five mentioned as having integrity; being trusted, being honest and credible, being willing to take responsibility for self and admit mistakes.	Five mentioned as not being trusted, being overly political, lacking integrity.
10. Confidence	Six mentioned as having a sense of personal security, communicating confidence, being decisive.	Six mentioned as being insecure, having no guts, being unwilling to make tough decisions, being unwilling to risk making enemies.

A problem with a competitor that is also a supplier.

News of an infringement on a patent for a major product.

Phone call from a customer wanting to buy one of the division's small businesses.

Phone call from a supplier who wants to sell a piece of equity in his business.

A proposal the GM made to headquarters to install a system of incentive compensation in the division. Corporate headquarters is resisting.

A $2 million claim against the company made by a customer in France. "We screwed them and now we have to negotiate."

A meeting with a supplier about a new product of theirs.

A meeting to troubleshoot problems with a pilot plant for a new product.

A bid from a major customer to buy large quantities of the company's product.

A decision on a price hike and how to increase its chance of being accepted.

How to deal with a federal regulatory agency over a new kind of product.

How to export a new product that is still prohibited in the United States.

A meeting with British representatives on incentives they will offer the company to build a plant there.

A personnel change in a key position.

A customer request for a price concession on a product that lost $16 million the previous year.

An investment opportunity outside the United States.

These and many other items of lesser significance constitute the daily fare of general managers. One GM told us: "Every hour is filled with these kinds of issues." Another said: "I am the focal point for day-to-day problems." Two things are apparent. First, the GM must be adept at taking action on tactical issues, alone or with the help of other people. Second, in the process of disposing of tactical issues, the effective GM keeps in mind the connection between these and overall strategy (Kotter, 1982a). This is much easier said than done, as attested to by one GM: "My days are taken up by the here-and-now. Dealing with future opportunities and problems is almost not part of life." But a GM whose strategy is product development via strong ties with customers will turn a complaint from a major customer into an opportunity to pick up a bit of intelligence on changes in its business. A GM concerned with keeping a finger on the pulse of a plant start-up in a new business will convert a chance encounter with the plant superintendent into a quick status report.

Think Multidimensionally

Part of what is meant by multidimensional thinking, which comes into play equally at strategic and tactical levels, is the familiar analytical ability to break down problems into their constituent parts and to see the relations among the parts. Because problems come to the manager in bunches and action on any one problem often has implications for action on others, multi-dimensional thinking also involves seeing the ties among problems (Isenberg, 1984). These ties may take the form of tensions that must be resolved or complementarities that can be exploited. Managers who think this way also tease out the implications of pregnant bits of information such as the implied competitive threat in the piece of corporate intelligence that a competitor is planning to develop a new product that could cut into market share of an existing product. Furthermore, multidimensional thinkers can make the leap from grand strategy to the day-to-day and back again. Executives with this capacity for cognitive complexity

> tend to see multiple implications even in single items of information. They consider various potential impacts of that information on a variety of future events and decisions. They are often strategists par excellence. They tend to plan long into the future, taking into account all possible events that can be anticipated, as well as the consequences of those events. . . . Their flexible, sensitive and strategic style is the basis of a superiority [with complex problems] which we have so often observed in these managers. (Streufert, 1983, p. 15)

The GMs in our sample frequently referred to the trade-offs they make in juggling the several factors bearing on a decision. They are well aware that decisions are not made in a vacuum; that if, for example, they decide to raise prices as a way of increasing profits, they may open the door to increased competition. One GM described the considerations that surrounded his decision on whether or not to create a manufacturing capability in Japan:

> I decided not to build manufacturing capacity in Japan. It is a low-price market with little chance to make money. Yet it is important to maintain a presence so we have credibility with Japanese contractors, our customers,

who are doing business outside of Japan—credibility that we can handle big jobs. Because of their culture, Japanese companies don't change suppliers unless there are major problems. I made the decision not to expand manufacturing into Japan despite the fact our salespeople wanted us to do it. The sales director in the North Pacific argued that it could help the relationship with contractors. He is probably right, but I've got undercapacity elsewhere. We convinced the contractors to accept a mix of local and U.S.-made products. It's a balancing act.

General managers' agendas are filled with tangled issues such as this one. (It is no wonder that some GMs come down with analysis paralysis.)

Use Large Networks

All managers have networks of contacts, ranging from close associates to mere acquaintances, upon whom they depend for the information, expertise, and support they need to do their jobs (Kaplan, 1984). What makes networks challenging to develop and maintain is that they typically consist as much of people outside the manager's "vertical channel" as those in it and, therefore, require managers to find means other than formal authority to get what they need (Sayles, 1979; Kaplan, 1984). What distinguishes the network of a general manager is its size and the facility needed to make use of it.

As Kotter (1982a, b) found in his intensive study of fifteen general managers, they can have networks with literally hundreds of people up and down the line, including superiors and their superiors; subordinates and their subordinates; peers and their peers' superiors and subordinates; members of corporate staff groups such as central engineering, central research, the legal department, corporate finance, and corporate personnel; individuals and outside the corporation including key people from among customers, suppliers, competitors, industrial or professional associations, and relevant government bodies. In large organizations, these people are usually geographically dispersed; in international organizations, they are dispersed worldwide. Many of these contacts are individuals of similarly high level in their own organizations. If GMs are lucky, they bring much of their network with them when they take a job and develop those relationships that become important in the new job. One GM spoke of his "vast switchboard," much of which he had assembled in 20 years of varied assignments throughout the corporation.

General managers use their networks to gather the information that forms the basis of their strategies, to build support for those strategies, to maintain movement in a strategic direction, to keep their finger on the pulse, and to get help in hacking through thorny issues (Kotter, 1982a, b). In responding to others' comparable demands on them, GMs create a reciprocity that sustains their own supply lines. The good ones maintain their network by making the experience of working with them productive and rewarding.

A key ingredient in GMs' ability to use their network is a "maze-brightness" that informs them as to who needs to be involved in what. A network is not a static thing. It is used and extended in highly dynamic fashion each time an issue arises. At their best, GMs employ a "court vision" that enables them, like basketball players breaking down court, to see the play developing and know how to position themselves in relation to the players on their own team and the opposing team (Halberstam, 1981). In technical terms, GMs dip into their network by consciously or unconsciously consulting their list of *stakeholders* in an item that has just arisen. One can think of the GM as being party to countless sets of intergroup relationships, each one of which revolves around its own issue or set of issues, with all issues overlapping (Alderfer, 1984). The enduring issues invoke more or less stable arrays of people with a stake in the issue. The more novel the issue, the more care is needed in scanning for people who can help or who may stand in the way. One GM talked about the awareness he brings to managing upwardly in a major corporation:

> As a new GM, you have to realize you no longer have one boss. You have a series of bosses who need to know things of importance to the business— the corporate controller, the people in planning, those in engineering (who are building plants for you). I bypass C [his boss, the group vice president] and go to M [the executive vice president] for understanding. S [the vice president of administration], D [the head of corporate personnel], and M— I have to see each of them as a boss. They influence the business; they need to know. I can't afford politically or businesswise to let them get blindsided about something affecting my business. I learned by offending some people, by making mistakes. I must sense whether there is a technical issue, a personnel issue in my business. If so, I must let the relevant person know. I call or meet or write a note; it depends on how important the issue is.

In addition to knowing who to involve, general managers need to know how to maneuver well at the point of involvement. This problem is compounded by the diverse collection of people the general manager has to work with. From the thumbnail sketches of effective and ineffective GMs (see table 9–1), we found that those cited as effective were in many cases seen as having good influence skills (e.g., the ability to sell, get support, get work done through others) and good interpersonal skills. Interestingly, two of the GMs regarded as effective had poor interpersonal skills and influenced others by negative means such as fear and intimidation. In Kotter's study, the better-performing GMs used a larger set of influence tactics and did so with greater skill. "The excellent performers asked, cajoled, praised, rewarded, demanded, manipulated, and generally motivated others with great skill in face-to-face situations" (Kotter, 1982a, p. 75). Their arsenal also typically included references to sports and family as well as liberal doses of joking and humor. One of the most valuable means of influence at their disposal is the ability to express themselves well, to articulate ideas, to explain complex strategies clearly and compellingly. Summing up the qualities of a good networker, one GM said "Effective people make it easy for other people to help them."

From our thumbnail sketches of effective and ineffective GMs, we obtained two relevant findings. (See table 9–1.) GMs cited as effective were in ten of twenty-one cases seen as having influence skills. Those cited as ineffective were in three of sixteen cases seen as not having good influence skills; one individual did well with superiors but at the expense of relationships with subordinates and peers. As to interpersonal skills, seven of the effective GMs were described as having them and five of the ineffective GMs as lacking them. Interestingly, two of the GMs regarded as effective had poor interpersonal skill and influenced others by negative means, especially fear and intimidation.

Encompass Scope

The multifunctional scope together with the sheer bulk of the general manager's domain pose a stiff challenge. By definition, the job requires the incumbent to grasp, though not necessarily master, the full range of functions (marketing, sales, manufacturing, R&D, finance) and at the same time to transcend a functional perspective to achieve a holistic view of the business. The GM must do something for which few managers in companies and other organizations are adequately prepared—be a generalist. GMs must, as one said, "learn to orchestrate all disciplines to get business results." The thumbnail sketches provide a data point here: six of the GMs classified as effective were seen as understanding the business as a whole, as taking a broad view; three of the ineffective ones were downgraded for not doing so.

The GMs we talked to all stressed the importance of getting a solid grounding in the business. One commented: "Experience in the business is critical. You must know your way around the territory. You must know the customers. [He had a marketing background.] I don't think that just being a 'good manager' means that you will succeed in any business." Another GM, who transferred into an unfamiliar business said: "It's hard to change jobs and enter a new business. You have to learn the business before you can effectively manage it." Consistent with what these managers said, Kotter (1982a) found that GMs on new assignments spent a minimum of 6 months learning the ropes. It is only then that they are in a strong position to take significant action (Gabarro, 1985). The GM just quoted also said that the business keeps changing and he has to keep up with it. So the job of knowing the business thoroughly never ends because it constantly evolves, gradually or rapidly, in repsonse to pushes from within or pulls from without. The GM must run to keep up with technical developments, changes in the economy, expansion into foreign countries, new products, new markets, and internal organizational changes. In this connection, four of the GMs classified as effective were given high marks for being curious or a "quick study" or accepting of change. None of the ineffective GMs were mentioned in this regard.

Because GMs usually have a better command of some functional specialties than others, they must rely on people more expert than they. This makes it important for the GM to know who can be trusted and who cannot and also to be sufficiently literate in those specialties to tell good ideas and information from bad.

But with the breadth of the job goes the sheer magnitude. Talking about their schedules, GMs made comments such as "no one can do it all" and "the routine could swallow anyone." The consensus among the GMs we interviewed seemed to be that the only way to survive was to dish out big chunks of responsibility to subordinates. Those who cannot delegate are doomed to fail. The consensus also seemed to be that in addition to achieving a "proficient superficiality" (Mintzberg, 1973), GMs need to pick a few key issues in which to invest themselves thoroughly. As one individual put it: "I spend a lot of time on four or five specific projects, especially those where the company can leverage its efforts. For these projects I keep 'hands on.'" Delegation came up a number of times in the thumbnail sketches, with six effective GMs getting credit for delegating well and six ineffective ones cited for failing to delegate well and for getting bogged down in detail. A related characteristic of the effective GMs is that four of them were mentioned for setting priorities well.

Thus, as a complement to the distance they assume in relation to much of what happens in the business, GMs inform themselves thoroughly about and take an active decision-making role in a handful of strategically important issues. One GM focussed on branching out into a business that several years ago had suffered an enormous defeat. He wanted $40 million to invest in the new business and knew that he would have to overcome top management's negative associations with it. Another GM in a growth-oriented end of the company put a lot of his energies into shepherding major new products to the marketplace. Still another spent a day a week for 14 months on a special assignment having nothing to do with the rest of his job. He headed a task force investigating the possibility of having the corporation generate some of its own energy.

GMs also tackle their large-scale operations by using structure. In conjunction with dealing directly with people, GMs resort to the indirect and impersonal method of shaping their organizations to influence things in the desired direction (Kotter, 1982a). A host of systems are available in most large organizations—management information systems, performance planning and appraisal systems, compensation systems, planning procedures, budgeting procedures, and so on. To supplement these, GMs can introduce their own. To place a priority on product development, one GM split that function out from each of the business units reporting to him. Another mounted a quality-improvement campaign involving staff in all functions and at all levels.

Handle the Potentials and Pitfalls of High Position

The GM position sits in the upper reaches of a corporation and carries with it some demands, prerogatives, and temptations not found in management jobs lower down. The watershed varies from one organization to the next, but beyond some cut-off point, upper-level managers take on the characteristics of a corporate aristocracy. The eleven GMs in our sample were among the top 75 people in a corporation with many thousands of employees. One GM described his passage into the upper echelon this way:

> When I joined a subsidiary company of ours in 1979, I was made a VP and became an officer. I had been a plant manager. It was obvious to me that in this organization, the officer group had an exalted status. They could do no wrong. I found that people down in the organization just didn't feel comfortable to sit down and talk.

Another talked about the mixed effects of elevated standing on his relationships:

> I find there's less truly personal conversation. I try, but my wife says I get into business modes. At this level, people are less willing to sit and chat. The positive side is I get more attentiveness from superiors. I'm listened to more. I also get more respect from industry outsiders. And there is more expectation from subordinates regarding my competence.

Just as the organization confers a special status upon the individual, individuals may come to regard themselves as members of the power elite. The power and prestige of the position together with the history of success that got a GM there may combine to foster an attitude of superiority and even of infallibility (Kaplan et al., 1985). One of our GMs described another GM whom he saw as ineffective.

> He assumed a holier-than-thou attitude, an air of royalty. He was really strong on "I'm the boss, don't question me." Matter of fact, if you questioned him twice, he'd tell you to go look for another job. Now, when you have a slim margin of error on decisions in the first place and you say "just do it, I'm the boss," then you make a lot of mistakes.

It is clear then that managers at this level who let their success and standing go to their heads run a number of risks—making misguided decisions, damaging their networks, becoming isolated from the rest of the organization, stunting their continued growth as executives (Kaplan et al., 1985). In its most innocent form, this mentality grows out of a track record so successful that it blinds individuals to their limitations. The result may be the "I-can-do-anything syndrome": the individual harbors the illusion of being capable of taking on any general-management assignment in any organizational situation—a perilous assumption (Kotter, 1982b). The thumbnail sketches turned up a characteristic that pertains here. The characteristic is "integrity," which includes being honest and able to admit mistakes. Five of the GMs cited as effective were described as having integrity or its equivalent; five of the ineffective GMs were described as lacking it.

On the other hand, incumbents may find the deference, trappings, and expectations that go with high position uncomfortable and even onerous. They may prefer to be just themselves rather than a symbolic figure, an organizational figurehead (Mintzberg, 1973). They may shy away from the limelight, the visibility, the speeches to large gatherings that come with the territory.

> The spotlight is always on you. They are always trying to get at you, to influence you. I'm uncomfortable being the center of attention. I escape to the men's room.

One of the general managers in our sample, while extremely effective in most respects, eschewed some of the ceremonial and status-conferring aspects of his role, and people spoke of him as "not being a typical executive."

The GM may also discover with some dismay the press for consistency that accompanies the visibility (Janis and Mann, 1977). It becomes more difficult to change one's mind, to reverse oneself, when one has gone public with a policy of position.

If we assume that a general manager's skills are not infinitely generalizable and will not guarantee effectiveness in *all* general-management assignments, then, by the same token, how generalizable is the set of GM job requirements we just laid out? The reason that GMs will not necessarily succeed in every setting is that they have come of age managerially in certain institutional settings, have adapted to those settings as well as to the GM job, and may or may not adapt successfully to the institution-specific requirements of a new setting. To the extent that the GM job is situation-specific, our set of job requirements is incomplete because it captures the central tendencies but not the variation. To say that to be effective, GMs need to operate strategically and tactically, contend with big-scope and large-scale operations, build and use a wide-ranging set of coworkers and other contacts, think complexly about the intersection of business problems and social processes, and assume high position without letting it go to their heads is to say a lot. But it is not much different from saying that baseball players need to hit, field, run, and throw. Knowing that a player could do all these things well enough to play major league ball would not tell you which position to put him in.[1] Likewise, knowing that a GM could meet the basic requirements of a job would not tell you in which situations the person would perform best. In what ways do GM jobs vary and what accounts for the variation? An answer to this question will help fill in the picture of what it takes for a GM to be effective.

Variants in the Job

Since all the GMs in our sample came from the same organization, it is convenient to inquire into variation in GM job requirements in that context. First, a few words about the corporation, which I shall call Signet. It is a Fortune 500 company that generates billions of dollars in annual sales and employs tens of thousands of people in numerous locations both in the United States and around the world. Signet grew up around a core set of businesses and has since diversified, to a large extent by acquisition.

Looking at the GM job at Signet, we noticed immediately how much the job varied. The factors that accounted for much of this variance are the type of business, formal lines of authority, the GM's superior, the GM's interpretation of the requirements, and time. These factors did not affect *whether* the basic requirements of the GM job apply, but influenced *how* they applied. The variants in the job are analogous to the woof, which is the set of threads woven across the warp to give the fabric color, texture, and composition.

Type of Business

At Signet, it makes a great deal of difference to the GM's job what piece of the business the job is located in. (Mintzberg, 1973, also determined that type of industry affected the makeup of senior management jobs.) Divisions within the core business are big and broad, each containing many different businesses, markets, and products. One of the major other divisions is equally big, but narrow, with just a few businesses and products and an essentially homogenous market. Most of the rest of the divisions are comparatively small and narrow. Obviously, the bigger and more diverse the division, the more difficult it would be to become knowledgeable about it and frame a coherent strategy around all of it or separate strategies around the disparate pieces. Mintzberg also found that organizational size had an effect on senior management jobs.

The divisions that GMs headed up also fall at various points in the organizational life cycle, from growth-oriented to mature to declining. Those GMs in our sample who are rapidly building new businesses on the basis of a heavy emphasis on R&D have very different jobs from those who are perched atop businesses whose markets are shrinking and are being "cashed out" or phased out. For example, the GM who was trying to start a business from scratch on the strength of a heavy emphasis on R&D had a strong background in R&D himself, something that GMs in charge of mature businesses lacked.

It also matters whether the business is a chunk out of the corporation's core business and, therefore, closely related to the processes and products of its sister businesses or, on the other hand, self-contained in a business sense and perhaps also in geographic terms. GMs in the self-contained units tended to be more autonomous and isolated, and their networks were less extensive.

The profound influence that the type of business can have is evident in the experience of one GM who ran a self-contained, high-growth business unit. He told us that he had adopted and encouraged in the organization "an informal style" that his kind of business necessitated.

> We're in a kind of business that if you don't do it that way, I don't think we'd ever get anywhere. We have a business that's made up of many, many pieces, no one of which will make you or break you, but collectively they will. Very different from this one group over here that has only three big customers. One customer buys 50 percent of the output. Well, in this case, we probably have 150–200 customers. It's not like we're selling retail, but the largest customer only buys 8 percent of the output. On the production side, we make products that are essentially tailor-made for every customer. Our, let's say, 200 customers each has fifteen different sets of specifications. And they're all different. Each of these has a little different manufacturing process, a little different selling price, a little different margin, a little different set of problems associated with it. So from a marketing point of view, you've got to keep all those balls in the air all the time because no one of them will break you, but it's having most of them handled correctly that makes everything work. And from a manufacturing standpoint, we've got five plants. They are working on probably 300–400 products going through our system at any given moment. In product development, we have so many things in the pipeline that each one has its own project manager, who coordinates the new product between research, engineering, and marketing.
>
> You try to keep your finger on a lot of balls at one time and to do that you've got to talk to a lot of people and try to keep it short. I have five people who report to me and I don't necessarily work all those questions through the appropriate chain of command. I go directly to the guy who's handling it.
>
> So this is a business of lots of bits and pieces, a business that requires a lot of coordination. If you don't have an informal way to handle those,

you can't get there. You never get all these messages back and forth if they have to go through the department heads. So what we have is a system that says that if somebody in technology wants to talk to somebody in marketing, don't run it through the chain of command. We're trying to respond to what the customer wants, and our customers move fast. So we've got a matrix organization that just won't stop.

This GM apparently prospers amid the fluid structure, the freedom that he and other managers have to go to whomever the task requires, the extremely fast pace, and the complex formal and informal frameworks set up to ride herd on the plethora of products and customers. To cultivate and participate in this kind of organic, participative internal structure (characteristic of complex, fast-paced organizations), to engage in this kind of freewheeling networking, to stay informed as the product mix proliferates, and to keep up with the intense pace would hardly be every GM's metier. This GM job is, in this respect, fundamentally different from one in a slower-moving business such as those found among the core Signet businesses, where the GM could expect to operate more hierarchically and to structure a more traditional organization. The markedly different context gives a different shape to the same basic set of requirements.

Lines of Authority

Besides type of business, the preceding example contains another factor that has sizeable impact on GM job requirements—a division's organizational structure and, in particular, the formal lines of authority it bestows upon the GM. Five of the GMs are embedded in a matrix that puts functional managers in sales, manufacturing, and R&D on a par with them. Although they remain the focal point and are at least informally awarded "an extra half stripe," they have a different relationship with the functional managers who in a traditional organization would be their subordinates. Frustration, although not universal, runs high. The GMs in this situation talk about the need to "buy manufacturing, technology, and selling services." They also have to compete for these services with the other GMs in their operating company. On top of this matrix, even though Signet assigns worldwide accountability to GMs, it has an international organization that is not under the GM. Thus, most GMs "have worldwide accountability without the authority." Their people outside of the United States report up the ladder of the International Division and have a dotted line to their GMs. Overall, the GMs in matrix arrangements complain about the time and trouble they must take to "gain the commitment of peers to implement programs, to see things as I do, to stick to agreements we have made." Another organizational variation is the hybrid case of two GMs who have marketing and R&D reporting to them, but not sales and manufacturing.

To whatever extent the GM must operate in a matrix, it puts a premium on a different set of networking skills, the kind necessary for lateral relationships where formal authority is not available (Kaplan, 1984). As one GM put it: "You have to make Signet work for you, not though administrative authority, but through logic, persuasion, coercion, stealing, and any other way I can get it." In contrast, the joy of running an organization without a matrix was captured in one GM's statement: "I don't have to check with five guys to go to the bathroom." Note that GMs also need to use logic and persuasion with subordinates.

The Superior

An important determinant of what is required of the GM (although nowhere is it stated formally) is the GM's boss. When our project team presented the results of our study to the GMs, the report did not mention the boss as a factor in how the GM job varies. Two groups independently corrected our mistake. The point they made was simply that the priorities of the GM's superior strongly influenced the GM's priorities. As a result, the GM will be more or less concerned with generating profit or investing in future growth, and with following the chain of command or taking an egalitarian approach.

Depending on the latitude given by the group vice president, the GM will have more or less influence over strategy making and the handling of critical midrange problems that spring up. Students of role sets have found the same thing—that the expectations for how a role should be performed are conveyed chiefly by a small set of people, prominent among whom is the person's superior (Kahn et al., 1964).

The Incumbent

No less important a determinant are the GMs themselves. GMs intentionally or automatically decide what to require of themselves. In defining the role, they are of course influenced by the situation in which they find themselves, which is why GMs form their agendas as they enter their roles (Kotter, 1982a). But in responding to the numerous things that could attract their attention and energies, they choose to work on some and not others. Why? One basis for choosing emerges clearly from the research: functional background (Gabarro, 1985). General managers with strong backgrounds in marketing identify a need to build or revamp the marketing function. The finance types pay particular attention to the numbers. Former international managers may reorganize their area into domestic and international organizations (Gabarro, 1985).

They see what they are attuned to see; they instinctively play to their strengths. The same job occupied by different indivdiuals would result in different definitions of the job requirements and different execution, as Stewart et al. (1980) found in their study of district managers in Britain's National Health Service. What is clear is that there is no such thing as a general manager's job independent of the incumbent. We must think of the phenomenon as the "person-in-job." In an almost artistic fashion, GMs shape the job requirements out of a rich interaction between the givens in the situation and the givens within themselves. As a GM remarked to us: "Every GM is individualistic. For new GMs, it's a problem because there are no rule books. You have to build your own nest." One GM, taking the corporation's interest in shifting from commodity products to specialty products and drawing on his own strong technical background and penchant for making change, adopted a strategy of developing new high-value-added products through an innovative program of collaborative research with leading customers. This strategy departed dramatically from that of his predecessor, which illustrates the difference that the incumbent can make in setting the specific requirements of the job.

This list of factors that produce variation in the GM job by no means exhausts the possibilities. With the passage of time, for example, the content of the job changes because of the dynamic nature of what happens within the GM's domain (a major acquisition one year, a long and bitter strike the following year, and the distorting effects of a strong dollar the next) and because of the dynamic nature of the larger corporation (which may be diversifying one year and divesting a few years later). The list is exhaustive enough, however, to make the point: the variation in what is required of GMs is sufficient to rival the elements in common. As one respondent said, "It is probably not possible to see the GM's job as having any consistency across different companies" (although in saying this, he allowed for consistency among the GM jobs within a company). The variations, however, do not cancel out the similarities. For example, the difference is not *whether* a GM networks, but *how* the GM networks. Similarly, all GMs have to operate strategically, but one may be plunked into an unformed situation that requires the GM to evolve a strategy and another may enter a situation in which the strategy is formed and the job is chiefly to execute it by keeping it front and center in the organization.

Measuring Overall Effectiveness

The question of GM effectiveness is further complicated if we expand the scope of the discussion beyond discrete criteria to an overall evaluation of the individual. GMs can be assessed on how well they match up against each of the several requirements of their jobs, but what about a global measure of effectiveness? Is there a threshold of overall effectiveness past which a GM, despite any rough spots or shortfalls in specific areas, would be declared effective? No GM has it all. Capable GMs come in all shapes and sizes, and no single individual's package of capabilities fits the contours of the situation perfectly. How flawed would a GM's performance have to be on one dimension to be considered ineffective overall? The importance of this question is brought home by the case given to us as an example of a remarkably effective GM (a person singled out by no fewer than three people):

> He took over the X business when it wasn't much of a business. Y product was an interesting opportunity, but no one knew how to make money with it. In five years he single-handedly evolved a strategy for commercializing and marketing Y, brought it into commercial development, and turned it into a big money-maker. He saw the opportunity, evolved the vision for the business, and put it in place in a short period of time. He delegated the day-to-day running of the larger business to a subordinate and did nothing but focus on Y.
>
> He was irascible, pompous, bright, and domineering—a synthesizer, a bulldog. There were two ways to do things: his way and the wrong way.

Another person held a similarly high opinion of this GM's entrepreneurial ability, but put his failings more graphically.

> His flaw was his kick-in-the-rear approach. Fear is why he and the division succeeded—fear, fear. Fear is a powerful motivator. People were afraid of him and his impact on their careers. He would shower verbal abuse on people in public. His version of a performance review was to go out to dinner and after two drinks he'd go around the table and tell each person what was rotten about them. Not a bed of roses. There were people who wanted him dead.

This case may be extreme, but it raises interesting pragmatic and moral issues. Does the end justify the means? This flaw has proven fatal to some executives' careers; abrasiveness was one of the leading causes for "derailment" in a recent study of executives (McCall and Lombardo, 1983). We can only assume that in this case, the general manager's successes were stunning enough to offset his blatant failing. Evidently, top management pegged him at a point beyond their cutoff for overall effectiveness. How would we researchers have approached the evaluation of this man's performance? Does *effective* mean to us that a general manager will score high on all major performance criteria for the job?

In baseball, good hitting is more important than good fielding, so that a superb hitter who cannot field well can make it in the major leagues. Catchers are important, so that a good catcher can be a miserable hitter and still have a career in the majors. On the other hand, any player other than a pitcher who hits less than .225 or so will not stand a chance. All major league players have the ability to hit, field, run, and throw, but many of them possess these abilities in unequal proportions. What are the minimums and how are those affected by maximums? What redeeming qualities can offset poor performance against another criterion? How do our theories of effectiveness take account of these imbalances in baseball players, general managers, and organizations in general? How well do our theories address *configurations* of strengths and weaknesses?

How the Job Is Defined

The picture of the general manager's job as it stands is incomplete because the job is represented as an essentially static thing, a fixed entity. As we have understood it so far, a given job is a product of the constants built into all GM jobs and the variation growing out of the particular circumstances surrounding it. As such, a given job simply *is*. But how does it *become* what it is and, having become that, how does it evolve into something new? So having seen the warp and woof of the GM job, we turn now to the *process* by which the fabric of the job is woven. In so doing we should reveal a dynamism that makes the static elements more real.

Implicit in the discussion at the end of the previous section is the fact that an underlying set of values defines what about an individual GM's performance is valuable to the system and what is dispensable. The GM job, embedded as it is in the system, is shaped by system values and reshaped as the values change. To see how system values are at the root of the GM job, we shall look at how a shift in overall strategy at Signet produced flux in the job.

A system's core identity determines what is most important to it. For every system, there are certain "critical contingencies," classes of activities upon which the success of the system is contingent (Salancik and Pfeffer, 1977). These critical contingencies are arranged in a hierarchy, with *the* vital function on top (Kanter, 1977). In a consumer products company such as Procter & Gamble, for example, marketing and advertising are preeminent. When Digital Equipment Corporation concentrated on selling sophisticated minicomputers in an industrial market, its engineering function predominated. The hierarchy of functions in an organization is reshuffled as the organization evolves and its priorities change.

Like many other large, established U.S. corporations, Signet wanted to renew itself by emphasizing innovation, by fanning its entrepreneurial spirit (Peters and Waterman, 1982). To do this, Signet decided to put its technical base to work in developing commercially successful new products. In this light, GM effectiveness did not mean any old GM effectiveness, but effectiveness in the service of an entrepreneurial, development-oriented company. This redefined purpose put a premium on the technical function and on its being represented at high levels. As one executive said: "To be a technologically driven company, you need people with technical backgrounds calling the shots." (The strategic change at Signet affected some business groups more than others. Those already pursuing a growth strategy predicated on R&D were not affected; they tended to be led by GMs with technical backgrounds. In fact, these units served as a model for the rest of the corporation.)

The strategic redirection came at a time when recent retirements had drained top management of most of its technically strong representatives. The problem was compounded by the fact that there were very few technically oriented candidates for general-management positions in the pipeline. The management succession plan revealed that only a small minority of the candidates for general manager had technical backgrounds and that the same was true of the pool of candidates for business director, a position one notch below GM.

In this way, the GM job at Signet was revised to include a larger technical component. Deciding to revise the job and implementing that decision, however, were two different issues. This is where dynamism in how the GM job is defined and redefined enters the picture.

Implementation via Selection

Basic to implementing an altered notion of the GM job is finding individuals to fill it. The rub at Signet is that, to oversimplify, there were roughly two types of people in the organization to draw from—those from the technical community and those from the business community. A vice president we interviewed offered capsule descriptions of the typical technical person and the typical business person.

Qualities of the typical business person that make for a good GM:

Proactive—pursues opportunities

Aggressive

Good interpersonal skills

Real world-oriented

Results-oriented

Ambitious, impatient for success

Short-term time horizon

Sells self and products (from a sales background)

Orchestra leader (learned by matrixing to sell products)

Knows strategy

Qualities of the typical technical person that do not make for a good GM:

Reactive—waits for opportunities

Abdicates responsibility for influencing business decisions

Passive

Has no interest in strategy

Finds science more important than next promotion

Spends all the time in the lab

Works on a project for 1 to 3 years

Fear of failure, professional pride; can't kill projects

No risk taking

Positive aspects of technical people:

Technically proficient

Long-term perspective

It is important to know that the vice president came from the business side. The view from the technical side did not coincide at every point with his. The technical managers we interviewed tended to see the GMs as action-oriented to a fault (losing sight of the long term) and as "presentation types" who were sometimes more concerned with style than substance. One of the bones of contention between the technical and business communities was the operational definition of a *strong technical background*. Influential technical people felt that it took a minimum of 10 years in the technical function to qualify. Commercial people disagreed. The split between the two camps boiled down to this: the technical side claimed that business types (including GMs) were hopelessly short-term in outlook, while the commercial side faulted the technical types for being hopelessly long-term in perspective.

The question of which type was best suited for the GM job was hung up in a tension between recent history and the call to the future. Top management had in the recent past generally emphasized short-term income generation more than long-term development. As the strategic redirection was being engineered, general managers at Signet felt pinched by a double message coming from top management—invest in the future and produce attractive short-term results.

The vice president just quoted recognized on the one hand that, with their technical proficiency and long-term perspective, technical people "could help Signet find high-technology niches for the future, a corporate priority." On the other hand, he believed that technical types would not generally work out as GMs because, although top management claimed it wanted technical leaders, it "rewards proactive commercial types and short-term results."

The definition of the GM job and who is best qualified for it was thus caught up in this tugging between the two communities and the two sets of values at Signet. The struggle had something of a political character in that the relative standing of functions at Signet hung in the balance. When we entered the scene, the business community more or less held sway, as evidenced by the fact that it made up the large majority of top management. Because of this, the commercial wing held an advantage in the debate over the GM job. The tide was shifting, however, as evidenced by the new emphasis on technically based growth. Commercial people were sensitive to the change. One executive told us: "If I leave Signet it will be because I am prevented from the top jobs because of my lack of technical background."

Implementation via Development

This controversy over selection of the best candidate assumed two distinctly different types of manager at Signet. If we consider the possibility that a new cross-bred type of manager could be developed, then we come to a second form of dynamism in the implementation of a revised job definition. One option was to develop a new breed of GM out of people with technical backgrounds. As one high-level person put it: "What is needed is a program of technological affirmative action." It was clear to everyone we spoke with that to prepare for the GM job, technical managers would need breadth of experience, which they could get by taking assignments with commercial responsibilities. Our interviews quickly made it apparent, however, that formidable barriers blocked the passage of technical managers to the commercial side. The business side rejected the typical technical manager as ill-equipped, for reasons given earlier. On the technical side, relatively few managers *wanted* to go over to the other side; their mixed feelings about being managers in the first place and their stereotypes of business managers hurt their motivation. The situation was aggravated by the assumption that it takes a minimum of 10 years to become strong technically, by which time the individual has missed the chance to ascend the ladder to GM.

Moving technical people to the commercial side was not the only way to develop technically proficient senior managers. Theoretically, you could start with nontechnical people and give them training and experience on the technical side. Three of the GMs we interviewed freely admitted that their lack of technical expertise hampered their performance. One said: "I'd be better off with more technical knowledge." A second said:

> I am asked to decide on research programs that will determine the success of this business 5 years from now. But I have to go on blind faith. I've picked up some technical background along the way. But ideally I'd have as much overall technical ability as commercial ability.

So there was an awareness of the value of technical preparation. Unfortunately, barriers comparable to the ones slowing down traffic in the other direction stood in the way of migration of nontechnical managers to the technical side. If anything, these barriers were higher. The general feeling was that technology was a "closed shop." Technologists "believe that you must have a technical background to manage technology." Apparently the demands were so stringent among scientists that "if you spend more than 2 years out of research, you lose your technical credibility."

Thus, both the structure of the GM job and the career structures to prepare people for that job were swept up in a less than optimal intergroup relationship. However unproductive for Signet, the situation illustrates nicely the messy social and political process by which a new definition of the GM job at Signet was hashed out and put into effect. The social order in organizations and elsewhere is a negotiated one (Berger and Luckmann, 1967; Pfeffer and Salancik, 1978). Because of Signet's corporate commitment to a technology-driven future, the technical ability of its GMs became an issue, one that could only be resolved through extended dialogue among the interested parties. Such resolutions are never permanent because the next stage in Signet's future will raise a fresh set of issues about the mix of requirements of the GM job.

Restating the Problem

Signet, then, conjured up a vision of its general managers—and higher-level management—of the future. The new generation of executives "would need to walk both sides of the street." "We want hybrids, and we can get them with early identification and cross-training." The hitch was that a program predicated on cross-grooming would run afoul of the relatively impermeable boundary separating the technical and commercial communities throughout much of Signet. Once Signet began to make cross-functional transfers, the culture would presumably loosen up. But what could be done to make the organization more receptive to transfers in the meantime?

Some people called for an all-out attack on the problem of relations among *all* functions, not just between technical and commercial. Their label for what they felt afflicted Signet was "functionalitis." This is a condition borne of the practice of having managers grow up primarily in one function. As a result, they are inclined to know only their own function well and to defer too quickly to the expertise of colleagues in other functions. They are also prone to expect their counterparts to defer, in turn, to their expertise— all of which breeds an unhealthy territoriality, a compartmentalization. The prescription of choice was the obvious one—to "encourage coordination, instead of islands." Some said that to put teeth into this encouragement, top management would have to get fully behind the program. When it came to transfers, for example, top management would have to be prepared to sacrifice some continuity in technical specialization in favor of functional cross-breeding.

We were led to the cultural issue as a way of clearing the way for a program of career development. But it occurred to us that perhaps we had the tail wagging the dog. If our concern was GM effectiveness, and if *that* depends on pulling the disparate functions together, then the culture is hardly just a vehicle for building in breadth as potential GMs climb the ladder. It is the milieu in which GMs operate, and it will powerfully limit their ability to operate effectively, especially with respect to joining a business's production/ selling capability with its product-development capability.

To emphasize development, Signet needed to shake off its compartmentalizing tendencies and begin practicing an "integrative management" that built strong ties between all the parties to the process of identifying, developing, producing, marketing, and selling commercially viable new products (Kanter, 1983).

To come up with the kind of GM needed for a redirected Signet, what is required is not only the indicated career-tracking but a corporate management culture that makes cross-training possible and, more than that, provides a milieu conducive to the GM's carrying out of the corporate mission. The revised definition of the GM job at Signet is a cog in the revised management structure at Signet. The two entities have a symbiotic relationship. The job, via its occupants, serves as a regulatory mechanism in the management structure—a vital steering function. The job, however, will not perform its function, especially the coordination of R&D and the business side, unless the larger structure unites these two sides of the house. Nor will potential GMs get the cross-training they need unless the two sides are sufficiently integrated to allow managers to transfer over. Thus, the fabric of the GM job takes its place in a larger tapestry.

Conclusion

Instead of summarizing the content of the GM's job, I shall extract several guidelines for approaching an understanding of the job.

1. Generalizations about the job are useful up to a point as long as we recognize that "particularizations" are no less important. Theories must be stated in accordance with local conditions (Dunbar, 1983) and in relation to time and place (Spence, 1985) and specific contexts (Sternberg, 1985). The dilemma is that the more abstract we make a theory of the job in order for it to encompass the wide range of instances of it, the further the theory retreats from accurately representing any concrete instance. Conversely, to the extent that a theory does justice to a concrete instance, it gives up generality. The inescapable conclusion is that generalizations about the job must be modified to fit local conditions. These conditions include type of "business," type of organization, stage in organizational life cycle, and so on.

Whatever common elements can be discerned in the GM job, the variation among concrete instances will always rival the central tendencies. Theories of GM effectiveness need to leave in the variance instead of stripping it away in an effort to find the lowest common denominator.

What we have in the GM job or in any social phenomenon is what philosophers call the problem of the one and the many. The phenomenon contains within it both a oneness that unites all instances and a plurality that encompasses differences among instances. The GM job is a single thing and a multitude of things.

2. Because of the variation in contexts, GMs cannot necessarily transfer successfully from one context to another (Kotter, 1982b; McCall and Kaplan, 1984). The more similar the situations, the easier it is to make the jump. If the situations are vastly different (e.g., different industry, different organization), then the GM who would make the grade must be blessed with an ability to form new relationships easily and a knack for learning new things quickly. Kotter (1982b) found that GMs are specialized; they have adapted to specific contexts and are therefore not necessarily well suited for different contexts. In fact, Kotter pointed out that the fit between GM and context can erode if the context changes—something that happened at Signet when the call came for technical competence in GMs. Similarly, intelligence (defined as the ability to adapt to or shape an environment or select suitable settings within it), which is a considerable part of what GMs bring to their jobs, is not the same thing across environments (Sternberg, 1985, p. 46).

3. The GM job needs to be studied in the context of its dynamic relation to the larger system of which it is a part. GM requirements flow from system requirements (you must always ask: effective at doing what?), which in turn can only be met if GM requirements are also met. As we saw, GM require-

ments grow out of a negotiated definitional process, one that cranks up every time the system changes its own requirements. The lesson: deal in the complexity around the job's membership in a larger, interactively causal set of relationships.

As important as any job (executive or otherwise) might be, it is important not to fixate on that job. At Signet, the GM job at first looked as if it were focal, but later revealed itself to be no more than a key piece of the larger management structure, with which it has a symbiotic relationship.

4. No GM job exists apart from its incumbent. No matter what requirements issue forth from the context and are mediated by the GM's superior and other influential individuals, incumbents inevitably shape their jobs in their own images. The only way to think of any given GM job is as the person-in-job. The job's requirements and the way the job is enacted are functi..is of the interaction between person and situation.

5. Whatever our criteria of GM effectiveness, very few concrete instances will meet all criteria and conform completely to any model of ideal GM behavior. Actual instances of anything are uneven, lopsided, and marvelously ragged around certain edges. I do not subscribe to the view that executives-to-be must encounter a cafeteria of positive executive virtues where they get to pick one of each. I will go so far as to suggest that our field brings a misplaced idealism to setting standards for effectiveness—an idealism that, expressed in mechanisms such as performance appraisal, could threaten to homogenize people. Is it possible that we project our ego ideal onto the people and organizations we study? High standards are one thing; perfectionism, another.

As Belbin (1981) said: "Nobody's perfect but a team can be." Human imperfection notwithstanding, systems can be robust if they compensate for one person's flaws with the corresponding strengths of others. A GM in our sample had no previous experience in a business but succeeded because, among other things, he was sandwiched by people who knew the business. I suspect that the field would benefit from putting more energy into understanding *configurations* of strengths and weaknesses in individual GMs as well as *constellations* of executives who together constitute an organization's top leadership.

The GM job is a critical post in large organizations, but one that has not received research attention commensurate with its importance. Historically, the behavioral sciences have been working their way up the organizational ladder. The field began by studying workers, moved on to foremen and supervisors, and progressed to middle managers. There is still little known about CEOs and what they actually do. But we are beginning to accumulate knowledge about general managers, who occupy the first rung on the executive ladder (Kotter, 1982; Gabarro, 1985). The study reported here was an effort to collect raw material on this job. As we fill in our understanding about what the role is really like, we will be in a position to select, develop, and facilitate the effectiveness of GMs.

Note

1. Bill Drath suggested the baseball analogy that appears here and later on.

References

Alderfer, C. P. (1984). An intergroup perspective on group dynamics. In J. Lorsch (ed.), *Handbook of organizational behavior.* Englewood Cliffs, N.J.: Prentice-Hall.

Belbin, R. M. (1981). *Management teams: Why they succeed or fail.* New York: John Wiley & Sons.

Bennis, W. (1982). Leadership transforms vision into action. *Industry Week,* May 31, 54–56.

Berger, P. L., and Luckmann, T. (1967). *The social construction of reality: A treatise in the sociology of knowledge.* Garden City, N.Y.: Anchor.

Dunbar, R. L. M. (1983). Toward an applied administrative science. *Administrative Science Quarterly, 28,* 129–44.

Gabarro, J. J. (1985). When a new manager takes charge. *Harvard Business Review,* May-June, 110–23.

Halberstam, D. (1981). *The breaks of the game.* New York: Knopf.

Isenberg, D. J. (1984). How senior managers think. *Harvard Business Review,* November-December, 81–90.

Janis, I. L., and Mann, L. (1977). *Decision making: A psychological analysis of conflict, choice, and commitment.* New York: Free Press.

Kahn, R. L., Wolfe, D. M., Quinn, R. P., Snock, J. D., and Rosenthal, R. A. (1964). *Organizational stress: Studies in role conflict and ambiguity.* New York: Wiley.

Kanter, R. M. (1977). *Men and women of the corporation.* New York: Basic Books.

Kanter, R. M. (1983). *The change masters: Innovation for productivity in the American corporation.* New York: Simon & Schuster.

Kaplan, R. E. (1984). Trade routes: The manager's network of relationships. *Organizational Dynamics,* Spring, 37–52.

Kaplan, R. E., Drath, W. H., and Kofodimos, J. R. (1985). *High hurdles: The challenge of executive self-development.* Technical Report no. 25. Greensboro, N.C.: Center for Creative Leadership.

Kotter, J. P. (1982a). *The general managers.* New York: Free Press.

Kotter, J. P. (1982b). General managers are not generalists. *Organizational Dynamics,* Spring, 5–19.

Kotter, J. P., and Lawrence, P. (1974). *Mayors in action.* New York: Wiley.

McCall, M. W., and Kaplan, R. E. (1984). *Whatever it takes: Decision-makers at work.* Englewood Cliffs, N.J.: Prentice-Hall.

McCall, M. W., Jr., and Lombardo, M. M. (1983). *Off the track: Why and how successful executives get derailed.* Technical Report no. 21. Greensboro, N.C.: Center for Creative Leadership.

Mintzberg, H. (1973). *The nature of managerial work.* New York: Harper & Row.

Peters, T. J., and Waterman, R. H., Jr. (1982). *In search of excellence.* New York: Harper & Row.

Pfeffer, J., and Salancik, G. (1978). *The external control of organizations: A resource dependence perspective.* New York: Harper & Row.

Salancik, G. R., and Pfeffer, J. (1977). Who gets power—and how they hold on to it: A strategic-contingency model of power. *Organizational Dynamics,* Winter, 3–21.

Sayles, Leonard R. (1979). *Leadership: What effective managers really do . . . and how they do it.* New York: McGraw-Hill.

Spence, J. T. (1985). Achievement American style: The rewards and costs of individualism. *American Psychologist, 40*(12), 1285–95.

Sternberg, R. J. (1985). *Beyond IQ: A trairchic theory of human intelligence.* Cambridge, England: Cambridge University Press.

Stewart, R., Smith, P., Blake, J., and Wingate, P. (1980). *The district administrator in the National Health Service.* London: King's Fund Publishing.

Streufert, S. (1983). The stress of excellence. *Across the Board,* October, 8–16.

Part IV
Overview

10
Integration and Overview of the Research on Work Facilitation

F. David Schoorman
Benjamin Schneider

The chapters in this book represent the independent research of scholars who have approached the work-facilitation issue from different perspectives. At the most general level, the unifying theme of the various approaches is a concern for identifying conditions and events that facilitate or inhibit effectiveness in organizations.

In our development of the research program on facilitators and inhibitors of effectiveness, we made an a priori decision to organize the program into three components: conceptual issues, measurement issues, and leadership and management activities that controlled the facilitators and inhibitors. This scheme is also reflected in the organization of this book. The researchers contributing their work were made aware of the three-part framework, and each contribution was intended to represent one of these components. However, as we discuss each contribution, it becomes apparent that the three a priori components are intricately related, with numerous chapters cutting across the three issues.

Conceptual Issues in Studying Facilitators and Inhibitors

The three chapters in part I address several critical aspects in conceptualizing facilitators and inhibitors of effectiveness. The integrative questions that we shall examine to explicate these conceptual issues are:

1. What are facilitators and inhibitors?
2. What is the appropriate level of analysis for studying them?
3. What is effectiveness?

What are Facilitators and Inhibitors?

At the most general level, all three chapters characterize facilitators and inhibitors as organizational conditions or events that have direct or indirect impact on effectiveness. Chapter 1 by Schoorman and Schneider uses the Katz and Kahn description of subsystems to develop a broad framework for categorizing facilitators and inhibitors. This framework encourages the study of conditions and events beyond such obvious issues as inadequate tools and equipment, shortages of raw materials, and ambiguous instructions. It emphasizes all three stages of the production process (input, throughput, and output) by examining how effectively each of five subsystems in the organization functions to promote effectiveness. This framework has the added diagnostic advantage of identifying the lack of facilitators in a particular subsystem by noting any conspicuous lack of data on conditions and events relevant to that subsystem. For example, the difficulty in identifying adaptive-subsystem items in the university sample suggests a lack of departmental adaptive facilitators among the departments interviewed and studied.

The approach based on Katz and Kahn's conceptualization can be contrasted to chapter 5 by Peters and O'Connor, who use an inductive approach to generate categories of inhibitors. Their approach relies on organization members' ability to identify conditions and events, and it typically results in the identification of conditions that are visible barriers to effectiveness. Their methods do not identify potentially positive conditions that have not existed. For example, one would expect a worker to note the many interruptions in the production process to do rush jobs, the necessity to substitute materials because the appropriate materials are out of stock, or having to sit idly because the equipment broke down. What this worker does not tell you is that the organization needs production scheduling, inventory control systems, and regular servicing of equipment. As one might expect, the Peters and O'Connor procedure leads to the identification of inhibitors rather than facilitators, an outcome consistent with their a priori decision to focus exclusively on inhibitors or constraints.

Guzzo and Gannett in chapter 2 conceive of facilitators and inhibitors as representing two different dimensions rather than opposite ends of a continuum. They argue that the absence of inhibitors does not mean that facilitators exist and vice versa. They further argue that these dimensions are independent and have different effects on performance. Specifically, they suggest that inhibitors restrict performance to a minimally acceptable level while facilitators push performance toward maximally attainable levels. This issue is not explicitly addressed in any of the other chapters, the underlying assumption across the other chapters being that inhibitors and facilitators are opposite ends of the same continuum.

For example, consider the following four events or conditions occurring in an organization, with respect to a particular machine:

A1: The machine breaks down.

A2: The machine does not break down.

B1: The machine is serviced regularly.

B2: The machine is not serviced regularly.

Obviously, A1 and A2 are mutually exclusive, as are B1 and B2. We can all agree that if A1 occurs, we have an inhibitor that will minimize performance. If A2 occurs, we do not have an inhibitor, but do we have a facilitator? Guzzo and Gannett argue that we do not. Their logic would be that since the machine not breaking down fails to facilitate maximally attainable performance, the machine not breaking down is not a facilitator.

We can probably agree that B1 (there is a service contract) is a facilitator, but if B2 is true, do we have an inhibitor? Once again, Guzzo and Gannett would say either you cannot tell or no. If B2 does not restrict performance to minimally acceptable levels, it is not an inhibitor.

What is interesting from the Guzzo and Gannett perspective is that these two sets of conditions (A1, A2 and B1, B2) are not independent. Thus, B1 decreases the probability of A1 and increases the probability of A2, while B2 does the opposite. This suggests that at least in the present example, the facilitators and inhibitors are clearly not independent. The approaches taken by Schoorman and Schneider and by Peters and O'Connor make two simplifying assumptions. First, they assume that facilitators and inhibitors are dependent and, second, the issue is one of relative effectiveness rather than absolute effectiveness. Specifically, they assume that the absence of an inhibitor leads to *higher* performance than the presence of an inhibitor, while the absence of a facilitator leads to *lower* performance than the presence of facilitator. In the Schoorman and Schneider chapter, the diagnostic described maintains the direction of the item consistent with the way it was reported in interviews: facilitators are worded as facilitators, while inhibitors are worded as inhibitors and reverse-scored.

Peters and O'Connor's decision to focus their investigation on inhibitors is in itself an interesting alternative. It certainly avoids the issue of whether facilitators and inhibitors are independent dimensions. It is generally easier for job incumbents to identify inhibitors since they are very salient, while there is often less awareness about facilitators that do exist and, perhaps, little or no awareness of potential facilitators. In their conclusions, Peters and O'Connor note that their research on inhibitors is based on the assumption that "resources are not so plentiful that their absence is improbable." This premise is that there is not so much slack in the organization that an inhibitor would go unnoticed. This poses an interesting dilemma. If, for example, a secretarial pool has two extra typewriters, then when a typewriter (or two) breaks down due to lack of proper maintenance (an inhibitor), there will be no resulting decrease in performance. The position adopted by the Schoorman and Schneider perspective is that the extra typewriters represent a facilitator and, in this example, the aggregate of facilitators and inhibitors in the same subsystem predict no net change in performance. Thus, the need for the assumption of no slack resources in the Peters and O'Connor model may be construed as evidence for the position that facilitators and inhibitors are mutually offsetting and therefore are opposite ends of the same dimension.

Chapter 3 by Kerr describes facilitators and inhibitors in terms of reward systems. Kerr justifies this view from an operant framework that would suggest that all behaviors (individual or group) are explainable through the rewards provided by the environment. The focus on rewards as the domain of facilitators and inhibitors is interesting when viewed in terms of the Schoorman and Schneider framework. In the Katz and Kahn subsystem model they use as their operating framework, the reward-system facilitators and inhibitors would correspond to the personnel-maintenance subsystem. It is interesting to note that in the development of the subsystem model, the preponderance of items in the maintenance subsystem led to its subdivision into equipment maintenance and personnel maintenance, and that the personnel maintenance subsystem evolved into the largest subsystem for facilitators and inhibitors. The reward system certainly represents an important domain for studying facilitators and inhibitors. Kerr treats facilitators and inhibitors as opposite ends of the same dimension, although he does argue that some rewards facilitate minimally acceptable behavior (attendance, membership), while other rewards facilitate maximally attainable behavior (performance-based behavior). This conceptualization is consistent with the views of Guzzo and Gannett discussed previously.

What Is the Appropriate Level of Analysis?

Several chapters in this book address the issue of the level of analysis. Ironically, the discussions of the level of analysis occur at different "levels" of abstraction. For the purposes of this integration, the level of analysis problem is discussed in three distinct domains.

1. The level of analysis is discussed as a conceptual issue where the researchers are concerned with the framing of the problem of facilitators and inhibitors. Should facilitators and inhibitors be studied at the organization, group, or individual level? At which of these levels is effectiveness most affected by facilitators and inhibitors? These issues are addressed by Schoorman and Schneider, by Kerr, by Guzzo and Gannett, and by Peters and O'Connor.

2. The level of analysis is discussed as a measurement issue. In this domain, the controversy centers around the aggregation of data. How does one

collect data at the appropriate level of analysis? What are the implications of aggregating individual responses to obtain group scores? These issues are addressed by Moeller et al. as well as by Roberts and Sloane.

3. The level of analysis can also be framed as a coordination issue. As different groups or levels contribute toward a common product, does that product exceed the simple aggregate of the group contributions? The consequences of effective and ineffective coordination among units of the same hierarchical level as well as across levels is explored by Roberts and Sloane. We shall discuss the conceptual aspects of level of analysis in this section. Measurement and coordination issues will be discussed later.

Chapter 1 by Schoorman and Schneider adopts the work unit as the level of analysis and focusses exclusively on facilitators and inhibitors at this level. On the other hand, in chapter 5 Peters and O'Connor accept the individual as the level of analysis and their research proceeds at the individual level. Guzzo and Gannett in chapter 2 explore the issues involved in studying facilitators and inhibitors at both individual and group levels. They observe that facilitators and inhibitors are qualitatively different at various levels. In reviewing the literature on facilitators and inhibitors, they argue that at the individual level, most of the systematic research has focussed on inhibitors, while at the group level, there has been more systematic research on facilitators. That is, we have tended to ask the questions:

What is it that prevents individuals from doing their jobs?

What can we do to help groups do a better job?

Why the issues come out this way is an unanswered question.

Kerr's view of the level of analysis issue in chapter 3 is consistent with Guzzo and Gannett, in that he sees facilitators and inhibitors as important issues at both individual and group levels. Reward systems can be tailored to individuals or to groups, and the resulting facilitation (or inhibition) of behavior will be at the targeted level. It is important to note that neither the Schoorman and Schneider approach nor the Peters and O'Connor approach rule out the alternative level on conceptual grounds, although Schoorman and Schneider do point to a frequent lack of significant findings in prior work at the individual level. Peters and O'Connor, on the other hand, indicate that the success of their research is based on the asssumption that individual performance is valued by the organization.

These arguments, taken together, suggest a potentially useful heuristic for determining the appropriate conceptual level of analysis. If the organization to be studied operates in a technology that reinforces independent, individual effort, the individual may be the appropriate level. If, on the other hand, the technology requires interdependence and interaction, while reinforcing group productivity, the appropriate level would be the work group. In either case, the literature suggests that a focus on both facilitators and inhibitors would be appropriate.

What Is Effectiveness?

The criteria or dependent variables of interest are important in any research program, but this is especially so in the study of facilitators and inhibitors since they are inextricably tied, conceptually and operationally, to the definition of effectiveness. For example, if you change the definition of effectiveness from meeting delivery schedules to maximizing quality, the requirement that critical production processes be verified (checked for quality) will change from being an inhibitor to a facilitator. It is not surprising, therefore, that each of the conceptual chapters addresses the issue of effectiveness.

In the Schoorman and Schneider chapter, the definition of effectiveness is unique to the three organizations being investigated. In the university sample, department teacher ratings are used; in the financial-services organization, unit sales data are the criteria; while in the military organization, a unique rating system is developed that gauges effectiveness in accomplishment of long-term and short-term goals. The philosophy of this approach is that each organization should identify its preferred outcomes against the facilitators and inhibitors that can be evaluated. Kerr points out a potential hazard to this reasoning: most organizations seem to articulate one set of preferred outcomes, but inadvertently communicate a different message to their employees through their reward system.

According to Kerr, this problem is frequently evident in organizations as a conflict between production criteria and membership or attendance criteria. He argues that organizations often lose control over their reward systems (and, therefore, the definition of effectiveness) by developing an elaborate set of policies and rules that govern the distribution of rewards. Kerr suggests that the solution to this problem is to verify the definition of effectiveness by comparing the response of the organization (management) with responses of the individuals (workers).

Guzzo and Gannett define effectiveness in terms of a continuum ranging from minimally acceptable performance to maximally attainable performance. They argue that inhibitors constrain performance to minimally acceptable levels, while facilitators push performance to maximally attainable levels. There is a potential inconsistency in their view that while facilitators and inhibitors are independent dimensions, they have an effect on opposite ends of the same effectiveness dimension.

Kerr's views about membership versus production criteria are compatible and consistent with Guzzo and Gannett's notion of minimally acceptable and maximally attainable goals. March and Simon (1958) argued (1) that maintaining membership in an organization requires individuals to perform at some minimally acceptable level and (2) that, if appropriately motivated to produce, people would work toward maximally attainable levels of performance. This suggests, however, that minimally acceptable performance is not the end point on the continuum, but rather is a noticeable distance above the bottom point. If this were the case, it would be possible to consider the facilitation of minimally acceptable performance (consistent with Kerr and inconsistent with Guzzo and Gannett).

Peters and O'Connor argue that their research (and, implicitly, all research on situational constraints) is based on the assumptions that (1) workers are assigned to tasks that require the use of abilities and motivation and (2) performance requirements are something above a minimal level. They argue that when the performance standards are minimal, the effects of constraints cannot be detected. In sum, while Guzzo and Gannett argue that minimal performance reflects the operation of inhibitors, Peters and O'Connor argue that it could reflect either inhibitors or low performance standards.

The issue of whether an indicator of effectiveness should be general enough to allow cross-organizational comparisons is a dilemma that has long occupied the attention of researchers in this field. It is interesting to note that Kerr articulates the desirability of having such a universal measure, but also laments the fact that it has been impractical, in that "each organization that has used the diagnostic has . . . for the best of reasons . . . altered its contents." Guzzo and Gannett argue that indicators of effectiveness should be situationally specific. In the Schoorman and Schneider and Peters and O'Connor research programs, the criterion measures are always specific to the organization being studied. Taken together, these chapters suggest that while general measures of effectiveness may have some theoretical advantages, they tend to be impractical and yield much less specific data than more specific measures about the impact of facilitators and inhibitors.

The Measurement of Facilitators and Inhibitors

The chapters in part II focus primarily on the measurement aspects of the study of facilitators and inhibitors. (As we have already noted, each of these chapters also contributed to our understanding of conceptual issues as well.) The questions that we shall focus on in this section are:

1. How does one identify facilitators and inhibitors?
2. How does one deal with the level of analysis (aggregation) problem?
3. How reliable are measures of facilitators and inhibitors?
4. How valid are measures of facilitators and inhibitors?

How Does One Identify Facilitators and Inhibitors?

A remarkable degree of convergence is achieved among the researchers on this issue. The unanimous response to this question is "Ask the workers." The Schoorman and Schneider research described in chapter 1 builds the facilitators and inhibitors diagnostic "ground-up" in each organization with specific items tailored to reflect the facilitators and inhibitors relevant to each organization. The common themes across organizations are captured at the higher level of abstraction where the six subsystems (categories of facilitators and inhibitors) are common across organizations. Similarly, Kerr's approach outlined in chapter 3 relies on the workers to identify facilitators and inhibitors in reward systems, while Peters and O'Connor's data on obstacles summarized in chapter 5 are obtained through surveys of workers.

This unanimity regarding the source of the data, however, masks a broader question of how open-ended the inquiry should be at each research site. Another way of stating this problem is in terms of the perennial dilemma in research of how much specificity one is willing to give up to gain generality. Peters and O'Connor discuss the early taxonomic studies that asked very open-ended questions in order to define the categories of inhibitors in organizations. In their later research, they seek to achieve more generality by using the previously identified categories and focussing the respondents' attention on a common set of stimuli. The obvious advantage of this approach is that it allows comparison across organizations. However, Peters and O'Connor point out that some constraint dimensions are irrelevant for certain jobs, and this complicates the process of developing a composite score to represent the total set of inhibitors.

Chapter 4 by Moeller et al. takes an approach a little more toward the specificity end of the continuum by developing unique items for each organization. Generality is achieved in this research at the level of the categories or subsystems, which are common across all organizations. Moeller et al. also discuss attempts to develop a set of generic items that require only minor modifications for each new organizational setting.

Kerr's research established different modules of questions regarding various reward systems, and in each organization a set of modules was selected for use. This strategy is similar to that adopted by Peters and O'Connor. Kerr notes, with some remorse, that organizations too often changed the content of the modules as well, further reducing the generality of the measure.

How Does One Deal with the Aggregation Problem?

The issues involved in the aggregation of data are addressed in the chapters by Moeller et al. and by Roberts and Sloane. Roberts and Sloane make a strong argument against the practice of aggregating individual level responses to obtain group level data. They argue persuasively that this procedure misrepresents the variable at the group level and misses an important aspect of the way individual parts are combined to create a whole.

Moeller et al. provide interesting and rare empirical data in chapter 4 that address the aggregation question. The data obtained from an aggregation of individual responses are compared with data obtained through a group-consensus procedure in terms of their criterion-related validity. The results indicate a very high correlation between the aggregated data and the concensus data for subsystems of facilitators and inhibitors (r = .80–.92) and very similar validity data for the two procedures. These data would seem to argue against the Roberts and Sloane position presented in chapter 6 that the whole is greater than the sum of the parts, although such an interpretation is not without its problems. Moeller et al. indicate that the interrater reliability in this sample is quite high (average r is approximately .70) using the James, Demaree, and Wolf (1984) procedure for estimating interrater reliability. This suggests that each of the raters in a group had a shared perception of the facilitators and inhibitors. This is consistent with the propositions expressed by Schneider (1983) with respect to the development of shared perceptions in organizations. What the data indicate is that when the assumption of shared perceptions among organizational members is valid, aggregation of individual responses achieves much the same result as a consensus procedure. The Roberts and Sloane position on the aggregation issue is based on a different set of premises and does not share the assumption of shared perceptions articulated by Schneider (1983) and observed in the Moeller et al. chapter.

What Roberts and Sloane suggest is that when the criterion of effectiveness requires interdependence among individuals and across levels for success, aggregating individuals' perceptions may yield incomplete information about facilitators and inhibitors. In contrast to the Moeller et al. study in which individual salespeople worked essentially alone, Roberts and Sloane attempted to capture the inherent multiperson, multilevel, nature of high-reliability systems. Perhaps, then, the aggregation problem is not an issue that is answerable as a yes–no response to the question "Should I aggregate?" What these chapters suggest is that there are boundary conditions (e.g., multiple levels of interdependence versus individual work) that should determine the answer.

Are Measures of Facilitators and Inhibitors Reliable?

The question of reliability takes on different forms as a function of the conceptual definition of facilitators and inhibitors and the level at which they are to be measured. In the Peters and O'Connor research, the inhibitors are categorized such that each category is conceptually a single dimension. Multiple items measuring each category are used to collect data at the individual level. This model suggests that the internal consistency reliability of each scale is an important issue and is used by Peters and O'Connor as evidence of reliability of measurement. Achieving a high coefficient alpha is facilitated by their ability to use a relatively large number of items plus their ability to assess each of the categories of inhibitors through an individually administered survey. Peters and O'Connor report good reliability evidence for their measures of inhibitors.

In the chapter by Moeller et al., the question of reliability takes a different form. The range of facilitators and inhibitors examined in this chapter is much broader, and the number of categories is approximately half that used by Peters and O'Connor. The subsystem framework for classifying the facilitators and inhibitors represents a categorization at a higher level of abstraction. The conceptual space of each subsystem is clearly multidimensional. One would not expect to obtain a high coefficient alpha for a multidimensional variable. In addition, the time restrictions imposed by the group consensus procedure effectively restrict the number of items that could be used to an absolute minimum, which virtually eliminates the opportunity to have many items measuring the same dimension (within a subsystem). Internal-consistency reliability is not to be expected in this study, and the data verify this. However, since the level of analysis is the work unit, and a significant issue at this level is the degree of shared perceptions, the interrater reliability is much more important. As noted earlier, the data indicate that the interrater reliability is high, suggesting that there is reliability in the measurement of facilitators and inhibitors.

How Valid are Measures of Facilitators and Inhibitors?

Peters and O'Connor report the criterion-related validity data from several studies of inhibitors. They report that inhibitors were consistently related to measures of dissatisfaction and frustration. However, the relationship between inhibitors and performance was observed in one study, but not in two others. One of the issues raised by Peters and O'Connor, as an assumption on which their research is based, is that people should not be able to make excuses to justify not meeting high performance standards. This assumption plays an insidious role when performance appraisals are used as the criterion data. When raters make a judgment about individual performance, they are often prone to make allowances for situational constraints beyond the individual's control that decrease the individual's performance. Thus, the variance in actual performance that would be accounted for by inhibitors may be cognitively partialed out during the performance-appraisal process. The residual, not surprisingly, is not related to the measure of inhibitors.

In chapter 4 by Moeller et al., the criterion data in both studies are not performance-appraisal data and therefore not subject to this bias. In both samples, a composite score for all facilitators and inhibitors was significantly related to the performance criterion. In examining the six individual subsystems, two are significant in one sample and three are significant in the other. It is important to remember that in both studies, statistical power was severely limited by the small number of cases, which resulted from using the work unit as the level of analysis.

Kerr's chapter provides some qualitative evidence of the validity of facilitators and inhibitors of effectiveness. His accounting of the consequences of good and bad reward systems provides examples that we often overlook in our analyses of organizations.

Peters and O'Connor propose a construct called "performance tension," which they argue is a necessary situational precondition for successfully observing the effect of inhibitors on performance. They argue that unless an organization is operating at or close to peak efficiency, the existence of an inhibitor would not necessarily affect performance. This is similar to the concept of a tightly coupled system that Roberts and Sloane use to describe complex organizations. A tightly coupled system is one that must operate at or close to peak efficiency, and the existence of an inhibitor could have serious consequences. Both these ideas suggest that organizations "operating on the edge" are more susceptible to observable decrements in performance due to the presence of inhibitors.

In sum, the evidence on the validity of facilitators and inhibitors is quite encouraging. While several of the chapters have identified assumptions and boundary conditions that must be met, the prospects for additional findings of validity in further investigations of facilitators and inhibitors are good.

Leadership and Management as Antecedents of Facilitators and Inhibitors

When the research program on facilitators and inhibitors of work-unit effectiveness was initially formulated by the present authors, the final phase of the project was conceived in terms of an effort to understand the mechanisms that control the existence of facilitators and inhibitors. It seemed reasonable, therefore, to focus on the role of unit supervisors and examine their behaviors in terms of leadership and management activities as potential antecedents of facilitators and inhibitors. The chapters in this section (1) focus on the job of managers, describing the leadership and management activities that make up their role, and (2) explore the question of how managers control the facilitators and inhibitors of work effectiveness.

What Are the Characteristics of the Manager's Job?

The chapters by Kaplan, by Moses and Lyness, and by Roberts and Sloane each provide a rich description of the jobs of managers. Although the contexts of each of these chapters are quite different, there are several similar themes that cut across the descriptions. Each author emphasizes the extraordinary complexity of the manager's job. Here are some examples of how they characterize that complexity:

> General managers' agendas are filled with tangled issues such as this one. (It is no wonder that some GMs come down with analysis paralysis.) (Kaplan)

> Many contemporary managers face changes that are much less predictable and can occur at a dizzying rate. Less time is available for response, and the interrelatedness of events results in a complex series of consequences and implications. (Moses and Lyness)

> The number and technical intensity of operational, logistic, and administrative functions that must be performed by the ship in order to accomplish its missions result in extreme complexity. It is not possible for any of the ship's decision-making officers to fully understand the entire process. (Roberts and Sloane)

For Moses and Lyness, the essence of a manager's job is how the person copes with ambiguity. The authors conceptualize ambiguity in chapter 8 as a pervasive characteristic of the situation. Ambiguity can be either a facilitator or an inhibitor of effectiveness, depending on the coping style of the manager. The manager can be characterized as having one of four predominant styles that are functions of comfort with ambiguity and skills for dealing with ambiguity. The success of the manager is conceived of in terms of a person–situation fit model, where managers with "matching" styles are more likely to encounter ambiguity as a facilitator.

Kaplan's chapter describing the general manager's job characterizes the job in terms of the features common across all general managers' jobs. He then points out in chapter 9 all the sources of variation that are functions of the specific organization in which the general manager works. Kaplan's attempts to describe the conceptual space of managerial behavior reflect many of the struggles and tensions noted in earlier chapters conceptualizing facilitators and inhibitors. For example, he struggles with the trade-offs between generality and specificity in the level of description of the manager's job. He argues that general theories about managerial work must be modified to fit specific conditions. These conditions include the type of business, type of organization, and stage in the organizational life cycle.

Another familiar tension apparent in the Kaplan chapter is the choice of the appropriate conceptual level of analysis. He addresses the need to simultaneously attend to the context of the job and the relationship of the job to the larger system. In chapter 6 by Roberts and Sloane, this theme of simultaneity emerges for the manager of handling the coordination or linkages between units at the same level and between hierarchical levels. The need for coordination is a function of the complexity of the system, which is defined in terms of the interdependence among units. As the complexity increases, particularly in a tightly coupled system, the manager's job of coordination becomes increasingly critical with no margin for error plus severe consequences for errors. This is certainly an environment where managers can develop conditions that can facilitate or inhibit success.

Chapter 7 by Schoorman et al. does not address this simultaneity problem. It develops a conceptual model that differentiates leadership and management behaviors. Leadership is defined as interpersonal interactions with subordinates, while all noninterpersonal activities and interpersonal activities with external constituencies are defined as management. The rationale for this distinction is based on the premise that managerial behaviors may be substitutable for leadership behaviors in the creation of facilitators and inhibitors in the work context.

Do Leadership and Management Behaviors Create Facilitators and Inhibitors?

The Schoorman et al. chapter explicitly tested this proposition in the context of a financial-services telemarketing organization. Although the results do not support the proposition, the authors indicate that the source of data on supervisory behaviors (self-reporting) may have contributed to the lack of significant results.

The chapters by Kaplan, by Moses and Lyness, and by Roberts and Sloane all provide qualitative and anecdotal data consistent with this proposition. For example, in the Roberts and Sloane chapter, the task environment on board the *U.S.S. Vinson* is one in which the manager's behavior can certainly contribute to conditions that facilitate or inhibit effectiveness. According to Moses and Lyness, the manner in which managers cope with ambiguity can create a facilitating or inhibiting environment.

While these chapters have not produced substantial evidence for the causal link between managerial behaviors and facilitators and inhibitors, there appears to be sufficient encouragement across the chapters for the continued consideration of such a linkage.

Summary

This chapter has attempted to integrate the nine chapters previously presented in this book, to identify the common themes across the research efforts, and to summarize the learning that has occurred through the experience of sharing these research ideas and data. It is clear that on some problems we have come a long way and learned a great deal, while on others we continue to struggle with very basic issues. The sources of contribution to our learning on each of the issues are outlined in table 10–1, while the learning that we have achieved can be summarized as follows.

1. *Conceptual issues.* We have made significant progress in identifying the issues involved in conceptualizing facilitators and inhibitors. The issues examined in this chapter were the definition and description of facilitators and inhibitors, the appropriate conceptual level of analysis, and the definition of system effectiveness. The integrative review revealed that there is a significant amount of rich thinking about the nature of facilitators and inhibitors of work effectiveness.

2. *Measurement issues.* The issues with respect to the measurement of facilitators and inhibitors examined in this chapter included the source of data on facilitators and inhibitors, the appropriate level of aggregation for studying them, and the reliability and validity of indices of facilitators and inhibitors. This chapter concluded that there is considerable agreement that job incumbents are clearly a useful source of data on inhibitors, but that the specification of facilitators may require persons with special expertise. While the general conclusion regarding level of analysis was that it should be driven by the characteristics of the specific study, several guidelines were discussed for making this judgment. The measures of facilitators and inhibitors were generally found to be reliable, and the criterion-related validity data (although not overwhelming) indicated substantial support for the validity of facilitators and inhibitors.

3. *Leadership and management.* The role of leadership and management activities as antecedents of facilitators and inhibitors was examined in terms of the conceptualization of leadership and management as well as in terms of their relationship to facilitators and inhibitors. While there was some convergence in terms of the descriptions of management activities, the available evidence did not support the proposed causal link with facilitators and inhibitors. Continued exploration of this issue was recommended.

It is probably appropriate to conclude this book with an observation regarding the level of analysis at which this integration and overview were conducted. As we examined the convergence and controversy with repect to specific issues and questions, we noted some significant gains, some modest gains, and some lack of any gains at all. However, there is little doubt in the minds of these authors that as we step up one level and reflect on the entire process of the meeting and sharing of research programs by fifteen authors

Table 10–1
Summary of Questions Raised by Sources of Response

Issue	Authors (Chapter Number)								
	Schoorman and Schneider (1)	Guzzo and Gannett (2)	Kerr (3)	Moeller et al. (4)	Peters and O'Connor (5)	Roberts and Sloane (6)	Schoorman et al. (7)	Moses and Lyness (8)	Kaplan (9)
Conceptual issues									
What are facilitators and inhibitors?	X	X	X		X				
What is the appropriate level of analysis?	X	X	X		X				
What is effectiveness?	X	X	X		X				
Measurement issues									
How does one identify facilitators and inhibitors?	X		X	X	X				
How does on deal with the aggregation problem?				X		X			
How reliable are the measures?				X	X				
How valid are the measures?			X	X	X	X			
Leadership and management issues									
What are the characteristics of the manager's job?					X	X	X	X	
Do leadership and management create facilitators and inhibitors?						X	X	X	X

and many other individuals, the overall experience was most stimulating and the gains substantial.

References

James, L. R., Demaree, R. G., and Wolf, G. (1984). Estimating within-group inter-rater reliability with and without response bias. *Journal of Applied Psychology*, 69, 85–98.

March, J. G., and Simon, H. A. (1958). *Organizations*. New York: John Wiley & Sons.

Schneider, B. (1983). Interactional psychology and organizational behavior. In L. L. Cummings and B. Staw (eds.), *Research in organizational behavior*, Vol. 5. Greenwich, Conn.: JAI Press.

Index

About the Contributors

Elizabeth Berney is an adjunct professor in industrial-organizational psychology at George Mason University in Fairfax, Virginia. She is also a consultant specializing in organizational change and development and health promotion. She has a Ph.D. and M.A. in industrial-organizational psychology from the University of Maryland and a B.A. in psychology from Yale University.

Barbara Gannett earned an M.A. in personnel psychology at New York University, where she is currently a Ph.D. candidate in industrial and organizational psychology. Her current research interests concern expectancy effects in organizations.

Richard A. Guzzo (Ph.D. Yale University) is associate professor of psychology at New York University. His research concerns the determinants of effective team performance, the impact on productivity of psychologically based management practices, and the dynamics of idealist organizations. Guzzo was formerly a member of the faculty of management at McGill University.

Robert E. Kaplan is applications director for the Executive Leadership area at the Center for Creative Leadership, Greensboro, N.C. Since 1984, he has done research on management and written a book with Morgan McCall called *Whatever It Takes: Decision Makers at Work*. For the past few years, he has engaged in research on what accounts for executive effectiveness and ineffectiveness and under what conditions executives do or do not continue to develop. He is currently writing a book with Wilfred Drath and Joan Kofodimos based on the notion that leadership and leadership development are highly personal expressions of the individual executive. He is also a management trainer and consultant, specializing in organizational change and executive development. He works closely with individual executives to help them assess and act on their developmental needs. He has an undergraduate degree in English and a Ph.D. in organizational behavior from Yale University.

Steven Kerr is dean of faculty and research professor of management in the Business School of the University of Southern California. He is on three editorial review boards, has authored nearly fifty journal articles and book chapters, and has coauthored two books. His major research interests are in leadership and in organizational evaluation and reward systems.

Karen S. Lyness is manager of personnel and field management research at Avon Products, Inc. in New York City, where her current research focusses on issues related to sales management positions, including personnel requirements, motivation potential, sources of stress, impact on nonwork lives, turnover, and evaluation of a strategic intervention designed to improve productivity. She is also an adjunct assistant professor in the Organizational Psychology Program at Columbia University. Previously, Karen worked at AT&T corporate headquarters, where she was director of operations for the Advanced Management Potential Assessment Program and conducted research on the identification and development of high-potential managers including the socialization of new managers, job analysis of corporate management positions (with Mirian Graddick), and research on how managers cope with ambiguity and change.

Anne Moeller (Ph.D., University of Maryland) is an assistant professor of management at the University of Colorado at Denver. Her interests concern the role of task activity in organizational effectiveness, relationships between organizational climate and productivity, and levels of analysis in organizational research. She is currently studying the management of work groups in service organizations.

Joseph L. ("Joel") Moses heads AT&T's New York–based psychological research unit, which examines complex individual and organizational behaviors. Active in the assessment center movement, he has pioneered many of AT&T's innovative programs. A Ph.D. from Baylor University, he is a fellow of the Society for Industrial and Organizational Psychology and holds a diplomate in industrial/organizational psychology.

Edward J. O'Connor is a visiting associate professor in the College of Management at the Georgia Institute of Technology. He received his M.B.A. from the Harvard Business School and his Ph.D. in industrial/organizational psychology from the University of Akron. In addition to carrying out research and consulting in numerous organizations, he has also served as president of WPRC, Inc., a financial services corporation located in Dallas, Texas. Dr. O'Connor's current research interests include human productivity, situational performance constraints, organizational revitalization and change, organizational culture, and entrepreneurial management. He has published numerous articles and book chapters in *Research in Personnel and Human Resource Management, Journal of Applied Psychology, Personnel Psychology, Academy of Management Journal, Academy of Management Review, Organizational Behavior and Human Performance,* and *Journal of Management.*

Lawrence H. Peters is associate professor of management at the M. J. Neeley School of Business at Texas Christian University in Fort Worth. He received his Ph.D. in industrial/organizational psychology from Purdue University in 1975. His current research interests include the study of employee retention, situational performance constraints, and applications of cognitive performance appraisal models. He has contributed numerous articles and book chapters in such leading publications as *Research in Personnel and Human Resources Management, Journal of Applied Psychology, Academy of Management Review, Organizational Behavior and Human Performance, Personnel Psychology,* and *Psychological Bulletin.* He currently serves on the editorial boards of *Journal of Management* and *The Industrial-Organizational Psychologist.*

Karlene H. Roberts holds a Ph.D. in psychology and is professor of business administration at the University of California, Berkeley. She has written in the areas of organizational communication and research methodology. Her current research concerns designing and managing high-risk technologies.

Daniel Schechter has an M.A. and is working on his Ph.D. in industrial/organizational psychology at the University of Maryland. He is also manager of staff development for GEICO Corporation in Washington, D.C. His special areas of interest concern leadership, organizational commitment, and the implementation of psychological concepts and findings into ongoing work settings.

Stephen B. Sloane is a retired captain in the U.S. Navy. He holds a Ph.D. in political science from the University of California Berkeley, and is on the faculty at St. Mary's College, in Moraga, California. His current research interest is organizational similarities and differences between the Spanish Armada's tactics and modern naval warfare.

About the Editors

Benjamin Schneider is professor of psychology and business management at the University of Maryland, College Park, where he received his Ph.D. under C.J. Bartlett in 1967. His research interests concern the role of person factors in organization climate and culture, the study of service, and service organizations, and the levels-of-analysis problem in organizational science. He has published widely in personnel and organizational psychology and believes the two subfields can be integrated. He has been president of both the Society for Industrial and Organizational Psychology (Division 14 of the American Psychological Association) and the Organizational Behavior Division of the Academy of Management.

F. David Schoorman is an assistant professor of organizational behavior and human resource management at the Krannert Graduate School of Management at Purdue University in West Lafayette, Indiana. He received his M.S. and Ph.D. in Industrial Administration from Carnegie-Mellon University. His research interests include organizational effectiveness, decision making, leadership, and management. He is the author of several book chapters and articles on these topics that have appeared in leading journals in the field. He was a coprincipal investigator on the grant from the Office of Naval Research that funded the research reported in this book.